The Media in Western Europe

SAGE Communications in Society

Dynamics of Media Politics
Broadcast and Electronic Media
in Western Europe
edited by Karen Siune and Wolfgang Truetzschler
for the Euromedia Research Group

New Communication Technologies
and the Public Interest
edited by Marjorie Ferguson

New Media Politics
Comparative Perspectives
in Western Europe
Euromedia Research Group
edited by Denis McQuail and Karen Siune

Television and its Audience
Patrick Barwise and Andrew Ehrenberg

The Media in Western Europe

THE EUROMEDIA HANDBOOK

Second Edition

EUROMEDIA RESEARCH GROUP
Editor: Bernt Stubbe Østergaard

SAGE Publications
London • Thousand Oaks • New Delhi

This edition published 1997

SAGE Publications Ltd
6 Bonhill Street
London EC2A 4PU

SAGE Publications Inc
2455 Teller Road
Thousand Oaks, California 91320

SAGE Publications India Pvt Ltd
32, M-Block Market
Greater Kailash – I
New Delhi 110 048

British Library Cataloguing in Publication data

A catalogue record for this book is
available from the British Library

ISBN 0 7619 5405 8
ISBN 0 7619 5406 6 (pbk)

Library of Congress catalog card number 97–67390

Typeset by Photoprint, Torquay, Devon
Printed in Great Britain by Redwood Books, Trowbridge, Wiltshire

Contents

Notes on contributors

Kees Brants, lecturer at the Department of Communication Science, University of Amsterdam, The Netherlands

Els De Bens, professor at the Department of Communications, University of Ghent, Belgium

Panayote Elias Dimitras, assistant professor of political science at the Department of Economics and Business (ASOEE), Athens, Greece

Karl Erik Gustafsson, professor of mass media economics, School of Economics, University of Göteborg, Sweden

Mario Hirsch, journalist, teacher and researcher on economy and policy aspects of mass media, Luxembourg

Olof Hultén, head of strategic analysis, Corporate Development, Sveriges Television, Stockholm, Sweden

Mary Kelly, lecturer at the Department of Sociology, University College, Dublin, Ireland

Hans J. Kleinsteuber, professor at the Institute of Political Science, University of Hamburg, Germany

Rosario de Mateo, professor at the Faculty of Communication Sciences, Universitat Autònoma de Barcelona, Spain

Gianpietro Mazzoleni, professor of sociology and communications at the University of Salerno, Italy

Denis McQuail, emeritus professor of mass communication at the University of Amsterdam, The Netherlands

Werner A. Meier, media consultant and lecturer at the Department of Mass Communication, University of Zurich, Switzerland

J.-M. Nobre-Correia, professor in information and communication at the Université Libre de Bruxelles (ULB, Belgium); also at the University of Coimbra, Portugal

Helge Østbye, professor of mass communication at the University of Bergen, Norway

Bernt Stubbe Østergaard, research director at Informedica, Copenhagen, Denmark

Michael Palmer, professor of communications at the Sorbonne University, Paris III, France

Vibeke G. Petersen, special adviser, Ministry of Culture, Copenhagen, Denmark

Karen Siune, professor at the Institute of Political Science, University of Århus, Denmark

Claude Sorbets, research director, CNRS, Institut d'Etudes Politiques, Bordeaux, France

Helena Tapper, researcher and lecturer at the Department of Communications, University of Helsinki, Finland

Josef Trappel, project manager and consultant with PROGNOS, European Centre for Economic Research and Strategy Consulting, Department for Media and Communication Research, Basle, Switzerland

Wolfgang Truetzschler, lecturer in communications at the Dublin Institute of Technology, Ireland

Jeremy Tunstall, professor of sociology at City University, London, UK

Introduction

This book gives a nation-by-nation introduction to historical media developments in Western Europe (EU countries plus Switzerland and Norway) after 1945 and a thorough presentation of the media landscape in each country. The book is the result of a concerted effort by media researchers to give a coherent presentation of the many-faceted media scene. It is a reference guide to press, broadcasting and new electronic media in each of the 17 countries, and enables the reader to make cross-national and cross-media comparisons. Each chapter follows common guidelines, developed over several years of cooperation.

Media developments in Europe in the 1990s have been characterized by internationalization, technological convergence and an on-rush of new multimedia, interactive services, leaving policy-makers and consumers more confused than they were in the 1980s.

Internationalization drivers have been technological, economic and political. Digitalization is putting voice and video services on the same footing and allowing innovative packaging of new (telecom and broadcasting) services, deliverable over a unified, inexpensive transmission system. DTH (Direct-to-Home) satellite television and extensive broadband cabling have given many European homes 10–20 television channels and new interactive telecom services to choose from.

German reunification, the enlargement of the European Community (when Austria, Finland and Sweden joined) and further economic integration in the European Union (EU), have created a 300 million pan-European mass media consumer market more open to international competition and commercial forces at the expense of protected national broadcasters. Defined as an essential growth industry by the EU, national parliamentary assemblies are accepting that the ethos of publishing and broadcasting is that they are to be profit-oriented services, much like films and books. Special programmes to preserve language and cultural identity are accepted, but basic public service ideals of democratic plurality are seriously challenged. Now that deregulation is no longer a question of if, but when, political assemblies seem to have lost the initiative. Where new telematic services in the 1980s were introduced from above through established broadcasting and telecom channels, the new multi-media and Internet-based services are being launched as commodities 'from below', leaving law-makers and consumers wondering what hit them. Although interactive technologies seem to have a long way to go before they pose any threat to established one-way conventional television, the regulatory climate is changing as a consequence of these still embryonic technological changes.

Not only are traditional media actors in press, publishing, broadcasting and telecommunications re-casting their products into comprehensive service packages, but they are doing so in new consortia that cut across national boundaries and technologies. It is still too early to predict which media/service scenarios will dominate, or how the household media budget will develop, but the on-going struggle will determine the parameters for future national media policies.

A coherent nation-by-nation presentation

The reader is offered here a coherent presentation of national press, broadcasting and electronic media. Authors of the individual chapters are noted national media experts, who over the past five years have met regularly in order to enhance the framework of this book, combining the diversity of media developments in all parts of Western Europe with an overall European perspective.

Each country chapter is introduced by a short summary of geographical and demographic features and the political situation in government and parliament. Then follows the developments in the printed press and electronic media since 1945, giving an overview of historical elements, the actors and the processes leading up to today's media situation in the country. The third section gives a more detailed description of the printed press, covering press legislation, the most important newspapers, ownership, financing, political affiliations and an analysis of the most important press issues, such as cross-media ownership, and how the press is investing in new media to retain market share. This leads on to a section on electronic media, beginning with national, regional and local radio and television. Here is information on the large number of private radio and television channels that have emerged in the de-monopolization process and the new services such as video-on-demand, pay-per-view and the re-invented Internet-based telematic channels (growing much faster than existing videotex and teletext). Each national author analyses these new channels and the new owners and their media strategies. In the chapter conclusions the authors sum up the important national trends in mass media developments. The salient issues and the policy problems facing the important actors in the media field are analysed in their national contexts.

Each chapter has a statistical section giving vital facts about media use and access, numbers and types of channels, the main newspapers and medial economics such as turnover, financing and ownership. Literature references are also given for further in-depth studies of national media developments.

Final revisions to contributions were made in early 1997 and changes after this time have not been incorporated, although developments are anticipated in the trends and issues discussions.

The Euromedia Research Group

The Euromedia Research Group was established in 1982 and has since met regularly to address the central questions of convergence in Western European media policy. The group now stands as one of the longest-established independent media research groups in Europe, accepting gratefully the goodwill and hospitality of the various universities with which the members are associated. The group's research findings were first published in 1986 in *European Media Policy*, published by Campus Verlag, and a comparative analysis, *New Media Politics*, was published by Sage. Five years later, the group again published its findings in two parallel volumes, *The Media in Western Europe* and *Dynamics of Media Politics*, presenting a comparative analysis of media developments and issues in Western Europe since 1985, both volumes published by Sage. This volume marks the third round of publications from the group.

Bernt Stubbe Østergaard

The Euromedia Research Group

The Euromedia Research Group was established in 1982 and has since [illegible] to address [illegible] central questions of media policy in Western European media politics. The group [illegible] is one of the longest established independent media research groups in Europe, [illegible] by the goodwill and hospitality of [illegible] institutions [illegible] [illegible] research and [illegible] [illegible]

[illegible]

[illegible]

1

Austria

Josef Trappel

National profile

Geographically, Austria is situated in the heart of Europe and is considered one of the 'bridges' between East and West because of its permanently neutral status since independence after the Second World War. With its small home market of around 8 million inhabitants living in a surface area of 84 000 km^2, Austria is not one of the powerful economic forces in Europe. Nevertheless, Austria plays a crucial role in international diplomacy and has influenced the policy of various international bodies. Several departments of the United Nations run their headquarters in the International Center in Vienna.

Austria shares borders with Germany, Switzerland, Italy, Slovenia, Hungary, the Czech and the Slovak Republics and Liechtenstein. Deriving from the time when Vienna was the capital of the Austro-Hungarian monarchy, there are still some language minorities today, living mainly in the southern and eastern parts of the country, but the majority share the German language with the country's large northern neighbour.

In 1989 Austria officially applied for membership in the (then) European Community. As negotiations were linked to similar requests submitted by the Nordic EFTA states, actual accession as a full member of the European Union took place on 1 January 1995.

Austria is a parliamentary democracy with a federal constitution. The president is the head of state, but he does not play a dominant role in daily politics. In parliament there are five parties, of which the Social-Democrats and the conservative People's Party are the largest. In the general election held in December 1995, the Social-Democrats (SPÖ) gained a relative majority of 38% against the People's Party (ÖVP) with 28%, the right-wing Freedom Movement (former National-Liberal Party, FPÖ) with 22%, the Green Party with 5% and the Liberal Party with 6%. Since 1986 Austria has been governed by a coalition between the two largest parties, SPÖ and ÖVP, predominated by the Social-Democrats, who have been in power since 1970.

Politics in Austria are marked by a strong tradition of democratic corporatism. The so-called 'social partnership' between the large groups in society has brought about a relatively stable social system. All major decisions in Austria are taken only after reaching a certain consensus among the social partners.

Since the mid-1980s Austria has undergone a period of changing orientation in economic policy. The long tradition of state-owned industry has come under discussion and proportions of shares have been sold to private investors. There are no major Austrian multinational companies. Because of the small domestic market and the hesitant policy towards foreign investment, Austria's enterprises are suffering generally from undercapitalization.

Development of the press and broadcasting since 1945

At the end of the Second World War, Austria was divided into four sectors, each governed by one of the Allies. There was no particular press law governing the remaining four newspapers in Vienna in 1945, a number which had dropped from 22 in 1938. Across Austria the press was obliged to start again with almost nothing to build on. It was the availability of paper which enabled publishers in the western and southern part of the country to start new newspapers earlier than in Vienna. A licence to publish had to be obtained from the occupying forces and this was only given to politically 'approved' persons. This might further explain why the process of founding new newspapers was so slow. However, the fully independent 'Second Republic' started in 1955 with 35 newspapers and more regional editions.

Since the Second World War developments have gone through four phases.

- From 1946 until 1957 there was a steady decline of newspapers and of their overall circulation. In 1957 an all-time low was reached, with a mere 1.2 million copies printed in the whole of Austria.
- From 1958 until 1973 the first round of concentration took place. With the start of a new mass medium – television broadcasting – the number of newspapers declined further but at the same time circulation expanded. Within 11 years the number of copies doubled from 1.2 million in 1957 to 2.4 million in 1969. By then only 24 newspapers remained. In 1973 the figure dropped to 19 (Institut für Publizistik, 1977).
- The period from 1973 until 1987 was marked by a stable supplier market on the one hand and a slow but steady increase of circulation figures on the other. Two newspapers dominated the Austrian market. The popular tabloid *Kronenzeitung* circulated roughly one million copies every day and, together with the *Kurier* (440 000 copies), accounted for more than half of all newspaper copies in Austria (1989). In this period papers of political parties substantially lost market share and were financially dependent on state subsidies and party funds.
- From 1987 to 1992 the press development was marked by a second wave of concentration and by foreign capital penetrating the market, assisting substantially in the creation of a dominant print market power (Mediaprint). In parallel, new titles entered the print market.

From 1992 to 1995 the Austrian press market was characterized by a phase of consolidation.

During the Second World War broadcasting was the central domestic propaganda instrument of the Nazi regime in Austria. Similar to the lack of 'hardware' (paper) in the print media, after 1945 broadcasters were confronted with serious problems in building up the necessary technical equipment for a regular service. All technical hardware was German property during the war and was handed over to the occupying Allies afterwards. French, British, American and Soviet forces started their own services and hampered the installation of nation-wide broadcasting (Fabris et al., 1990). Only in 1954 was an agreement reached in which broadcasting was declared a national matter. Therefore the ORF (Österreichischer Rundfunk – Austrian Broadcasting Company) was founded and in 1955, when Austria regained full sovereignty, the first television experiments started. In 1957 the Council of Ministers constituted the ORF as a public service company.

The first broadcasting legislation after the war came into force in 1967 and restructured the sector. Three radio programmes and two television channels were defined as a minimum obligation for the ORF. Up to 1996 the ORF remained the only legal programme provider for radio and television within Austria.

The press

Policy framework

Apart from the European Convention on Human Rights (1950; art. 10) and the Constitutional Law (Staatsgrundgesetz 1867, revised 1982; art. 13), which ensures freedom of expression and prohibits all kinds of censorship, press legislation is based on two pillars: The Press Act of 1922 and the Media Law of 1981. The Act of 1922 states that the freedom of the press is guaranteed. In the interest of national security, health and morality, and in the event of an infringement of territorial rights, this otherwise absolute freedom may be limited. There are certain obligations deriving from the Media Law of 1981: each periodical has to carry a clear indication concerning the owner, the publisher and the general political or ideological orientation. In addition, a certain amount of copies must be delivered free of charge to the National Library and advertising must be clearly separated from the informational part of the paper. There is a right to reply, protection of privacy and, of course, copyright legislation. Journalists enjoy 'freedom of opinion', which includes their right to refuse collaboration on a piece of work which does not conform with the personal opinion of the journalist. They also can claim a 'shift in the general orientation' of the paper and can then quit their job without losing the right to severance pay.

Newspapers and most of the periodicals enjoy three different kinds of state support: first, there is a reduced VAT on printed products; second, they can apply for postal distribution at a much lower rate than ordinary mail; third, they can apply for direct state subsidies.

As indicated above, the Austrian newspaper industry was and is characterized by a far-reaching concentration process. With this process in mind, in 1975 a law concerning press subsidies was passed, stabilizing the industry for a couple of years. The fundamental concept was to re-balance the burden of the VAT back to the newspapers, but the total amount was reduced substantially in the following years. An amendment in 1985 directed the subsidy into two channels: the *ordinary* subsidy is granted to every applicant daily newspaper and distributes a certain amount of money every year to each newspaper, regardless of its economic performance, while the *special subsidy for the maintenance of diversity* is granted in addition to papers specifically contributing to the diversity of opinions and which are publishing less advertisements than 22% of their annual printed pages.

In 1996 state subsidies to the daily press amounted to AS230.5 m (17.1 m ECU), of which AS65.5 m went to the ordinary subsidy, varying from AS2.3 m to AS4.9 m (170 000 to 363 000 ECU) per daily newspaper, according to the size of the paper. More important and significant is the special subsidy, distributing AS165 m (12.2 m ECU) among seven papers, ranging from AS13.8 m to AS33.8 m each. In addition to these annual subsidies, the federal government has on several occasions financially supported investments of the media in technical equipment, data transmission, print shops etc. Over the years, the subsidy system has not prevented the closing down of newspapers, but its withdrawal would put several papers, in particular the smaller papers receiving special subsidy, immediately at stake.

Structure, ownership and finance

At the end of 1995 there were 17 newspapers on the Austrian market. Seven of them are published in Vienna and account for 73% of the (estimated) nationwide circulation of 3.08 million copies. The three biggest newspapers are the *Kronenzeitung* (1 075 000), *Täglich Alles* (540 000) and the *Kurier* (325 000). It is to be noted that the three market leaders do not publish their circulation and sales figures and they do not participate in the 1994 founded circulation control system. Therefore, these figures are estimations.

Between 1987 and 1991 five *party papers* disappeared from the market. In 1987 a conservative partisan newspaper (*Südost-Tagespost*) and a socialist paper (*Tagblatt*) shut down their presses, followed first by another small conservative party paper in 1990 (*Volkszeitung*) and, in 1991, by the famous *Arbeiterzeitung*, formerly a partisan paper of the SPÖ and sold to private owners in 1989, and then by the communist party paper *Volksstimme*. By 1996, only three party papers are left and none exceeds a circulation of 55 000. However, most of the formally independent newspapers have a more or less declared political affiliation. Seven of the ten papers outside Vienna are deemed to sympathize with the conservative People's Party.

Media concentration in terms of ownership control was boosted in 1988 and the following years. The two owners of the highly profitable *Kronenzeitung* decided to dissolve their agreement and the one partner had to take over the shares of the other. Unable to find sufficient financial backing in Austria, he finally sold 45% of the company to the German *Westdeutsche Allgemeine Zeitung* (WAZ, 1.1.1988). Six months later, in June 1988, the WAZ landed its second coup when it bought 45% of the *Kurier*. Consequently, the two newspapers together formed the company Mediaprint for joint operations in printing, advertising acquisition and distribution. The interlinked conglomerate subsequently gained control of the leading opinion-makers (weeklies *Profil* and *Wirtschaftswoche*) and some of the most successful general interest magazines (e.g. *Basta*).

In 1988 the German company Springer Verlag decided to enter the Austrian press market by taking 50% of the shares in the newly founded quality paper *Der Standard*. Springer reinforced its engagement in 1992 by investing a 50% share in a newly launched weekly news magazine (*News*) and the acquisition of (finally) a 65% share in the *Tiroler Tageszeitung*. By 1991 the circulation share of daily newspapers published in cooperation with German publishers had reached 31% (Bruck and Melcher-Smejkal, 1993: 77).

The trend towards higher concentration of the daily press market was paralleled by the founding of three new titles. The 1988 launch of the quality paper *Der Standard*, the first launch of a new newspaper for 16 years in Austria, animated competition in the quality newspaper market. *Der Standard* competes with the well-known *Die Presse* and the *Salzburger Nachrichten*, the latter launching a nationwide edition in 1989 with more emphasis on politics and economics. Similarly, the quality paper *Die Presse* increased its journalistic staff and its coverage of foreign affairs and economic matters considerably. Contrary to some expert warnings concerning the small size of the Austrian market for quality papers, all three newspapers succeeded in at least maintaining their level of daily reach in the following years. In October 1995 another quality paper was launched. Importing the idea of business daily papers from Sweden (*Dagens Industri*), a consortium of Austrian publishing houses and the Swedish Bonnier group started the *Wirtschaftsblatt* in a promising market niche. Competition in the Austrian quality paper market segment has therefore significantly increased during the first half of the 1990s.

But the boulevard market was also affected by turbulence. Since April 1992 the leading *Kronenzeitung* faced a serious competitor. The former co-owner of the *Kronenzeitung* aggressively launched *Täglich Alles*, printed entirely in colour and sold at less than half the cover price of the other newspapers. Printed on one of Europe's technically most sophisticated presses, the boulevard paper rapidly gained market shares and within only one year ranked second in circulation, without, however, seriously challenging the market leader. This new competitor has put heavy pressure on the *Kurier*, for decades the second largest paper. In 1993 the *Kurier* was relaunched with an entirely new layout and extended coverage of national and international current affairs and with the strong intention of becoming one of the quality papers, thus reinforcing competition in this segment.

Outside Vienna there is no real choice of newspapers. Most of the Austrian *Länder* have one dominant newspaper in a more or less monopolistic position challenged only by the regional edition of the *Kronenzeitung*. In Upper Austria, Styria, Carinthia and Vorarlberg there are two papers, but the second has a marginal circulation compared to the market leader. Market access for new papers in the regions is extremely difficult. This fact is best illustrated by the 1990 launch of a paper in Lower Austria (*Guten Tag Niederösterreich*), in an area where no single regional daily papers exist. After only four weeks the financial backing crashed and the paper collapsed.

Newspapers account for the largest market share of advertising revenue and that share is increasing. The 1996 market share reached 32% with an annual growth of 5% (according to Focus Media data). Advertising is the main source of income of Austria's newspapers: 42% of the budget comes from sales and 56% from advertising. This ratio has been fairly stable for 15 years (Lankes, 1990; Schrotta, 1981), but depends largely on the size of the newspaper, smaller papers having a higher proportional income from sales (Aiginger and Peneder, 1993).

Readership

The Austrians are not a nation of avid readers. For the first part of the decade, however, newspapers have slightly increased their reach from 72% (1990) to 77% (1996) of the population, outscored by television with 78% (1996) and radio with 80% (1995), according to *Media Analyse*. There exist strong disparities between the newspapers. The *Kronenzeitung*, with its circulation of more than a million copies, reached 42%, *Täglich Alles* reached 12% and the *Kurier* some 12% (all in 1996). With the exception of the *Kleine Zeitung* (11%), all other papers reach some 5% or below of the population. This illustrates the high level of concentration not only in ownership and circulation but also in the political influence and power of the popular boulevard press in Austria. It still holds that the Austrians love easy reading and watching television.

However, during the first five years of the 1990s the trend towards slightly higher reach of the quality papers continued. All quality papers with nationwide circulation have increased their readership. In 1990 the *Presse*, the *Salzburger Nachrichten* and *Der Standard* reached 3.3%, 3.4% and 3.8% of the population respectively. In 1996 they had increased their reach to 4.7, 4.3 and 5.4% respectively (*Media Analyse*, 1990 and 1996). During the same period, the *Kronenzeitung* lost 1% and reached in 1996 some 42% of the population despite fierce competition from *Täglich Alles*. This dominant position does not depend on age or wealth, as the reach of the *Kronenzeitung* among the richest part of Austrian society amounts to 42% and among young adults from 14 to 19 years, to 39% (*Media Analyse*, 1994).

Electronic media

Legal framework

Austria's broadcasting is basically governed by two laws: The 'Federal Constitutional Law to safeguard the Independence of Broadcasting' and the 'Broadcasting Act concerning tasks and organization of Austrian Broadcasting', both of 1974. The Constitutional Law defines broadcasting as a 'public service', to include both terrestrial and cable operations, and prescribes the passing of legislation which will guarantee objectivity and impartiality of the coverage, the variety of views and the independence of the institutions and individuals concerned with broadcasting.

By law the 'Austrian Broadcasting Corporation' (ORF) is the only institution licensed to transmit television programmes within Austria. Thus the *de facto* monopoly is not set up by the Constitutional Law but derives from the fact that only one Broadcasting Act has been promulgated. As regards radio, the Regional Radio Act of 1993 enabled the granting of licences to private operators. The ORF, still the only television provider in Austria, must operate commercially but on a non-profit basis. Its organizational and control structure is designed to ensure that all significant views of society are fully and fairly represented in its operations. The supreme governing body, the Board of Trustees (*Kuratorium*), is composed of 35 representatives: 9 members are appointed by the federal government, 6 according to the relative strength of the political parties in parliament, one by each of the nine Austrian regions (*Länder*), 6 by the Council of the Viewers and Listeners and 5 by the employees. Along with control duties and investment decisions, the main task of the Board of Trustees is the election of the Director-General (*Generalintendant*) every four years, who enjoys far-reaching competencies. During this election campaign it usually becomes apparent that the Board of Trustees is composed entirely of party members or individuals with strong political party affiliation. At least at the level of the Director-General, the ORF appears to be dependent on party bargaining.

The ORF is required by law to operate at least three radio and two television channels with the obligation to make transmissions technically available to the largest possible extent to all citizens on Austrian territory. To this end, the ORF operates an extensive network of transmitters all over the country. Furthermore, the ORF runs the short-wave radio channel Radio Austria International at the request of the federal government.

The Council of Viewers and Listeners was constituted under the Broadcasting Act without any executive power but with the purpose of representing the interest of the public. It has the right to propose programme adjustments, demand information from the Director-General and suggest technical improvements. Furthermore, the Head of State (*Bundespräsident*) has to appoint a Commission with 17 members, which is convened by the Federal Chancellery to supervise the ORF's operations in accordance with law. The Commission also decides on alleged violations of rights of individuals by ORF programmes.

Since the early 1980s cable networks have been installed all over Austria carrying foreign programmes to the connected households – without any specific cable legislation. Consequently, there are no legal restrictions on whether a particular programme is eligible for re-transmission or not and there is no explicit must-carry rule for the programmes of the ORF. However, programme creation by cable operators was illegal until July 1996. Until then they were only licensed to re-transmit programmes simultaneously and without any editing (§20 Rundfunkverordnung 1965). Observers criticized that regulation. 'There was, and basically still is no vision of the social, cultural or political function of cable TV.' (Latzer, 1996). By August 1996, however, a decree of the Constitutional Court entered into force, enabling cable operators to produce their own programmes as long as the parliament does not enact new legislation. Within several months, all over Austria cable operators started their own programming, mainly low-profile transmissions with local content. In March 1997 parliament adopted new cable legislation, implementing a simple registration procedure for such programmes without any licensing requirement. Cable programmes simply have to respect the general legal framework, including the Television Directive of the European Union.

Prior to this legal but unlawful situation, several small cable operators started their own regional or local television programmes without explicit authorization, claiming that no clear demarcation line might be drawn between freeze-frame and animated sequences. Apart from these small-scale programmes, all major German and Swiss channels are distributed by cable networks. The Austrian cable market is highly concentrated, with Philips (Netherlands) and Siemens (Germany) controlling over 60% of the market. In Vienna, in economic terms the most interesting region in Austria, with a household cable penetration of 48%, Telekabel holds the local de facto monopoly.

Structure, organization, ownership and finance

The ORF has its headquarters in Vienna and operates a radio and television studio in every *Land*. Since the broadcasting reforms in 1984 there is more emphasis on regional programme production, and in May 1988 all the regional studios of the ORF started producing local television news, a reaction to the international trend towards localization. The radio channels are directed at different target groups. The first and national channel broadcasts classical music and high quality information programmes. The second channel is mainly devoted to popular Austrian folk music transmitted by the regional studios. The third channel is nationwide and broadcasts light entertainment and pop music targeted to the youth sector. The fourth channel, Blue Danube Radio, is also transmitted all over Austria, with programmes in foreign languages; it was originally planned to serve the international community of employees of the United Nations in Vienna and their families. During the debate on the new Regional Radio Act 1993, the existence of this fourth channel was challenged, as private radio operators claimed the frequencies for their purposes and the Broadcasting Act foresees only three ORF radio channels – without, however, preventing the ORF from extending this minimum.

As regards language and ethnic minorities, the ORF is obliged by the Broadcasting Act to cater for the expression of their culture in its programmes.

Because of the size and geographical location of the country, some 15% of households are able to receive foreign television and radio (terrestrial reception). As early as 1956 the first cable network was established in the most western part of Austria to make pilot broadcasting transmissions available to the public. Steady growth of cable-connected households started in the early 1980s, reaching by early 1997 some 36% of television households (22% in 1990). Together with the rapidly expanding satellite reception in Austria (36% at the beginning of 1997 from 2% in 1990), more than three-quarters of all Austrian households receive foreign television channels one way or another.

In the aftermath of political change in Austria's eastern neighbouring countries, new programme suppliers have entered the electronic media market. Based in (then) Czechoslovakia and Hungary, some private Austrian business people started pirate radio stations, following the example in southern Austria. Since the early 1970s some pirate stations have conquered audience (and advertising) market shares in Carinthia, where they have even managed to provide an Italy-based television channel. While these pirate radio stations were considered marginal, since they did not manage to reach the central area of Vienna, the pirates from the East competed on almost equal footing with the third ORF radio channel. When in 1993 the Regional Radio Act was released, most former pirates grouped together and applied for regular Austrian licences. In parallel, authorities in the Slovak Republic refused the extension of the frequency contracts, resulting in the disappearance of most of the pirate radios.

With an annual turnover of some AS9.8 bn (726 m ECU; financial year 1995) the ORF is financially rather large compared to the public service broadcasters in other small states in Europe. Forty-four per cent of the income is derived equally from licence fees and from advertising, with the latter having progressively grown (40% in 1989). With some 2758 employees and several thousand freelance workers, the ORF is by far the largest media company in the country. However, as a result of financial constraints the company has reduced its permanent personnel by almost 15% between 1989 and 1997 (from over 3200 to below 2800).

As regards advertising, the ORF (radio and television) gained in 1996 some 34% of all advertising revenue in Austria, with newspapers and magazines taking 59% of the cake. Compared to other west European countries, the share of television (23%) is relatively low. During the first half of the 1990s the overall advertising market has expanded at an average annual growth rate of some 10%. Within a decade advertising expenditure per capita has tripled from AS654 in 1983 to AS1997 in 1994 (according to Nielsen data).

Programme policy

ORF has expanded its daily transmission substantially over recent years. Since March 1995 both television channels are broadcasting for 24 hours each. This decision was taken by the Director-General, appointed in 1994 together with far-reaching programme reforms. One channel is now dedicated almost entirely to light entertainment, talk shows and movies, while the other channel fulfills the classic requirements of a public service broadcaster. The concept is based on the slogan '*One programme on two channels*' and is clearly oriented towards private competitors from Germany available in Austria by cable and satellite – with growing market shares.

Austrian adults spent in 1996 on average 148 minutes every day watching television, 43 minutes more than in 1989 and representing almost two thirds of the freely available leisure time. At the national level (adults), the market share of the ORF declined from 77% in 1991 to 62% in 1996. In cable and satellite households, channels from outside Austria increased their market share up to 57% in 1996. However, the strongest foreign competitor, RTL, reached 9% while ORF1 and ORF2 still hold the lead with 20% and 28% respectively in 1996 (ORF Medienforschung, 1996). Also in terms of daily reach the two ORF channels are doing rather well, with 44% and 46% of the population, with RTL following third with 25% (adults in cable and satellite households 1996).

As regards the programme schedule (before the reform of 1995), some 37% of broadcasting time is allocated to entertainment, 21% to news and culture and 9% to sport (1994). This distribution is by and large paralleled by consumption habits, with 43% of all viewing time dedicated to entertainment programmes, 27% to news and culture and 13% to sport (adults 1994).

Resulting from constant expansion of air time, the ORF has been forced to buy inexpensive programmes of the international series type, produced in the USA, Germany or the UK. 'This has led to the "self-commercialisation" of the public service' (Fabris and Luger, 1986). This tendency has continued from 1986 to 1995, most significantly with the 1995 programme reform. For the majority of the population, TV is used mainly for entertainment. The most popular programmes, with a reach of over 50%, are Austrian folk music shows, international crime series and game shows, mainly produced in West Germany.

Radio programming is much more decentralized in Austria. Each of the nine *Länder* studios produces its own programmes carrying regional and local content for the second channel. Programme reform in 1990 changed the radio schedule radically; aiming to meet the needs and habits of the population better, more time was dedicated to local affairs, and on the popular third channel the structure is now more oriented towards that of the successful private commercial radio stations in Switzerland and Germany.

Local TV and radio

In Spring 1993, the government presented a Bill on Regional Radio, which was adopted by the parliament in July 1993. The Act enables the licensing of one radio broadcaster in each of the Austrian *Länder* (two in Vienna) to transmit radio programmes to the regional audience. The law distinguishes between regional and local radio stations, the difference being that regional radio has the right to cover the whole of a *Land*, while local stations will simply address the programme to the local area of their transmitter. This law took over 10 years to come into being, although the result is not convincing. Not only can regional newspaper publishers apply for licences within their region of distribution (up to 26% of the shares), they can also participate as shareholders in other stations (up to 10% of the shares). Despite the fact that the Austrian media market is one of the highest concentrated world-wide, the Regional Radio Act provides for more cross-ownership. Furthermore, the Act excludes all kinds of non-commercial radios on the regional level, as all frequencies are dedicated to applicants financed by advertising. The journalists' association and the opposition parties criticized the law for enforcement of multi-media and cross-ownership concentration.

By the end of 1996, the frequencies for the regional stations were allocated. In all but one case, the applicants represented by the dominating regional newspaper were chosen by the Regional Radio Office, set up by law. By January 1997, however, only two regional radio stations were on air, because unsuccessful candidates decided to contest the decisions of the Office before the Austrian Constitutional Court. In the cases of Styria and Salzburg, the competitors for the licences entered into agreement with the licence holders and therefore these radio stations were permitted to broadcast. In May 1995 the Constitutional Court decided to suspend all other licences. The Court held that the economic harm that this judgment might do to the successful candidates appeared less serious than would be the effects of competition on the present unsuccessful candidates if new grants of licences were to be made. In October 1995 the Court furthermore dismissed parts of the Regional Radio Act as unconstitutional, making it necessary to start the whole licensing procedure again. Parliament passed the necessary legal amendment in March 1997.

In anticipation of private competitors, the ORF re-adjusted the radio programme schedule as early as 1989 to emphasize local coverage. Local radio programmes had been introduced in 1981, with local television operated by the ORF following in May 1988. There is a half-hour local television feature daily at 1830 h on the second channel produced by the *Länder* studios.

Foreign media availability

Austria's media market is traditionally penetrated by press products from Germany. While the magazine and book market is particularly under firm control of German producers in terms of market shares, rather the opposite is true of television and radio. The audience still prefers the domestic channels even when foreign channels are available. By 1997 some 25 television channels were available on cable networks, only two of them being Austrian. The most important competitors as regards market share are the German-language private and public service channels RTL, SAT1, PRO7, ARD and ZDF. Channels broadcasting in languages other than German are available (CNN and MTV being the most successful), but account for insignificant market shares.

Policies for the press and broadcasting

Main actors and interests

Efficient media policy is unknown in Austria for at least two reasons. First, there is no central administration like a 'Ministry of Communications' acting as a powerful regulator. Competencies are spread over several ministries, including the Federal Chancellery. No standing committee or commission constantly observes the media landscape. What prevails is policy directed by powerful interest groups and lobbies without transparency, making carefully balanced policy measures according to principles of common sense or public interest literally impossible.

Second, media policy in Austria is one of the areas where corporatist structures predominate over market forces. The 'iron triumvirate', consisting of the political parties, the ORF and the Publishers' Association, has kept all developments under its firm control for decades. Neither the government nor the parliament have so far consequently adopted a coherent and active media policy. As early as 1964 – when broadcasting was still in its infancy – the publishers declared their interest in the relatively new medium. They launched a referendum concerning the organization and programming structure of the ORF. All further developments in the electronic sector can be seen as the result of the search for compromise and agreement between publishers and the ORF. In both of these organizations party interests are strongly represented. In 1985 the Publishers' Association and the ORF signed an agreement concerning the division of advertising between the media. The ORF extended its weekly advertising time to include Sundays and public holidays, but agreed to accept no regional advertising to the benefit of the print media.

Public debates on media policy virtually do not take place. Not even the Regional Radio Act in 1993 provoked a fully fledged policy orientation debate, despite being an essential ingredient for a democratic society. Actually, media policy is limited to efforts aimed at maintaining the monopolistic position of public service television – with lip service being paid to deregulation – on the one hand and leaving the print media and their subsidies undisturbed on the other.

Main issues

Opportunities to start a more comprehensive debate were offered frequently during the early 1990s:

- Following the 1990 elections, there was a government declaration on the gradual opening of the monopoly broadcasting system in Austria, renewed after the parliamentary elections in 1994. There was no significant follow-up.
- In 1992 a federal government report on satellite broadcasting, an issue which formed part of the working programme of the government, stated that the cultural and economic benefits of transmitting ORF channels over satellites would not justify the operational costs.
- The amendment of the Cartel Act in 1993 made mergers above a joint turnover of the involved companies of AS3.5 bn (250 m ECU) compulsorily notifiable, with a considerably lower limit for mergers in the media sector (joint turnover of AS17.5 m, 1.3 m ECU). The Court also has to examine the possible threat to media diversity and pluralism, but this amendment came at a point in time when the important mergers in the Austrian media market had already been effected (Mediaprint, *Kronenzeitung*, *Kurier*).
- The Regional Radio Act and the amendment of the Broadcasting Act transposing the European Union's Television Directive 89/552/EEC, were both adopted by parliament in 1993. The amendment to conform with European standards was necessary following the accession of Austria first to the European Economic Area (1994) and later to the European Union (1995). As the Austrian Broadcasting Act did not differ in substance from the EU Directive, the changes were relatively insignificant.
- On 24 November 1993 a judgment of the European Court of Human Rights in Strasbourg went against Austria in the case of Informationsverein Lentia. Five applicants went to the Court after having exhausted the national institutions, claiming the right to transmit sound broadcasting (radio) and in one case television broadcasting, based on art. 10 of the European Convention on Human Rights. The Court held finally that the exclusivity of the ORF in Austria is a violation of art. 10. The Court

pointed out in its justification of the judgment that the principle of pluralism is an important and legitimate feature of state media policy, but the monopolistic position of a single broadcaster is a means which '*imposes the greatest restrictions on the freedom of expression, namely the total impossibility of broadcasting otherwise than through a national station* . . .' (quote from the judgment). Consequently, the Austrian broadcasting legislation is to be considered as violating the European Convention on Human Rights, but there are no immediate legal consequences for the Austrian legislature and the government has resisted political pressure to bring forward legislation in line with the Convention so far.

- Finally, first the granting of licences to regional radio operators and then the declaration of the Regional Radio Act and the frequency plan was deemed unconstitutional by the Austrian Constitutional Court in 1995.

All these events failed to convince either the political parties or the government of the need to present a comprehensive vision of the media in the future. Only the appointment of a new Director-General of the ORF dominated the public debate for weeks, but this is very much in the Austrian tradition of regarding media policy mainly as personal policy.

Policy trends

Generally, the Austrian media system is fully integrated into the European media order by its participation in the European Union and its membership in the Council of Europe and the Audiovisual EUREKA. However, the implications of these institutions for the national media policy have been fairly limited during the 1980s, whilst becoming more important in the early 1990s. As national media policy did not present visionary or at least conceptional policy guidelines, it became increasingly the courts where the initiative finally was taken. First there was the 1993 judgment in Strasbourg, declaring the Austrian broadcasting policy inconsistent with the European Convention on Human Rights, then in 1995 the national Constitutional Court dismissed parts of the first new broadcasting (radio) law since 1974 as unconstitutional.

Austria entered the European Union with an economically quite healthy media system, with strong national actors at the level of the press and at the level of the public service broadcaster. The fact that there was at the time of accession no competition in the broadcasting market enabled the ORF to adapt its programming to changing consumption habits without being challenged by a national competitor. It would have been the right time to discuss in detail and in an open forum a new policy concept for the development of a media system in Austria, capable of dealing with the challenges of the upcoming Information Society.

Statistics

(1 ECU = 13.5 Austrian schillings, AS)

Population (1995)

Number of inhabitants	8.05 million
Geographical size	84 000 km^2
Population density	95.2 per km^2
Number of households	3.25 million

Broadcasting (1997)

Number of national TV channels	2
Number of regional TV channels	0
Number of national radio channels	4
Number of regional radio channels	2

Household media equipment	1997	1994
Households with TV sets	96%	96%
VCR	69%	62%
Cable households	36%	35%
Satellite households	36%	27%
PC/home computer	28%	14%
CD player	67%	52%
Car radio	75%	72%

Source: ORF Radiotest, Optima Analyse

The press (1997)

Number of daily newspapers 17

Readership and circulation for the 10 biggest newspapers (1995/1996)

	Readership (1996) '000	(1996) %	Copies printed	Copies sold
**Neue Kronenzeitung*	2700	42.2	1 075 000	N.A.
**Kurier*	807	12.3	325 000	N.A.
**Täglich Alles*†	800	12.2	544 000	N.A.
Kleine Zeitung	748	11.4	298 000	233 000
Der Standard	354	5.4	93 500	63 000
Oberösterreichische Nachrichten (OÖN)	348	5.3	127 000	107 000
Tiroler Tageszeitung	318	4.8	99 000	84 000
Salzburger Nachrichten	281	4.3	93 000	62 000
Die Presse	311	4.7	103 000	72 000
Vorarlberger Nachrichten	206	3.1	73 500	64 000

* These papers no longer publish figures on circulation or sales and they do not participate in the Circulation Control System in Austria, therefore the circulation figures are from the publishers themselves.
† Figure for printed copies from 1993. N.A., not available.

Source: KOMDAT, Media analyse 1996, ÖAK, VÖZ

Advertising – total spend and division between media (1996)

	AS bn	ECU m	%
Daily newspapers	5.39	399	32
Regional/magazines	4.47	331	27
Special interest			
Press total	9.85	731	59
Radio	1.78	132	11
Television	3.83	284	23
Electronic media total	5.61	416	34
Outdoor	1.17	86	7
Total	16.64	1.233	100

Source: Focus Media

References

Aiginger, Karl and Peneder, Michael (1993) 'Ökonomische Grundbedingungen der Printmedienbranche. Endbericht'. Research Report, University of Salzburg, p. 52.

Bruck, Peter and Melcher-Smejkal, Iris (eds) (1993) 'Printmedien'. Institut für Publizistik, pp. 57–91.

Fabris, Hans-Heinz (1989) 'Kleinstaatliche Medienentwicklung im Europa der "Großen". Das Beispiel Österreich', *Rundfunk und Fernsehen*, 2–3: 240–50.

Fabris, Hans-Heinz and Luger, Kurt (1986) 'Austria', in Hans J. Kleinsteuber, Denis McQuail, Karen Siune (eds), *Electronic Media and Politics in Western Europe*. Euromedia Research Group Handbook of National Systems. Frankfurt/New York: Campus, pp. 1–16.

Fabris, Hans-Heinz, Luger, Kurt, and Signitzer, Benno (1990) 'Das Rundfunksystem Österreichs', in Hans-Bredow-Institut (ed.), *Internationales Handbuch für Rundfunk und Fernshen*. Baden-Baden: Nomos, pp. D168–D183.

Institut für Publizistik und Kommunikationswissenschaft der Universität Salzburg (ed.) (1977, 1983, 1986, 1993) *Massenmedien in Österreich-Medienbericht*, I, II, III, IV. Vienna.

Lankes, Gertraud (1990) 'Österreichs Pressemarkt im Umbruch', in Verband österreichischer Zeitungsherausgeber und Zeitungsverleger (ed.), *Pressehandbuch 1990*. Vienna, pp. 11–13.

Latzer, Michael (1996) 'Cable TV in Austria: Between telecommunications and broadcasting', *Telecommunications Policy*, 20(4): 291–301.

Luger, Kurt and Steinmaurer, Thomas (1990) 'Die Medien-Megamorphose. Österreichs Medienlandschaftim Umbruch', *Rundfunk und Fernsehen*, 2: 242–58.

Muller-Rabler, Ursula (1996) 'Austrian Information Highway initiatives in the stage of disillusionment', *Telematics and Information*, 13(2/3): 111–21.

ORF Medienforschung (1996) *Daten und Fakten zur Fernsehnutzung in Österreich*. Vienna: ORF.

Paupié, Kurt (1960) '*Handbuch der österreichischen Pressegeschichte 1948–1959*', vol. 1. Vienna.

Pürer, Heinz (1988) 'Österreichs Mediensystem im Wandel. Ein aktueller Lagebericht', *Media Perspektiven*, 11: 673–82.

Schrotta, Werner (1981) 'Die wirtschaftliche Entwicklung der österreichischen Tageszeitungen nach 1945', in Amt der OÖ. Landesregierung (ed.), *Das älteste Periodikum der Welt*. Linz, pp. 57–60.

Steinmaurer, Thomas (1996) 'Das Rundfunksystem Österreichs', in Hans-Bredow Institut (ed.), *Internationales Handbuch für Hörfunk und Fernsehen 1996/7*. Baden-Baden: Nomos, pp. C168–C180.

Trappel, Josef (1992) 'Austria' in Bernt Stubbe Østergaard (ed.), *The Media in Western Europe*. The Euromedia Handbook. London/Newbury Park: Sage, pp. 1–15.

2

Belgium

Els De Bens

National profile

Belgium is a small and densely populated country: 10.068 million people inhabit an area of 30 528 km^2 (330 inhabitants per km^2). Almost 909 000 people are foreign nationals (9%). Because Brussels is also the capital of the EU and of NATO, more than half the foreigners are European or American citizens; the majority of the other foreigners are migrant workers from southern Europe, the Magreb and Turkey.

The largest part of the population (5.825 million, i.e. 58%) lives in the Flemish region; 3.225 million (i.e. 32%) in the French-speaking part; 68 000 (i.e. 0.6%) in the German-speaking region, and 950 000 people (i.e. 9.4%) live in the bilingual area of Brussels. The population is relatively old (15% aged over 65 years); many families are childless and only 37% of the inhabitants belong to the active working population.

As a result of a number of constitutional reforms, Belgium has developed more and more towards a federalized country. This has led to a devolution of power from the central government to the regional governments (the Communities). Belgium today has a very complicated state structure, with a multitude of departments and services, so that bureaucracy is omnipresent.

Belgium has a multi-party system with a preponderance of Christian democrats in Flanders and socialists in the Walloon part. No party has a clear majority, so that coalition governments prevail.

Belgium is a highly industrialized country, with a high standard of living. More and more multinational companies have established their administrative headquarters in Brussels.

The gross national product in 1994 was Bfr7660 bn (201.6 bn ECU), which is Bfr760 826 per capita. Belgium has a good social security system; 13% of the active population is unemployed.

Development of the press and broadcasting since 1945

Print media

The Second World War caused many shifts in the world of the Belgian press. Newspapers that had appeared during the war were brought before special courts in the post-war period of repression, which was much harsher than after the First World War. Not only collaborationist papers were prohibited, because they had acted as active propaganda outlets, but also newspapers that had only opted for a policy of 'being present'. All journalists who had worked for a paper during the war were prosecuted and had to submit to a ban on writing. This led to the eventual discontinuation of many pre-war papers and caused the disappearance of a complete generation of journalists.

Additionally, the state of inactivity during the four years of occupation proved fatal for a fairly large number of newspapers. In this way, tens of papers disappeared indirectly as a result of the war.

Of the 65 pre-war newspapers, only 39 continued to appear after the war. Even so, a number of new initiatives were taken to fill the gaps. Between 1944 and 1947, 20 newspapers were launched, but 17 of them had disappeared again by as early as 1947. The number of titles continued to decrease over the years: by 1997 only 26 daily newspapers were being published by seven newspaper groups!

The concentration phenomenon in Belgium manifested itself mainly after 1945, more particularly from the 1960s onwards. Originally, the large newspaper groups were owned by individual families but gradually they became the property of financial holdings.

Belgium has always had a press with a clearly distinguishable political opinion. In Flanders it was the Catholic press that always dominated. Between the world wars the socialist newspapers thrived to some extent in both communities, but after the Second World War the socialist press lost its hold. The so-called neutral press was only successful in French-speaking Belgium. In the period 1975–7 there was a drastic fall in circulation for almost all newspapers. This sudden change can probably be explained by the large price increases for newspapers and by the onset of an era of economic crisis. After 1977 the papers regained their circulation of before 1975.

After the Second World War the Flemish press gradually caught up. From 1975 onwards it prevailed over the Walloon press (51% vs. 49%). The tendency became even more pronounced in the following years and as of 1997 the proportions are 60% (Flemish) vs. 40% (Walloon).

The broadcasting system

After the Second World War the public broadcasting system in Belgium was given an absolute monopoly. Television broadcasting was introduced fairly late (1953) in Belgium, which was largely due to the fact that Belgian television sets needed to be very complicated because they had to be able to work with both the French 819 line system and the European standard of 625 lines used elsewhere.

In May 1960 a new law was passed creating two autonomous broadcasting institutions, one for Flanders (BRT) and one for Wallonia (RTBF).

Another new law in February 1977 created the Belgisches Fernsehen und Rundfunk (BFR) for the German-speaking part of Belgium.

As radio and television commercials remained illegal (until September 1987 in Wallonia and February 1989 in Flanders), licence fees constituted the sole source of revenue for the PSB. Over the years the BRT and RTBF have received only a fraction (50–60%) of the revenue from licence fees. Every year the budgets of the PSB had to be accepted by the Flemish and Wallonian governments.

An important factor that determined the audiovisual landscape of Belgium was the setting up of the cable networks in 1960. By the middle of the 1970s half of all households had been connected to a cable network. Today Belgium is the most densely cabled country of the world (94% of all TV households). Initially the cable companies only distributed the national programmes, but very soon the output of foreign TV stations was distributed as well. At first, only the foreign public service channels were given access to the cable, but gradually some commercial stations were admitted as well.

As TV commercials were forbidden, the law provided for the cable operators to cut out the commercials! In practice, no such thing ever happened. In point of fact, cutting out commercials is contrary to the EU stipulation of 'the free exchange of services' (art. 59 and art. 60 of the EC Treaty of Rome). Moreover, the European Court of Justice decided in its decree of 30 April 1974 that all television programmes – including commercials – are to be considered 'services'. Legal action taken in Belgium against the cable companies by consumers' organizations failed to change this situation.

The attitude displayed by the Belgian authorities in this affair was one of hypocrisy. The first commercial station to be allowed on the cable was RTL. In 1983 the RTT (Regie van Telegrafie en Telefonie) even supplied an extra microwave link so that RTL would be able to reach Flemish TV families more easily. This apparent indulgence of the Belgian authorities towards RTL may stem from the fact that the Groupe Bruxelles Lambert (GBL) has a long-standing majority participation in RTL, through its holding company Audiofina. When the Belgian banker and media tycoon Albert Frère took over GBL in 1982, RTL became even more 'Belgian', and enjoyed considerable success, taking away a large part of the audience, especially from RTBF.

The factual monopoly of the PSB was indirectly undermined by the cable networks, which were offering an increasing number of TV stations. RTBF was losing viewers to RTL and the French channels, BRT to the Netherlands and to a certain degree to France and Germany and Great Britain.

The issue of TV advertising became a crucial one. The political parties were divided over it. BRT and RTBF joined the debate: they demanded at least a partial, but preferably the exclusive right for radio and television advertising. It was not inconceivable that the decreasing audience ratings would be seized upon as a pretext to cut the allocated percentage of licence fees. Meanwhile, the ever-growing politicization of the PSB created a climate of public opinion in which the monopoly position of the PSB was increasingly resented: political pressure stifled the broadcasting system; job promotions were not awarded according to qualifications, but because of party loyalty.

The public broadcasting systems themselves were partly to blame: they had readily joined the political game, and as a result of their many years of 'inapproachability' in Belgium, both BRT and RTBF occasionally gave evidence of paternalistic and conceited traits. The permanently appointed employees, moreover, enjoyed the status of civil servants, and especially in the creative sectors this has proved too rigid and bureaucratic, often nipping creativity in the bud.

All of these factors created a climate of public opinion in Belgium that became more and more receptive to the idea of a breaching of the monopoly. A number of private enterprises, and the world of finance at large, stimulated the introduction of radio and television advertising.

The PSB monopoly was first undermined by the illegal local radio stations. In September 1981 these stations were legalized in Wallonia, and in May 1982 the same happened in Flanders. The monopoly of RTBF and BRT came to an end. Advertising remained illegal at first, but under political and commercial pressure, the ban on radio advertising was lifted in December 1985. The television monopoly was broken in law in 1987. The legal framework and the development of the new commercial channels together with their impact on the public broadcasting system will be dealt with extensively below in the section on the present situation of the electronic media.

The press

Policy framework

Belgium's constitution guarantees the complete freedom of the press. Articles 14 and 18 prohibit any form of preventive censorship, and repressive measures can be taken only if freedom of speech is revealed to have been abused.

In the case of offences against the press code a special guarantee is provided in art. 98, which provides that such offences do not fall within the competence of an ordinary criminal court, but must be referred to the Court of Assizes, the so-called 'People's Court', where a jury is to pass judgment. This procedure obviously protects the journalist, since public opinion is more likely to side with the press.

The law does provide for a number of restrictions on the freedom of the press. They are derived from fundamental rights, such as the individual's right to privacy and the individual's protection against defamation. Further restrictions are based on the need to safeguard the public interest (national security, moral standards, the monarchy etc.).

When ownership concentration hit the Belgian press in the 1960s, no specific antitrust legislation was enacted in Belgium. Belgium has no cross-ownership regulation. The only measure taken to preserve the pluralistic character of the press was the establishment of a system of subsidies. In fact, the government had been helping the Belgian press indirectly since the end of the Second World War, by means of reduced rates (mail, telephone, railway transport, paper and zero VAT rate). In 1974 non-selective direct subsidies were introduced.

From the outset the system misfired, since all newspapers, including the prosperous ones, initially received the same amount. This non-selective direct subsidy system, therefore, did not change the existing imbalance. Moreover, the sum to be distributed was small, about Bfr200 m (5.3 m ECU) and insufficient to save newspapers in distress. Later, a complex and partly selective system was adopted, giving small papers a trifle more than their larger and stronger colleagues. In the meantime, however, the overall subsidy itself had gradually become smaller.

The major groups

Not only has the process of concentration resulted in a lower number of newspapers, it has also led to an even stronger decrease in the number of independent papers. Of today's 26 papers, a mere 10 are truly autonomous; the remaining 16 papers are parallel editions of the main papers, and differ only slightly from them.

In Flanders the market is controlled by three groups: VUM (*De Standaard, Het Nieuwsblad, De Gentenaar, Het Volk*), De Persgroep (*Het Laatste Nieuws, De Nieuwe Gazet, De Morgen*) and RUG, a new alliance between two newspaper groups – NV De Vlijt (*Gazet van Antwerpen*) and NV Concentra (*Het Belang van Limburg*).

The two latest takeovers, that of the leftist daily *De Morgen* and the Christian-democratic *Het Volk*, again raised the question of whether the pluralism of the press is threatened.

In 1986 the socialist party decided to cut its financial support for *De Morgen*. The reasons for the party's decision were twofold: on the one hand, the party was losing its hold on the editorial staff, which wanted to steer a more independent course; on the other, the paper's debts were becoming quite a burden. Once the decision was taken, the editors sounded the alarm and succeeded in setting up a heroic rescue operation, in which it was mainly the readers who raised money. The paper managed to hold out until the end of 1988, when the financial losses were discovered to have become even larger, and in January 1989 the paper was bought by the centrist-liberal group NV Hoste-Van Thillo (De Persgroep). A deal was struck with the new owner that the paper was to be allowed to maintain its progressive image, but it remains open to discussion whether this arrangement will stand the test of time.

In November 1994, the Christian-democratic Het Volk newspaper group was taken over by the Flemish market leader VUM (De Standaardgroep). This takeover was resented because *Het Volk* still had a circulation of about 164 000, although over the years sales figures had diminished (in 1985 the circulation was 200 000). Revenue from advertising had also declined, so that the Christian trade union decided to get rid of the newspaper.

After the takeover of these two newspapers, the remaining press groups have strengthened their monopoly position. If the two dailies had not been taken over by the press groups they might, of course, already have disappeared. This is one of the dilemmas that media policy has to face. The recent alliance between NV De Vlijt and NV Concentra, both publishers of mainly regional newspapers, was caused by the financial problems of NV De Vlijt; the newspapers of both groups will keep their editorial autonomy.

Belgium's French-language press is dominated by only three large groups: NV Rossel (*Le Soir, La Meuse, La Lanterne, La Nouvelle Gazette, La Province*), SIPM (*La Libre Belgique, La Dernière Heure*) and Vers l'Avenir (*Vers l'Avenir, Le Jour/Le Courrier, Le Courrier de l'Escaut, L'Avenir de Luxembourg, Le Rappel*). In 1986 and 1987 three smaller independent papers had to close down or were taken over: the Brussels Catholic paper *La Cité*, the Catholic group around *Le Rappel* (based in Charleroi, along with *l'Echo du Centre* and *Journal de Mons*) and a neutral independent paper in Verviers, *Le Jour*, were bought by the group Vers l'Avenir. The main shareholder of Vers l'Avenir is the diocese of Namur. In March 1995 Vers l'Avenir obtained 32.3% of SIPM (*La Dernière Heure, La Libre Belgique*), so that the francophone press is approaching a duopoly situation: Rossel and SIPM/Vers l'Avenir.

The socialist newspapers have small circulation figures: *Le Peuple, Le Journal de Charleroi* and *La Wallonie* have been integrated in the Rossel group but with editorial autonomy; all three newspapers still have close links with the socialist party.

Initially, all the seven newspaper concerns were family enterprises, but gradually they came to be controlled by financial holdings and banking institutions. Their ownership structure continues to be Belgian, with the exception of the Rossel group: in 1989 Hersant succeeded in acquiring a 40% stake in the group.

All these groups have tended to become multi-media enterprises in the past few years. Quite a number of newspaper groups publish weeklies and free-distribution advertising papers. Most Belgian newspapers have participated in local radio and regional TV. They have also achieved participation in the new commercial television stations.

Grenz-Echo is published in the German-speaking part of Belgium. It was founded in 1927 and is a Catholic newspaper, published by an independent publishing house. The circulation is 11 000. Recently (1996) 50% of the shares were taken over by Rossel.

Belgium has two financial dailies: *De Financieel – Economische Tijd*, a Flemish independent daily, and *L'Echo*, the francophone financial newspaper of which Rossel has obtained 14.5% of the shares, SIPM 9.09% and Vers l'Avenir 4.5%.

Financial aspects: circulation, advertising and marketing strategies

In 1996 the overall circulation of the Belgian press amounted to 1 884 591, the Flemish press taking 60.06%, while the French-language press share was 39.3%.

Belgians do not subscribe to a newspaper in great numbers (only 36%), so by far the bulk of the circulation of the Belgian dailies (some 70%) is sold in single copies. This implies that the publishers are always left with a substantial number of unsold copies, and in the case of smaller newspapers this number is relatively high, since a sufficient number of copies have to be presented at the sales outlets anyway.

Circulation figures have been declining slightly in the past five years. Young people in particular read fewer newspapers. Dailies that have recently succeeded in increasing their market share owe this to a more popular tabloid strategy. As competition becomes severe in a saturated daily newspaper market, most dailies have tried to develop a 'new look', have added new columns, new inserts, new and better distribution systems.

Production costs have increased (especially for wages and promotion activities): between 1988 and 1994 costs had risen by 31%. Publishers who were confronted with cuts in sales revenue also had to face declining revenues from advertising. Commercial advertising had to cope with the competition of commercial TV; classified advertising fell as a result of the economic recession. In Belgium the share of classified advertising is low in comparison with other European countries.

Publishers again have reacted and developed strategies to make their newspapers more attractive to advertisers. In spite of the success of commercial TV, the print media still have the highest market share of advertising – 44% for print media versus 34.6% for TV advertising – but 10 years ago the advertising share of the print media was 70.1%. De Standaard-groep (VUM) as well as *Le Soir* (Rossel) are the market leaders for both sales and advertising revenues.

Quality and popular press

Belgium does not have genuine popular papers or tabloids such as the UK's *Sun*, or quality papers such as *Le Monde* in France. *De Standaard* and *De Morgen* as well as *La Libre Belgique* and *Le Soir* assume a somewhat more serious attitude; the others tend to present a more popular image.

The Belgian press is strongly characterized by its political leanings. Only the Rossel group publishes 'neutral' newspapers.

In Flanders, 71.93% of the newspapers have a Catholic orientation, whereas 24.16% are liberal and 3.89% socialist. The share of the Catholic press has continued to increase in recent years.

In French-speaking Belgium 28.70% of the papers belong to the Catholic press, 24.99% are liberal, 5.55% are socialist and the majority, that is 40.74%, are neutral, not following any party line.

Clearly, there is a striking discrepancy between how Belgians vote and what newspapers they read: the share of the Catholic newspapers in the overall circulation figures of the Flemish press is larger than the number of people who vote for the Flemish Catholic party, and the socialist parties in Flanders as well as in Wallonia have more voters than there are readers of socialist papers.

As a result of commercial pressure, newspapers pay less attention to the analysis of political and socio-economic news; editorials have disappeared from the front page or from the newspaper altogether. More human interest news, more extensive sports pages, bigger titles, smaller articles and more, often very sensational, pictures fill up the papers.

Distribution and technology

The large newspaper enterprises rely partly on direct distribution. In addition to direct distribution they also use the services of a specialized distribution agency, Agence et Messageries de la Presse, which enjoys a near monopoly in Belgium.

In view of the recurrent train strikes and the less than perfect postal service, the large concerns are trying to build up distribution systems of their own. Hence, the distribution of the papers adds a substantial element to the cost price of the newspapers.

All Belgian papers have changed over to on-line systems. The switch-over was carried out fairly smoothly in nearly all cases and certainly did not lead to serious social unrest, as was the case in the UK.

Broadcasting

Legal framework

The legal framework of the public broadcasting system has already been discussed above in the historical overview. The different causes which led to the break-up of the PSB monopoly have been explained as well.

Although Wallonia had established the legal framework for commercial television by means of the law of 28 January 1987, and Flanders with the law of 17 July 1987, a considerable period of time was to elapse before the new commercial stations could actually start their operations.

In order to make commercial television possible, a new law had to be passed allowing commercial TV advertising. Belgium has a very complex government structure, and since at the time commercial advertising was still within the national jurisdiction, it was the national government that first had to establish the legal framework. This was done by means of the law of 6 February 1987. However, the law was vague on many points: it was 'forgotten' to stipulate how much, when and how television advertising had to be programmed. A supplementary Royal Decree (3 August 1987) detailed that commercial advertising had to be grouped in non-consecutive blocks, of which the total duration should not surpass an annual average of 12 minutes per hour of broadcasting, while each individual block should last no longer than 6 minutes maximum.

As a consequence of the constitutional reforms, the authority over commercial advertising was transferred to the Communities from 1 January 1989 onwards.

The launch of commercial TV stations

In the French-speaking part of Belgium the preparations for the establishment of a new commercial station had been going on long before the decree of 17 July 1987. RTL had been the unofficial Belgian commercial station for many years, as one of the main shareholders is a Belgian bank holding. In the past RTL obtained more than half of its advertising revenue from the Belgian advertising market.

In 1986 negotiations between RTL and the Executive Council of the French Community led to an agreement. After the passing of the law on commercial advertising (6 February 1987) and the decree of 17 July 1987, everything went very quickly; RTL-TVi received its licence as expected. RTL has a 66% stake and Audiopresse (the Belgian Francophone dailies group), 34%. The Walloon decree refers to 'private television stations', in the plural, which contradicts the national law of 6 February 1987. For the time being, however, there is no danger to the monopoly of RTL-TVi. The licence has been granted for nine years. In return for its advertising monopoly RTL-TVi has to invest in the audiovisual industry of Wallonia.

A fairly rosy future was originally predicted for RTL-TVi, because it could fall back on an existing audience and on the large film and television archives of CLT. Moreover, participation in national commercial television projects fits in perfectly with the new media strategy of CLT. Instead of becoming the big pan-European channel, CLT has opted for decentralization: RTL (Germany), RTL-TVi (Belgium), RTL4 (The Netherlands) etc. The international advertising world is clearly more interested in segmented national TV markets than in one all-encompassing pan-European one.

RTL-TVi did, however, encounter unforeseen competition. The privatized French channel TF1 attracted more and more Belgian viewers with its popular programming. In January 1996 the French stations TF1, FR2 and A3 attracted 40% of the Belgian French-speaking TV viewers as against 18.3% for RTBF and 23.5% for RTL-TVi and Club RTL (see below). The rest of the viewing share went to other channels. The revenue for RTL-TVi kept diminishing. RTBF, which had always claimed the right to broadcast advertising and was losing viewers to TF1 in the same way as RTL-TVi, made a deal with RTL-TVi.

In June 1989 a decree granted RTBF permission to broadcast television advertising together with RTL-TVi from 1 September 1989 onwards. This 'amalgamation' did not lead to the hoped for result because, instead of an increase in the advertising volume, part of RTL-TVi's advertising was simply transferred to RTBF. In a clever arrangement RTL-TVi had anticipated this possibility and had made sure that part of the revenue would go back to RTL-TVi, which left the RTBF as 'poor' as before: advertising revenue was distributed 24% to RTBF and 76% to RTL-TVi. In 1997 the collaboration of RTBF and RTL came to an end and RTBF now has its own advertising service.

In February 1995 RTL launched a new commercial channel Club RTL, with an overall programme, offering at least one feature film every night.

In Flanders the cable decree of 17 January 1987 legalized commercial TV but it took a considerable period of time before a national Flemish commercial station could start its operations. The decree envisaged several types of non-public television station, but on the national level the monopoly was given to a single channel – VTM – and for 18 years at that! (RTL-TVi received a licence for only nine years.) The lobby of the Flemish daily and weekly press was given satisfaction to a large degree: the law stipulates that 51% of the shares in the TV company have to be owned by them. Later, it turned out that the VTM shares were owned almost 100% by the press!

The EU disapproved of the 51% rule as well as of the TV advertising monopoly of VTM; both regulations are in contradiction of the EU free trade directive. The 51% clause was abolished and since 1993 the Dutch publisher VNU (main publisher of periodicals in the Netherlands and Belgium) has obtained 44% of the VTM shares (VNU also participates in the Dutch commercial station RTL-4, with a 34% shareholding).

VTM has undoubtedly become a success story in all respects, in contrast to RTL-TVi. The financial success of VTM is inextricably linked to its high ratings. During the first launching month the target market share of 20% was surpassed: in February 1989 the viewing percentages rose to 27% and in December of that year 40% was reached. The success continued, with the audience share of VTM being approximately 44% in 1995, whereas the share of the PSB TV station BRTN fell to [illegible]. VTM's success is mainly due to a policy of popular programming: the emphasis is on entertainment and fiction (drama).

In 1994 VTM unexpectedly got a competitor. The American–Swedish group SBS announced the launch of a new commercial Flemish station, VT4. The new station is located in London so as not to collide with VTM's official 18-year monopoly. Very soon the cable operators announced that they were willing to distribute VT4 in spite of the fact that the Minister of Cultural Affairs refused to grant a licence. The Flemish newspapers market leader VUM (De Standaardgroep) took a share in VT4. The channel started up in February 1995 and from the start all cable operators distributed its programmes! The Minister of Cultural Affairs' attitude was disapproved of by the State Council (Raad van State/Conseil d'Etat).

In order to compete with VT4, VTM launched a second channel, Ka2. The result is that Flanders today has two commercial stations – VTM, with two channels, and VT4. An important question is whether the Flemish advertising market is big and flexible enough to 'feed' those three commercial channels. The two new channels, VT4 and Ka2, have very small audience shares – Ka2 3.4% and VT4 7.7%. In 1996, the commercial stations announced that their advertising revenues had diminished and that they had financial problems.

The PSB (BRTN and RTBF) cornered

Both BRTN and RTBF have tried to counteract the success of their commercial competitors. It is obvious that no broadcasting system can remain indifferent to a sharp decline in viewers. In addition, both BRTN and RTBF feared that the strong decrease in viewers might be used against the public broadcasting system. Reference has already been made to the difficult position of the public stations: too few resources (only 51% of the licence fee goes to the PSB) and the detrimental influence of a system of politicization that stifles creativity.

Even before VTM and RTL-TVi were set up, the public stations were faced with strong competition from foreign stations that reached viewers via the cable networks (on average 23 foreign channels are available to viewers in Belgium). However, the PSB stations did not change their proportion of 'serious' programmes: the mix of 'popular' versus 'serious' programmes remained virtually unchanged during the period 1970–87. What did change was the timing of the programmes: serious programmes were relegated more and more often to the early and late evening hours, while prime time was reserved for entertainment, mainly drama.

The advent of RTL-TVi and VTM, however, has led the public stations to adopt a levelling down strategy. 'Serious' programmes are no longer scheduled at disadvantageous hours, they have simply been discontinued. The amount of drama and entertainment has risen.

Both public stations are urgently in need of a new strategy in which a proper and new profile is presented. In the past the public stations in Belgium have always been financed exclusively with public means, i.e. without using revenue from advertising. This in itself is an excellent model if those resources are adequate. The model was abandoned not so long ago for RTBF and cooperation with the commercial channel was chosen instead. In Flanders, a first step towards commercialization of the PSB was made when advertising was allowed on BRTN radio in 1990.

The PSB television channels in particular are under pressure. In 1995 the Director-General of the BRTN was dismissed and replaced by a manager, selected by a head hunting bureau; a further 60 executives were dismissed. PSB radio stations have suffered less from the competition of private stations. This is the result of a successful strategy of segmentation aimed at different target groups. BRTN and RTBF each have five radio stations.

Private stations operate on a local level: in 1995 Wallonia had approximately 189 private local radios, Flanders about 281 (see discussion of private radio below). The public service radio stations continue to have much higher audience ratings and to attract more advertising.

In the German-speaking part of Belgium, the public service broadcast company BRF (Belgischer Rundfunk) offers a daily radio programme. Since September 1993 a short TV programme (quarter of an hour) is broadcast every day. Nine private radio stations also broadcast regularly.

Pay-television: initiatives from abroad

As early as 1985 Filmnet was given permission to start up a pay-television service in Flanders. The legal framework for it was not created until the cable decree of January 1987.

Filmnet, which offers pay-TV in the Netherlands, Belgium and the Scandinavian countries, soon turned out to be not very successful. After 10 years of operation, the Flanders Filmnet has about 120 000 subscribers.

In 1993 Filmnet launched a second channel, 'The Complete Movie Channel' with a non-stop movie supply whereas the first channel (Filmnet Plus) also broadcasts talk-shows, sport and pornography. In 1995 Filmnet launched a pay sports channel, 'SuperSport'; this channel has exclusive contracts with the Belgian Football (soccer) Association. The first channel is now called 'Filmnet'.

Filmnet, which belonged to the Swedish group Esselte, was sold in 1993 to the Swiss group Richmond and a South-African partner, Rupert. In 1997 Filmnet was sold to Canal Plus; Richmond and Rupert are still shareholders (±20%).

In Wallonia, Canal Plus Belgique (daughter company of the French Canal Plus) was started up in 1989. Many concessions were demanded: Canal Plus France had to agree that possible dividends would be reinvested in Wallonia and that it would participate in co-productions in Wallonia for a yearly amount that could not be lower than 80 000 million Belgian francs. In addition, Canal Plus had to give RTBF the opportunity to participate in every production planned in French-speaking Belgium.

Filmnet on the other hand did not have to fulfil as many requirements: for the first 4 years 5% of its productions were to consist of its own Flemish cultural productions. After 4 years this percentage was to rise to 7.5%.

The break-even point of Canal Plus Belgique is estimated to be about 80 000 subscribers. In 1994 Canal Plus Belgique had 123 000 subscribers. Canal Plus Belgique also made agreements with the Belgian Football Association.

In Europe, Canal Plus seems to be the most successful pay channel. The growth of Filmnet as well as of Canal Plus Belgique has been slow and pay channels that mainly offer movies will, in the near future, face competition from an increasing number of commercial stations, which broadcast a lot of movies, as well as increasing penetration of VCR. There will be competition from pay-per-view, video-on-demand services which offer more 'à la carte' programmes.

Private radio

The first illegal local radio stations started to appear in Belgium around 1980. These 'pioneers' had a number of common characteristics: they dreamt of small-scale, non-profit operations and profiled themselves as environmental and campaign stations.

They broadcast at irregular hours, operated illegally and carried on a campaign to break the BRTN–RTBF monopoly. The idealistic pioneers were, however, quickly joined by commercially inspired groups that turned the local radio stations into non-stop pop stations.

Legalization was bound to follow: technical norms were determined by the law of August 1981.

The norms with respect to content were accepted by the Walloon Community on 8 September 1981 and by the Flemish Community on 6 May 1982. Both decrees had many characteristics in common: the old 'pioneering model' was to be legalized – small-scale, regionally oriented and in interaction with the listeners. The decrees did not stipulate anything on financing, however; the resources therefore had to be looked for among fans, in charity actions etc. This obviously turned out to be untenable in the long run.

The commercially oriented local radio stations continued to broadcast advertising illegally. Advertising became legalized in 1985 and networks developed from then on (newspapers often participated). During this period local commercial radio networks were quite profitable, but a new law limited networking, and at the same time radio advertising was allowed on PSB radio so that many local private radio stations disappeared.

In spite of this, many local radio stations are still active: there are 281 in Flanders and 189 in Wallonia. Recently the Flemish Minister of Culture decided to halve the licensed number of private stations in order to give them a better chance of survival; networking, however, will remain forbidden.

In Wallonia networking has produced a strong position for five radio networks: Contact, Bel RTL, Nostalgie, NRJ and Fun. They monopolize half of the allotted frequencies; the PBS radio stations of RTBF only have 23% of the radio market share.

Regional private television

In Wallonia as well as in Flanders regional television has a somewhat identical legal framework. The geographical reach is limited, as well as the number of licensed regional stations (max. 11 in both Wallonia and Flanders). The amount of broadcasting time is limited (max. 200 hours, but most of the stations produce a 20–30 minute programme a day). The programmes have to be oriented towards regional topics. Regional advertising is allowed, but public funding can also be one of the sources of revenue. Regional TV has become a complementary, alternative medium. Especially in Flanders, the regional stations have high ratings; one of the reasons for their success is that the daily regional news programme is distributed by the cable networks 24 hours a day by means of the 'carousel system' (cf. CNN) so that viewers can watch their regional station 'à la carte'.

In 1987 Wallonia licensed its 11 regional TV stations (after an experimental period that started in 1976); in Flanders the first regional station was started up in 1988, but only in 1994 did the 11 stations become operational. Audience surveys have revealed that viewers are in favour of regional private stations; if the regional advertising market is large enough and if local and municipal authorities are willing to support these stations, they will be able to survive.

New electronic media

In Flanders, teletext distribution has increased over the past few years. The teletext service is provided by the public broadcasting system. In comparison with, say, the Netherlands and the UK, the number of pages is rather limited. An increase in the number of pages will probably lead to increased use. In Wallonia, teletext was unable to gain a foothold because French-speaking Belgium chose the French Antiope system. Antiope is a very sophisticated form of teletext but the system is far too expensive. Recently RTBF decided to get rid of Antiope and adopted the British standard, which is used worldwide.

Videotex domestic use in Belgium is not successful. Since 1988 the RTT has offered a videotex service, but the number of subscribers is very limited.

Recently audiotex has become very successful. The number of services and of users has increased rapidly, Internet is expanding in Belgium and many media institutions offer websites.

Convergence of telecom and cable networks

In Belgium the PTT (Belgacom) has always been a public monopoly. In 1996 it was partly privatized: the main shareholders (49%) are Ameritech (USA) and Singapore Telecom.

Most cable networks are owned by private companies in which municipal authorities have a share. Cable networks are only licensed to distribute TV signals; all other telecom services are a PTT monopoly. As a result of the EC policy, cable networks want to expand their activities to offer all kinds of telephone services. The convergence of telephone and cable networks will be realized in the near future. The Flemish government has announced that 'Telenet Vlaanderen', using the cable network infrastructure, will offer television and telephone services and as such will compete with Belgacom (PTT). Political and economical motives as well as technical innovations (digital compression) will blur the traditional distinction between telephone and cable companies. Belgacom, in order to counter the telecom strategies of the cable networks, has decided to introduce a video-on-demand trial project.

Policy trends

Belgium has never been in the forefront as far as a meaningful media policy is concerned. A lot of media law has only confirmed situations that were already in existence. Many media laws are ambiguous and can be interpreted in different ways. In the past few years media policy has been strongly oriented towards liberalism: new private initiatives have been supported, such as commercial radio, pay television, new commercial television networks. Advertising regulations have been neglected, with no government interference, and the quotas on cultural productions have been side-stepped by means of games and quizzes. No measures have been taken against the increasing concentration of the media, or to counter cross-ownership movements. Newspaper holdings have even been incited to participate in private radio and TV.

Supportive measures for the press, such as direct government grants, have no effect whatsoever: the amounts are too small and the selection criteria not selective enough. This has led to the situation that prosperous papers also receive a share of the very small overall amount available for subsidies. Indirect support measures such as lower rates for telephone, post, no VAT etc. are of course important.

The public broadcasting stations' situation is becoming ever more difficult: they suffer a lack of funds, the stifling effect of political patronage and bureaucratic inertia, and a loss of viewers. The commercial stations seem to have dragged the public stations along with them in a down-market process.

Statistics

1 ECU = 40 Belgian francs, Bfr

Population (1995)

Number of inhabitants	10.068 million
Geographical size	30 528 km^2
Population density	330 per km^2

Broadcasting (1995)

Public service	
Number of national TV programmes	4
TV1, TV2, RTBF1, RTBF21	
Number of radio programmes	10
BRTN, 5; RTBF, 5	

Commercial (national)
Number of TV programmes — 5
VTM, Ka2, VT4, RTL-TVi, Club RTL

Commercial (local)
Number of TV programmes — 22
Flanders, 11; Wallonia, 11
Number of local radio — 470
Flanders, 281; Wallonia, 189

Financing of the broadcast systems
PSB: Licence fees

Flanders	Bfr7.45 bn (0.20 bn ECU)
Wallonia	Bfr6.20 bn (0.16 bn ECU)

Audience share (%)	PSB		Commercial	
Flanders	TV1	17.5	VTM	37.1
	TV2	5.1	Ka2	3.9
			VT4	6.1
Wallonia	RTBF1	15.7	RTL-TVi	23.5
	RTBF2	12.6	TF1, A2, FR3	40.0

Transmission and AV equipment

Telephone	87.1%
Cable	94.0%*
TV sets	97.3%
VCR	52.9%

(* This implies that only 6% of TV households rely on terrestrial transmission.)

The press

Circulation according to groups

Titles published	Circulation	Ideology
VUM		
De Standaard, Het Nieuwsblad, De Gentenaar	373 124	Catholic
Het Volk	154 934	Catholic
De Persgroep		
Het Laatste Nieuws, De Nieuwe Gazet	303 993	Liberal
De Morgen	36 375	Socialist
RUG		
Gazet van Antwerpen, Gazet van Mechelen	171 380	Catholic
Het Belang van Limburg	110 688	Catholic
NV Uitgeversbedrijf Tijd		
Financieel Economische Tijd	42 786	Neutral
SA Rossel		
Le Soir	182 798	Neutral
La Meuse/La Lanterne	120 408	Neutral
Group La Nouvelle Gazette	98 820	
La Nouvelle Gazette		
La Province		
Le Journal de Charleroi		Liberal
Le Peuple		Liberal
*La Wallonie**	48 200	Socialist

SIPM		
La Libre Belgique/Gazette de Liège(*)	87 557	Catholic
*La Dernière Heure/Les Sports**	104 024	Liberal
SA Vers l'Avenir		
Vers l'Avenir, L'Avenir de Luxembourg, Le Courrier de l'Escaut, Le Jour/Le Courrier, Le Rappel	147 899	Catholic
L'Echo	27 956	Neutral
Grenz-Echo		
Grenz-Echo	11 739	Catholic
TOTAL	2 022 681	

* Figures from the publisher.

Source: CIM bulletin, 1995

Total Flemish press circulation	1 192 396 (61.3%)
Total French-speaking press circulation	753 263 (38.7%)
Total German-speaking press circulation	11 739 (0.6%)

Advertising

Division/media (1994)	
Newspapers	18.8%
Magazines and regional weeklies	25.2%
Total print	44%
TV	34.6%
Posters	11.9%
Radio	8.7%
Cinema	0.8%

References

Boone, L. (1978) *Krantenpluralisme en informatiebeleid*. Centrum Communicatiewetenschappen, Katholieke Universiteit Leuven.

Burgelman, J. (1989) 'Political parties and their impact on public service in Belgium. Elements from apolitical-sociological approach', *Media Culture and Society*, April, no. 2: 167–93.

De Bens, E. (1986) 'Cable penetration and competition among Belgian and foreign stations', *European Journal of Communication*, 1(4): 477–92.

De Bens, E. (1988) 'Der Einfluss eines grossen ausländischen Programmangebotes auf die Sehgewohnheiten. Belgische Erfahrungen miteiner dichten Verkabelung', *Publizistik* (Special issue: *Sozialisation durch Massenmedien*), 33 (2–3): 352–65.

De Bens, E. (1989) 'Audiovisual media in Belgium. Political, social, cultural and economic developments', *Soziale Konsequenzen einer europäischen Medienpolitik*, vol. 2. Hamburg: Studie für GDV der Europäischen Gemeinschaft, pp. 1–34.

De Bens, E. (1996) 'Das Rundfunksystem Belgiens', in *Internationales Handbuch für Hörfunk und Fernsehen 1996/97*. Baden-Baden: Nomos, pp. 24–30.

Gol, J. (1970) *'Le monde de la presse en Belgique'*. Brussels: CRISP.

Heinsman, L. and Servaes, J. (1988) *Hoe nieuw zijn de media. Een mediabeleid met een perspectief*. Leuven: Acco.

Herroelen, P. (1982) *1, 2, . . . veel? Kroniek van 20 jaar Belgische radio en televisie*. Leuven: Acco.

Lentzen, E. (1985) ' "La CLT", Courrier Hebdomadaire', *CRISP*, 18 January, pp. 8–18.

Luykx, T. (1973) *Evolutie van de communicatiemedia*. Brussels: Elsevier.

Maertens, H., Neels, L., Voorhoof, D. (1994) *Medialex 1994*. Antwerp: Kluwer.

Van Der Biesen, W. (1990) 'Vlaanderen en zijn 5 dagbladen' and 'Persconcentratie', *Mediagids*, Part 13 and 15, Deurne.

Verstraeten, H. (1980) *Pers en macht. Een dossier over de geschreven pers in België*. Leuven: Kritak.

Voorhoof, D. (1987) 'De nieuwe mediawetgeving: krachtlijnen en knelpunten', *Communicatie*, 1: 3–20.

3

Denmark

Vibeke G. Petersen and Karen Siune

National profile

Denmark has a population of 5.2 million spread over 43 069 km^2. The number of households is 2.4 million. Danish is the language spoken by all except a limited number of guest workers. Compared to many other countries, Denmark is a relatively homogeneous society with respect to culture and values.

Denmark has been a member of the European Union (EU) since 1973, but there is an old tradition for cultural and political affiliation with the Nordic countries, and Scandinavia is often considered as one unit. There are many similarities with the other Scandinavian countries with respect to media structure and media politics.

The political system is a multi-party system, with more than 10 political parties contesting national elections. No single party has a majority and compromise decisions are a feature of the political system. The Social Democratic Party has for decades been the largest party, with more than one-third of the vote, and it has very often formed the government, mostly in coalition with smaller bourgeois parties. From 1982 to 1993 Denmark had bourgeois coalition governments under the leadership of the Conservative People's Party in strong cooperation with the Agrarian Liberals. A number of smaller parties have participated in the coalitions. From the 1990 election until 1993 the two major bourgeois parties, the Conservative People's Party and the Agrarian Liberals, alone formed the government coalition. At the beginning of 1993 the Social Democrats returned to power with two of the minor bourgeois parties, the Centre Democrats (who left the government at the end of 1996) and the Radical Liberals.

Media policy is an issue for debate in Danish society, and all political parties have views on the media structure. Media politics has, however, never been the main election issue.

The Danish economy is basically capitalist and the state has very limited involvement in industrial production, but traditionally has much to say regarding the electronic media, radio and television. The standard of living is high, as is the distribution of consumer goods. Denmark is one of the leading examples of a welfare society.

A relatively high level of unemployment (10%), and problems with the balance of trade and the balance of payments, have been issues on the political agenda for many years. These issues have an impact on the debate on media policy as well as other policy areas related to economic growth and employment. The development of new technology suitable for export and thus increased employment opportunities has been influential in relation to Danish media politics, as described by Siune (1986).

Development of the press and broadcasting since 1945

In Denmark, telecommunications has been taken care of by the state or by concessionaries. The national Post and Telegraph (P&T) has distributed ordinary mail since 1711, and is responsible for telegraphy, telex and national telephone services (competition introduced in 1995).

In 1926 a monopoly on broadcasting was given to Statsradiofonien. This institution changed its name in 1959 to Danmarks Radio (DR) but kept the monopoly on all radio broadcasting till the 1980s. In 1953 DR started broadcasting television. The organization of DR has always been regulated by law.

From the very beginning of Danish national broadcasting the precondition was that it should be financed by licence fees; the costs for broadcasting should not burden the state budget as such. No commercials were allowed. DR was given the status of an independent public institution. The responsibility for broadcasting has been placed with a variety of ministries: starting out in the Ministry of Transport, it was moved to the Ministry of Education. In 1961 it went to the Ministry of Culture, where it has stayed except for five years (1988–93) in the Ministry of Communications.

DR's monopoly on national broadcasting ended in the second half of the 1980s with the establishment of a second national television channel, TV2. Independent local television and local radio were allowed as experiments in 1983 and later made legal permanently (see below).

A second television channel had been debated for years before it was finally decided upon in 1987. The issue had been handled by the government Commission for Mass Media, set up in 1980 to propose an overall media policy. A large majority of the Commission recommended in 1983 the establishment of a second national television channel independent of DR. TV2 was created as a reaction to the challenge from foreign channels broadcast to Denmark via satellites and transmitted to households via cable.

The law establishing TV2 in 1987 was passed in the Danish parliament, Folketinget, with a majority of just one vote. The opposition, the Social Democrats and the Socialists, were against the proposal because it introduced commercial financing of national television. The small centre party – the Radical Liberals, traditionally opposed to bourgeois cultural policy – supported the government's proposal in return for a decisive influence on the regional structure of TV2.

The ideas behind the new channel were several: to break the monopoly of Danmarks Radio was a prominent one, to introduce commercial television a second, presenting another Danish alternative to the foreign channels a third. Thus, the main arguments were based on a wish to protect Danish culture. The intention was also to give the Danish production companies a chance to produce for television.

In summary it can be said that broadcasting in Denmark has expanded a great deal in the period after the Second World War, but that the national expansion has always been heavily regulated. Local radio and television stations have emerged, now licensed locally and financed by advertising and private means. These stations are owned and operated by private broadcasting associations, companies and the like. They can also be owned by the press (more about local radio and television below). So private radio broadcasting has expanded during the 1980s, regulated, but with far fewer obligations than national broadcasting.

The vast increase in broadcasting outlets has taken place against the background of a drastic decrease in the number of daily newspapers since the Second World War. With the dwindling number came a restructuring of the press in provincial towns from competition to monopoly.

Since 1945, 84 newspapers have died, leaving 39, of which 10 are national papers published in Copenhagen. About half of the 84 ceased to appear before 1960, and the most recent large-scale close-down happened in the early 1970s when the Social Democrats decided to give up publishing independent dailies in all but two provincial areas (they still have close relations to one national daily). During the 1980s the concentration process has slowed down; a few new papers were launched but failed within a year.

In the provinces, where most of the closures took place, the post-war era meant the end of the traditional 'four-paper' system according to which each of the four major political parties (the Social Democratic Party, the Conservative People's Party, the Agrarian Liberals and the Radical Liberals) ran their own newspaper. This situation of diversity and competition has given way to one of monopoly nearly everywhere; only three towns have more than one daily. Close behind came the 'liberation' of most of the remaining papers from their party affiliation. It is commonly acknowledged, however, that more than 90% of the Danish press is to be found at the centre/right of the political spectrum.

The relatively stable period of the past 20 years or so has mainly been characterized by a stagnation/decline in the circulation of provincial dailies, while the national papers have increased theirs.

The press

Legal framework

Freedom of the press goes back almost 150 years to the Constitution of 1849. It gives everybody the right to impart information, and it prohibits censorship. Other laws specify and set the limitations of this freedom, notably the press law, the penal code and procedural law. The legal framework of the press does not encompass monopoly regulations, but it does provide for a (modest) state subsidy scheme.

Among the most important issues the laws deal with are editorial responsibility, the right of reply, the right to privacy, libel, defamation, incitement to crime, and the right of journalists to protect their sources. In addition, a set of voluntary ethical rules about journalistic practice were incorporated in a new law in 1991.

The main purpose of this law is to extend the press law's system of editorial responsibility to broadcasters and to expand the right of journalists to protect their sources.

Press legislation is the prerogative of the Prime Minister.

Structure and organization

When the Prime Minister in 1980 set up the Media Commission to look into the development of the media and to recommend policy initiatives, one of the first tasks it took up was an analysis of the economic status of the press. It was recognized then, as it is now, that the press operates largely on the same conditions as private business (in contrast to electronic media).

Unlike the other Nordic countries, Denmark does not have a tradition of active political intervention in the newspaper business, as, for instance, through direct subsidy. The existing exemption from VAT and cheap postal rates are difficult to evaluate precisely. It is generally valued at about Dkr500 m annually (40 m ECU). But although this form of subsidy helps the industry by enabling it to sell its product relatively cheaply, it does nothing to change structural problems.

As mentioned above, one such structural problem is the disappearance of competition at the local level. A number of idealistic attempts during the 1970s and 1980s to establish new papers or revive dead ones have shown that it is practically impossible to reverse the movement towards a monopoly structure.

Since 1970 a modest direct subsidy has been channelled to needy papers through the Finance Institute of the Press. On recommendation from the Media Commission, a large majority in parliament decided in 1984 to increase the annual state subsidy to the Institute from Dkr4 m to 14 m (320 000 to 1.1 m ECU). The money has been used as collateral for loans in connection with modernization of newspaper production, planning and establishing new papers and supporting financial reorganizations of existing papers.

The stated goal of such press policy initiatives is, of course, to further diversity and plurality. The political rejection of more substantial direct intervention in the financial affairs of the press stems from fear of cementing the existing press pattern. By keeping alive papers that would die in the market place because of inefficient management, the state would only delay the necessary adaptation to modern society, the argument goes. Newspaper proprietors have consistently (if not always unanimously) added to this that direct subsidy would make the press dependent on the state in an unacceptable manner.

The Danish press is almost entirely privately owned, mostly in the form of limited liability companies, and often organized as foundations in order to prevent hostile takeovers. The companies typically have extra income through related activities such as publication of free sheets and other printing business. But the bulk of their finance comes from the sale of copies and of advertising space in roughly equal proportions.

It is generally recognized that financing of the press increasingly will have to rely on a more efficient use of existing resources. Advertising volume went down between 1987 and 1989 by an average of 6.5% and up between 1990 and 1995 by 18%. The well-established connection between macroeconomic conditions and the advertising industry makes newspapers particularly vulnerable to these trends in society. It is no consolation that readership patterns show that young people increasingly choose to do without a daily paper.

The fall in advertising volume in the press between 1987 and 1989 coincides with the introduction of broadcast advertising, which came about during 1988. For years no serious attempt was made to establish a connection between the two or to draw policy conclusions, except at the local level. The press was allowed to own local broadcasting stations when commercial financing became possible. This, however, had more to do with giving the press an opportunity to participate in the electronic development of information exchange than with compensating them for lost advertising revenue. But in 1993 the issues were brought up by the Prime Minister himself, and a new committee was set up in 1994 under his ministry to look into the interplay between the many different media (more below).

Circulation

The total circulation of the 39 existing dailies is about 1.61 million. During the past 10 years dailies have seen their circulation fall by about 11%. The two tabloids alone have lost 25%. The 11 Sunday papers, which are Sunday editions of the daily papers, have a circulation of about 1.5 million. Also the division between different groups of papers has stayed much the same during the 1980s, with the 10 national papers taking about 55% and the 29 local papers, 45%. Within the group of national dailies, the two biggest newspapers, both tabloids, account for about one-third of the daily circulation.

Nine out of ten Danes read at least one daily newspaper. More than eight of them buy it. But the numbers are slowly going down: 25 years ago more than 100 copies were sold for every 100 households, so more people now confine themselves to just one paper, and, what is more problematic for the industry, the rise in the number of households is not reflected in the total circulation of dailies. Perhaps most worrying is the fact that it is young people who are dropping out of the readership, and owing to this, younger Danes' media use has been one of the salient themes on the agenda for the Media Committee of 1994.

Electronic media

Since 1988 Denmark has had a dual system of broadcasting: Danmarks Radio, the old monopoly, running one national terrestrial television channel, one satellite channel (since mid-1996) and three radio channels, and TV2 running one national television channel with eight regional 'windows'. The whole population can receive the DR channel and 98% can receive TV2.

All national broadcasting is regulated by law no. 1065 of 23 December 1992 with later amendments – the most recent dates from 27 December 1996. In the same law the community antenna network and other types of cable network are regulated, as well as satellite broadcasting and local broadcasting.

Organization of Danmarks Radio and TV2

Danmarks Radio is organized as a central unit and located in the capital, Copenhagen. It has one provincial TV production department. In contrast to this rather monolithic set-up, there are nine regional radio stations under Danmarks Radio. Due to political decisions, TV2 has been placed outside Copenhagen to make it pay more attention to provincial life, and it has eight regional television stations, each responsible for regional news and for providing the national channel with regional programmes.

According to the law, a board of governors consisting of 11 members directs DR, and a board of governors consisting of 11 members directs TV2. These two boards are appointed by the Minister for Culture. The boards are not composed in the same way: the board of DR has nine members selected by the parliament, one representative from the employees and a chairman appointed directly by the Minister. The board of TV2 has eight of its members appointed by the Minister and together they must represent knowledge about the media, business management and culture. One member is selected by the staff, and the regional stations select two members. Appointments last four years. The two boards are to be apolitical and active politicians – defined as members of the Danish parliament – are not allowed on the board. Besides the board of governors there are separate advisory programme committees for DR and TV2, also appointed for four years.

The financing of DR and TV2

DR TV and DR radio channels are all financed via licence fees, while TV2 from the outset was financed by advertising (66%) and by licence fees (34%). This balance has since shifted somewhat, increasing the dependence on advertising. There are strict regulations of the amount and insertion of commercials and, although the regulations have become less restrictive, they have not disappeared. In 1990 programme sponsorships were allowed on both channels.

Also regulated by law is the size of the licence fees, jointly collected for the two broadcasting organizations. The budgets for DR and TV2 are drawn up by the boards of governors, which also propose the size of the licence fees, however, these must be approved by parliament. Until 1990 the size of the licence fees was decided annually, but now the law gives the broadcasting organizations four-year budgets. The longer budget periods came as a response to a plea from the broadcasting institutions which suffered from the annual problem of not knowing the size of the budget until very late. The licence fees were increased by 2% annually for the three-year period from 1991 to 1993 and increased by 2.5% from 1994 to 1997. In 1996 an annual increase of 3.3% until 2001 was passed by parliament.

Programme responsibility

DR is an independent public institution, responsible for broadcasting radio and television programmes (news, information, entertainment and art) to the whole population. Quality, diversity and plurality are the main objectives. Fairness and impartiality are mentioned as objectives in relation to the transmission of information.

TV2 is labelled an independent institution, while the word public is absent. Programme responsibilities are described in much the same way as for DR, with an emphasis on quality, diversity and plurality. The purpose of TV2 is to produce news and current affairs, while all other programmes are to be bought from independent producers. Commercials are allowed. Both stations must account for their fulfilment of the public service obligations.

Television is watched daily by 70% of the population and the total amount of time spent by the Danes watching the Danish channels is a little under 2 hours per day. There has been an increase in the amount of daily viewing time, and a decrease in the amount of daily time spent reading newspapers. This is reflected in the issues of the public debate (see below).

Local TV and radio

Local radio and TV started in Denmark in 1983 as a three-year experiment. The Ministry of Culture gave licences and seed money to a limited number of stations and at the height of the experimental period, in 1985, 90 stations and 34 TV stations were on the air. The radio stations were run on limited incomes, advertising was banned and most of the money came from voluntary contributions, just as most of the broadcasters were unpaid amateurs. At present there are about 250 local radio licensees.

When the time came to replace the experiment with a permanent system two things were clear. There was a great deal of interest in local radio on the part of new broadcasters as well as listeners, therefore many new applications for licences were to be expected. And some form of secured financing would be required if the stations were to survive after the first bout of philanthropic support dwindled.

There was political agreement that the new system should be decentralized as far as possible, and that only frequency scarcity should limit the number of licensees. There was not, however, agreement on the issue of financing. The conservative minority government favoured advertising and no state support, whereas the liberal/social democratic/socialist opposition wanted partial public subsidy and no commercial income.

The resulting compromise law did not last very long. It did not allow advertising, it gave no state support and it opened up the field for new entrants. The consequence was that large numbers of people applied for a licence, convinced that time would work for the commercial proponents. To nobody's surprise they were right, and in 1988 local radio was allowed to carry advertising within certain limitations: a maximum of 10% of daily broadcast time and a maximum of 6 minutes per hour. As of mid-1990 they can also receive income from sponsorship.

The regulation of local radio is light, but whatever rules there are aim to keep it local and to make a sufficient number of licences available for everybody to join in. Frequencies are allocated by the Ministry of Culture but all other licensing and supervision is done by local committees, who are obliged to hand out licences until there is no more broadcast time left (the licensees have to share frequencies, and they have to use the time allocated if they want to keep it). Only local associations with radio broadcasting as their sole goal can obtain a licence. (Special provision is made for municipalities, which can run an information and/or open access channel.) It should be noted that the stations are allowed to be commercial, i.e. to earn money for their owners. Business interests may not have a dominant influence on a station (newspapers are excepted from this rule). Up until 1997 networking was forbidden except in very special cases.

The arrival of advertisements was accompanied by measures to counter some of the predictable effects of commercial financing, most notably that of killing off small or 'narrow' radio stations. A 'Robin Hood' fund was established to channel money from the rich to the poor stations by way of a levy of 10% on all income. Radio stations earning below a certain fixed amount of money per broadcast hour were entitled to subsidy from the fund for up to 28 hours of broadcasting a week. The actual amount was calculated on the basis of what was available in the fund, which did not have any state money coming in. From the start of the fund in August 1988 up to the end of 1989 a total of about Dkr16.5 m was paid to eligible radio stations, about 150 in all. The fund was discontinued in the early 1990s. In 1994 a new fund was set up, this time financed by the Ministry of Culture. The fund distributed Dkr7.5 m annually, mostly to non-commercial local radio stations. The political will to increase the state support for local media – TV as well as radio – seemed strong, however, and it resulted at the end of 1996 in a substantial subsidy scheme of Dkr50 m annually (to be shared with local television stations). At the same time networking was allowed for radio news and for all broadcasts between 11pm and 6am.

As there is no regulation on programme content, such as local/home production, not much is known about this. During the experimental period when the law required 'a substantial' amount of programmes to be local, music accounted for about 50% of broadcast time on average. The percentage is probably higher today. Whatever the content actually is, it seems to be in agreement with listeners' wishes. Almost the whole population has access to at least one local station, and on average more than half listens weekly.

Local TV

The law on local broadcasting governs TV as well as radio, with a few special provisions concerning advertising particularly. Local TV was only allowed to carry advertising in 1989, a year later than radio. As of mid-1996, 50 local TV stations were 'on the air'.

As in the case of local radio, there is little information available on programme content in local TV. No local quotas were imposed by law until the end of 1996. A subsidy scheme for local non-commercial TV was introduced for the first time by the law of 1996. That law also allowed for networking between commercial stations.

New electronic media

Teletext, in Denmark called Tekst TV, was started in 1985 and is now to be found in 75% of all households. The service is now organized by Danmarks Radio and by TV2 independently, and it consists of several hundred pages of information about news, sport, television and radio programmes, weather, traffic, business and leisure. A successful experiment on TV2 has offered job information on teletext on regional television. The service is free of charge for the consumers and considered a natural part of the public service. Teletext has never been an issue for discussion, and there is no special regulation of this service.

Government policy on videotex has been to let it develop according to market forces. It is now a liberalized telecommunication service, managed by the former telephone companies, which have joined forces in Tele Danmark. The number of subscribers has increased in the 1990s but it is still relatively limited.

In the law of 1996, Danmarks Radio and TV2 have been allocated means to enter into the digital age. They have also each been promised two digital channels on the future digital terrestrial network – one channel for parallel broadcasting of the existing analogue channel and one for new programming. This digital network will be established, if the broadcasters so decide, by converting an available, but unused, third UHF channel. No concrete plans have been made for going digital, however.

Following withdrawal from plans for a Nordic satellite in 1981 there was no DBS policy or plan in Denmark, until the discussion was opened in 1995 about the use of a satellite for joint Nordic distribution of television signals from the national television channel DR. As mentioned above, DR launched a satellite channel, DR2, in 1996 as a supplement to its terrestrial channel.

Foreign media availability

Foreign channels reach Danish households via satellites and cable. As of the end of 1996, Danes have an average of 25 channels to choose from. Every second household can watch Swedish television, and German television can be watched by more than one in three. The Danes watch Danish television more than foreign channels during the hours when it is available, but the use of foreign channels increases dramatically at the end of the day, when the Danish channels go off the air. TV3, the commercial Nordic channel broadcast to Scandinavia by satellite from London, is among the most popular foreign channels. According to surveys, 67% of Danish television viewers watch TV3 at some time during a week, and according to analyses in 1995, TV3's share of viewing time is increasing. Other channels, broadcast via satellite and reaching most Danish households via cable, like Eurosport and RTL, are viewed for approximately 10% of the total viewing time.

Direct-to-Home antenna dishes (DTH) are used for reception, but only in 13% of households according to estimates. The majority of households receive the foreign channels via cable, and the hybrid network transmits up to 20 channels to the households connected. Altogether, close to 70% of Danish households can receive foreign television channels either via the cable networks, via private antennas or over the air. At the end of 1996, approximately 60% of all households were connected to the hybrid network or to private networks.

There is a local pay TV channel, Kanal 2, in Copenhagen. Danmarks Radio and TV2 will launch a pay-TV service, mainly broadcasting sports and run in cooperation with the telephone companies' hybrid network, in March 1997. From 1991 the telephone companies, now Tele Danmark, in cooperation with the Swedish Esselte Entertainment, Nordisk Film and Sky News, offer Danish households connected to the hybrid network a 24-hour service of American films and news.

Policies for the press and broadcasting

During the 1980s the Danish media structure experienced a great many changes, in relation to newspapers as well as to broadcasting. More than anything it is the breaking of the TV monopoly that has changed the debate. Television is on the agenda more than any other medium, but in comparison with other issues, media are not very significant in the political debate. The public debate is very much focused on the two national television channels.

How much are they viewed, and how do they compete? How should they be financed and how should they be regulated?

TV2 has been a great success. Within two years the new channel managed to get half the Danish population as daily viewers. At the beginning of 1991 daily reach was 64% for both channels. In 1996 the numbers are 59% for TV2 and 53% for DR. Ratings are an ongoing issue for debate, especially related to the issues of programme structure and the size of licence fees. Share of viewing time was at the beginning of the 1990s almost equal for the two channels, whereas TV2 has 41% against DR's 27% in 1996. Danes are news freaks more than most; more than one-third of the population watch the daily news on TV2 and half of them also follow the later main news programme on DR TV. On top of this comes the amount of time spent on foreign channels, but foreign channels still are much less watched than the Danish channels.

Regarding radio, the eventual establishment of a fourth national channel has been under discussion, the question being whether it will be allocated to DR, TV2 or to private investors, possibly to newspapers. In 1995 the Media Commission recommended that it should be given to Danmarks Radio, as a supplement to its existing three national channels. The issue has not yet (mid-1997) been resolved.

The issue of broadcasting content is very old in itself, but at the same time it is typical of a nation where commercial channels are relatively new. The discussion is closely related to the ideals of public service broadcasting organizations versus commercialized media.

Commercialization has been debated, and so has the threat to Danish culture from an increase in foreign programmes broadcast to all Danes. But Denmark was not in favour of the EU regulation requesting European programme quotas of 50%, the main reason being a negative attitude from the political parties to EU regulation of national culture, an area that was considered to be outside the EU Treaty.

New technology was on the agenda at the beginning of the 1980s, and media policy at that time was closely related to issues like optical fibres, the broadband network and the hybrid network, which combined coaxial cables and optical fibres. Expectations were high, but in the later 1990s the Danish debate on media politics is very down to earth. Nevertheless, there have been several developments. A pilot ISDN project was started in 1989, and a commercial ISDN service was started in 1992. Meanwhile the issue of 'Danish culture at stake' has staged something of a comeback on the agenda for public or political debate.

The population and the different actors, such as the political parties and broadcasting institutions, have generally all adjusted to the new media structure; only changes in viewing patterns resulting from the new competition from more broadcasting outlets are debated. The Danish debate is still dominated by economic concerns, how to finance DR and TV2 in the future, and new communication technology is no longer as prominent as it was during the 1980s, even if its importance continues to be recognized.

The discussion on the consequences of digital technology for the media has started. Issues such as multi-media and the convergence of computer, broadcasting and telecommunications technology are dealt with at a rather abstract level but have entered the public debate. The first report on the electronic media by the Prime Minister's Media Committee, published in October 1995, illustrates this: it deals predominantly with the fate of public service broadcasting.

This fate was also at the centre of political discussions leading up to the law of 1996. As a consequence of the increased competition in the media market, the public service broadcasters have now been allowed to offer telecommunications services (only those services that can be likened to TV services, however) and other audiovisual services. As the law takes effect as of 1997, it is too early to predict the outcome of the new and wider scope of these operations.

In summary, it can be said that regulation and steering of the media structure in Denmark have not decreased. We do talk about deregulation, but there has been a series of re-regulations, some giving more freedom than before. Altogether, the amount of regulation counted in number of pages of law is far greater today than it was 10 years ago (Minke, 1990), and the plans for the new media laws continue this trend.

Statistics

(1 ECU = 7.90 Danish kroner, Dkr)

Population (1995)

Number of inhabitants	5 210 100
Geographical size	43 069 km²
Population density	118 per km²
Number of households	2 400 000

Broadcasting (1996)

Number of television channels	2 + 1 satellite
Number of radio channels	3
Regional TV stations (TV 2)	8
Regional radio (DR)	9
Local TV	50 (estimated)
Local radio licensees	250 (estimated)
Households with VCR	70%
Households with satellite receivers	13%
Cable connected households	60%
Financing of the broadcast systems	
Licence fees	
Colour TV (1996)	Dkr1664
Black & white TV (1996)	Dkr1070
Radio (1996)	Dkr246

Advertising	
Total media advertising spend (1994)	Dkr8.8 bn
Print media	82%
of this daily press	41%
Audiovisual media	18%
of this TV	81%
Radio	11%

Source: Reklameforbrugsundersøgelsen i Danmark, Dansk Oplagskontrol

The press

No. of main independent national and regional newspapers	39

Circulation of principal newspapers (1st half of 1995)	
Ekstrabladet	168 000
Jyllands-Posten	161 000
B.T.	155 000
Politiken	150 000
Berlingske Tidende	133 000
Det Fri Aktuelt	40 000

Source: Dansk Oplagskontrol

References

Andersen, O.E. (1995) *Medieudbud og Medieforbrug i Danmark 1983–1994*. Medieudvalget. Copenhagen: Ministry of State.

Boesen, B. and Lund, E.B. (1989) *Få styr på udviklingen*. Aarhus: Danmarksjournalisthøjskole.

Frøbert, K.A.A. (1983) *Massemediernes frihed og ansvar*. Copenhagen: Akademisk Forlag.

Jauert, P. and Prehn, O. (1995) *Lokalradio og lokal-TV, Nu og i fremtiden*. Copenhagen: Ministry of Culture.

Mediekommissionen (1983) 'Mediekommissionens betænkning nr. 3, Betænkning om de trykte mediers økonomi og beskæftigelse'. Betænkning no. 972, Copenhagen.

Mediekommissionen (1985a) 'Mediekommissionens betænkning nr. 5, Betænkning om et øget dansk TV-udbud'. Betænkning no. 986, Copenhagen.

Mediekommissionen (1985b) 'Mediekommissionens betænkning nr. 6, Betænkning om dansk mediepolitik'. Betænkning no. 1029, Copenhagen.

Ministry of Communication, Committee on Local Radio and TV (1990) *Status over ordningen for lokal radio og TV* (Overview of local radio and TV). Copenhagen: Ministry of Communication.

Minke, K. (1990) 'Media structures in Denmark, media structures in a changing Europe', *Innovation*, 3(2): 253–67.

Notkin, A. (1990) *Dansk Presse 1988/89*. Odense: Pressens Årbog.

Siune, Karen (1986) 'Denmark', in H. Kleinsteuber, D. McQuail and K. Siune (eds), *Electronic Media and Politics in Western Europe: A Euromedia Research Group Handbook of National Systems*. Frankfurt: Campus Verlag.

4

Finland

Helena Tapper

National profile

Finland has a population of 5 million and an area of 338 145 km^2. The country has a Swedish speaking minority population of 6%, and two official languages, Finnish and Swedish.

In the 1995 elections the Social Democratic Party won 63 of the 200 seats in the parliament, the Centre Party 44 and the National Coalition Party 39. The present Cabinet is historically exceptional, comprising a large coalition including the Social Democratic Party, the Green Party, the National Coalition Party and the Left-wing Union.

Finland joined the EU at the beginning of 1995, representing a major change in its history. Located as it is between the East and the West, it was for centuries ruled by Sweden and a part of the West. Then for a hundred years it was ruled by Russia, till independence in 1917. Today Finland embodies both cultures, but with rapid changes in politics, culture and economy, the country must seek out a new identity. Finland needs a new political–economic identity to enable it to participate in the global system.

Development of the press and broadcasting since 1945

The deregulation of electronic media and increasing competition for audiences and advertising money is characteristic of the Finnish media system today. Rapid changes in communication technology, like digital radio (DAB) and television, the Internet and other information network services change the media landscape and media policy, as the competition increases. New technology also opens new channels for new operators. Thus issues like the role of public broadcasting and the role of national or international ownership become matters of media policy.

The increasing competition produces polarization and concentration of media ownership. Foreign ownership of the electronic and other media will increase competition in the near future.

The press

The main change in the Finnish media system has been the switch from newspaper-dominated media to electronic media. The number of newspapers has decreased dramatically over the past 20 years. The polarization of the press has led to the dominance of big dailies and, at the same time, a strong role for local, small newspapers, which still have a large readership. There are 56 newspapers published 4–7 times a week and 158 local titles published 1–3 times a week.

The decreasing number of papers and the loss of circulation can be explained by the growing audience of electronic media – local radio, cable channels and TV – and media concentration. However, the role of the print media is still strong in Finland, compared to many other countries in Europe. Since 1994 the newspapers have lost about 2% of their circulation annually. The newspaper publishers operate today increasingly in the electronic media as owners of local radio stations, cable and TV companies and electronic information services over the World Wide Web (WWW).

The biggest newspaper in Finland is *Helsingin Sanomat*, published by Sanoma Corporation. *Helsingin Sanomat* has a circulation of 466 700, *Ilta-Sanomat*, an evening paper by the same publisher, a circulation of 219 700. The second largest newspaper is *Aamulehti*, published by the Aamulehti Corporation, with a circulation of 129 700. This company also publishes an evening paper, *Iltalehti*, with a circulation of 108 100. The third newspaper is *Turun Sanomat*, published by Turun Sanomat Ltd, with a circulation of 111 600.

These three companies have bought shares or a majority of shares in regional newspapers, especially Sanoma Corporation. Thus the concentration of newspapers has greatly increased. The biggest newspaper publisher was divided into two companies: Sanoma Corporation, which publishes the two biggest newspapers, the *Helsingin Sanomat* and the *Ilta-Sanomat*; and Helsinki Media, which publishes magazines and books and is a cable and TV operator. Additionally, in autumn 1997 Helsinki Media will launch a fourth national commercial TV channel, to be called Four. The latest venture of Helsinki Media is into the freesheet market. In the summer of 1997 it will start to issue a freesheet in Helsinki called *Quarter* (meaning quarter of an hour). It will be distributed in subway stations and on public transport throughout the Helsinki area. Helsinki Media will also launch a new economic periodical. The major newspaper publishers also operate in the electronic media, with involvement in local radio and cable television, and in the new national TV channel.

International operators have also shown increasing interest in the Finnish press: Marieberg (Sweden) has become the biggest shareholder in the Aamulehti Corporation. In Spring 1997 the Aamulehti Corporation became the biggest shareholder of the commercial national channel, MTV3. Thus, there are three large media companies in the country: the Finnish Broadcasting Company, Helsinki Media and the Aamulehti Corporation.

Another development has been that the press subsidies have decreased or have been cut severely, and therefore the dependency on advertising income and paid circulation has become more important.

Broadcasting

The public radio broadcasting was dominated by the Finnish Broadcasting Company (YLE) until 1985 when private, commercial, local radio stations were licensed to broadcast. Television was dominated by the YLE as well, though from the very beginning Finland has had a private commercial television company, MTV Finland, which has operated through the YLE's TV1 and TV2. Since 1993 it has had a channel of its own, MTV3.

Generally, the media field follows the general development of deregulation in Europe where the broadcasting monopolies have been broken and competition has been opened for electronic media.

Since joining the EU in 1995 Finland follows the general EU media recommendations, and competition is becoming prevalent in the electronic media. The major changes have been produced by new media technology; digital radio (DAB) technology is ready to be used, while the digitalization of TV is an issue of policy debate. The technology is available for its distribution but the financing remains to be resolved.

A new broadcasting law was enacted in 1994. There is legislation for cable and video (1987). Commercial cable TV companies have since moved towards networking, so the main debate today concerns the competition for advertising money between the commercial national television channel, MTV3, and the newspapers. With the entry of the newspapers into electronic forms of distribution of information, like the commercial TV channel (Helsinki Media was given a licence for an analogic, commercial national TV channel in 1996), there is increasing competition in TV advertising. Also, the Swedish commercial TV company, TV 3 (Kinnevik) and the Scandinavian Broadcasting System (SBS) are planning to start commercial TV distribution via satellite to Finland.

A new national commercial radio channel started in 1997, called Radio Nova, owned by News Radio Finland. It is owned by the MTV Group, Aamulehti newspaper and communication companies.

Following the development of information technology, where strong competition is expected in the near future, the political debates surrounding telecommunications regulation centre on who has ownership of the trunk lines, and who should be allowed to lease the lines for voice and data transmissions. The new law on telemarkets (1997) opened up full competition. Thus Finland has one of the most liberated telemarkets in the world. The newspaper publishers have announced plans for electronic data and voice transmission, in order to publish in electronic form. Many newspapers are already available in Internet (WWW) editions. The big publishers are following the latest technology (digital radio and television), and will enter that market as well.

Technological development changes the media landscape as more channels and operators enter the market. Thus issues like the role of public broadcasting, the fragmentation of the audiences and commercialization will continue to be debated. The digitalization of media, and new operators entering the market, are issues of media policy.

The structure of the electronic media has changed through deregulation: the national channels (TV and radio) are operated by the YLE, and the third national commercial TV channel is operated by a private company, the Mainos Television Group. The new entrant on the scene, operating Four, the new national TV channel, is the newspaper company Helsinki Media.

Another general trend has been the networking of the local radio stations and the cable TV companies.

Changes in public broadcasting

The role of public broadcasting is a matter of discussion in today's competitive environment. The increasing audience for commercial television and local radio, and the role of public broadcasting generally in today's society (whether postmodern or information society), were some of the reasons given for a reform of the Finnish Broadcasting Company in 1994 (replacing previous legislation from 1934).

The organizational structure of the Finnish Broadcasting Company (YLE) was changed, with four main units: television, radio and two smaller Swedish radio and TV units. The main purpose of the reorganization was to emphasize programme production and lighten the organization.

The 1994 Act clarifies the role of public broadcasting in an increasingly competitive environment. YLE should promote the universality principle, should make programmes accessible to all citizens and support democracy, following the general principles of the European public broadcasters. According to this Act, 30% of YLE shares, owned by the state, should be sold off. At present the state owns 99.9% of the shares.

The Act reaffirms the Finnish Broadcasting Company's right to public broadcasting with an Administrative Council nominated by the parliament. The Council nominates the Board and the President of the company.

Radio

The Radio Unit of YLE has three national channels: YLE1, Radiomafia and Radio Suomi. YLE1 is a culture and classical music channel, Radiomafia is a popular music channel and Radio Suomi a regional, news programmes channel and a national popular music channel. YLE's 20 regional channels operate through Radio Suomi. The Swedish language radio has two regional channels covering the coastal areas of the country. Additionally, there is the News Department, serving all radio channels. Radio Finland is an English- and German-language channel for global distribution, and Sami Radio a channel for Lappland. The digital radio plans will enable operation of six national radio channels.

Today there are about 59 local radio stations; they are mostly private and commercial. The licence for broadcasting is given for five years at a time by the Ministry of Transport and Communications.

The local radio stations have become a permanent and important part of the Finnish broadcasting system. They have increased their share of the audience, and are increasingly networked in their programme production, like the news, and also other programmes. Foreign ownership has increased slightly, though their share is still small. Classic Radio in the Helsinki area is an example of foreign ownership.

Digital radio will bring major change in the future.

Television

The change of television system in recent years has been a major one. In 1993 the MTV Finland group started to operate on its own channel, MTV3, and it was given an independent operating licence, valid until 1999.

In 1997 a new analogue TV channel will start, owned by one of the biggest media companies in Finland, Helsinki Media. This commercial channel is called simply Four, as the fourth channel. Until 1997 there have been three national TV channels. The YLE, as a public broadcasting company, has operated two national TV channels (TV1 and TV2), and the commercial MTV3 operated through YLE's national channels until it became fully independent. Getting its own channel caused major changes in the programme structure and operations of MTV Finland, as it began competing with YLE for the same audience. Both are full service companies, although MTV transmits mainly fictional material, news and entertainment.

The ownership of the MTV Group changed in April 1997. The Aamulehti Corporation became the biggest shareholder, and the Swedish media company Marieberg, through Aamulehti, the biggest owner. The YLE sold its shares in MTV to major publisher Yhtyneet Kuvalehdet. The rest is owned by Sanoma, central organizations of commerce and insurance companies.

Historically, deregulation of television started in 1986, when a purely commercially financed channel was given an operating licence. This company, Channel Three, was owned by MTV Finland, the Finnish Broadcasting Company and Nokia Ltd. The media political reasons for opening that channel were to attract more advertising revenue for television, though the cultural policy argument was to open a TV channel for domestic (independent) production. The latter argument failed in reality, but MTV3 today is a result of the integration of MTV Finland and Channel Three.

As a public broadcaster, YLE faces on one side the obligations to meet the needs of a large audience, and on the other side competition from MTV Finland's soap operas, game shows, light entertainment and news, which have given MTV the largest audience. The major competition will take place between the YLE and MTV Finland. The latter is paying an annually agreed fee to the YLE for using its distribution network. As a commercial company, it also needs to attract advertisers with programmes attracting large audiences.

YLE's financing is based mainly on the licence fees (76.6%) and secondly on MTV Finland's payments for usage of the YLE distribution network

(20.6%). About 3% is based on state funding and other income. The two commercial TV companies are paying a public service fee, which is partly used to finance YLE.

YLE has additionally a teletext service, and transmits Swedish domestic programmes for the Finnish audience through TV4, a channel which can be seen in southern and western Finland. YLE wants to rent that channel to an operator, as the audience is very small and the channel is expensive.

Cable television

The cable companies have continued to increase their penetration of households in Finland. Today, about 38% of households (780 000) are connected to cable networks. The cable companies are mainly distribution systems for satellite TV, YLE and MTV Finland. The biggest cable company, HTV, established in 1990, together with cable TV companies from Tampere and Turku, have set up a programme network, PTV, to cooperate in purchasing, marketing and advertising. Almost 50% of households with cable connection belong to this network.

The cable companies are generally owned by newspaper publishers together with local, private telephone companies. It has been expensive for the companies to produce their own programmes, so their own production is minor. PTV shows mainly soap operas, game shows and news. It is financed by audience fees and commercials and has a pay-TV service. Today in the Helsinki area there are 24 satellite channels to be seen on cable.

Cable licences are issued by the government through the Ministry of Transport and Communications. Domestic production should be 25% of the total programme time for large cable TV companies. Commercials may not be more than 11% of the programme time.

Generally, the audience has stayed with the national television channels, and satellite and cable TV has a minor share of the audience. The small role of independent producers has been a concern lately. Independent producers of programmes have little access to TV distribution, only if the TV companies have jointly produced programmes with them or they have been able to sell their products to TV companies. The cultural policy has been to support them financially and thus give them access to production and distribution. Their position is, however, problematic.

Television and radio audience

The national TV channels gain the major share of the audience. The YLE channels reach daily 65% of the audience (over nine years old). The average total viewing time was 2 hours 30 minutes in 1996, with YLE's programmes taking up 48.2% of the viewing time (TV1 25.4%, TV2 21%, FST 1.7%); MTV3 gained the largest share of the audience, 44.4%. In general the viewing time has increased. Satellite and cable viewing comprise 7.4% of the viewing time.

Radio reaches 82% of the audience daily. Out of that, the commercial local radios reach 39% of the audience and the YLE 62%. YLE1 reaches 13% of the audience, Radiomafia 18% and Radio Suomi 42%.

Issues of the future

Through membership of the European Union, from 1 January 1995 Finland has been covered by the communal agreements on TV and radio. The main issues are the TV Directive and copyright. Technological development will be rapid through integration of telecommunications and broadcasting. This affects distribution technology initially and receivers afterwards. Digital radio and TV are the technologies of the near future.

European integration and technological development produce challenges for a television and radio system seeking to follow both European and domestic media policy. The domestic media policy needs to be rediscussed, since the structures of ownership and the media landscape are changing. Foreign owners will have greater interest in Finnish local radio, cable TV and national TV networks. Major foreign companies currently operating in Finland are the Swedish Marieberg, the SBS (the Scandinavian Broadcasting System), which is a shareholder in local radio stations already, the Swedish Kinnevik and American United International Holdings.

The main growth in the media will take place in telecommunications, in data and voice transmission. The deregulation will continue, and competition will increase. The growth of mobile phones and the Internet is very strong; the number of daily users of Internet more than doubled from 1995 to 1996.

Since the civil society and local issues will have more importance in the future, the local media will also possibly gain greater prominence, as will the increasingly important issue of media globalization.

Statistics

(1 ECU = 5.84 Finmark, FM)

Population (1996)

Number of inhabitants	5 132 320
Geographical size	338 145 km^2
Population density	17 per km^2
Number of households	2 198 791

Broadcasting (1996)

Number of television channels	4 + 1
Number of radio channels	6

Source: YLE

Local TV	3
Local radio licences	59
Cable connected households	780 000 (38%)

Radio
YLE
R1: culture and classical music
R2: popular music
R3: regional programmes, news
R4: Swedish national channel
R5: Swedish regional channel
Radio Nova
Local radios

Television
YLE: TV1, TV2
TV4 (Swedish programmes)
MTV3
Four
Local TV
Cable TV

Advertising (1996)

Total media advertising spend	FM4.5 bn
Print media	72%
of this daily press	54%
Audiovisual media	25%
of this TV	21%
Radio	4.0%
Internet	0.1%

Source: Gallup-Media Finland

No. of main independent national and regional newspapers	56
Circulation of principal newspapers	3.3 million

Source: Newspaper Publishers' Association

5

France

Michael Palmer and Claude Sorbets

National profile

Occupying a surface area of 549 000 km^2, metropolitan France has a relatively small population (about 56.6 million inhabitants) and a low population density (102 inhabitants per km^2). Eighteen per cent of the population live in and around the capital. Traditionally, France has proved difficult to govern, because of its geographical diversity and socio-economic and cultural variations and disparities.

With the parliamentary victory of the Right in 1986, the pendulum swung towards liberalism and privatization, after the socialist-led nationalization phase of the early 1980s. Between March 1986 and May 1988, a socialist President of the Republic 'cohabited' in an uneasy peace with the new right-wing government of Jacques Chirac. In May 1988, François Mitterrand was re-elected President. In the new National Assembly, the socialists emerged with a relative – not an absolute – majority. This imposed constraints on the government headed by Michel Rocard, a (democratic) socialist: no more companies were to be nationalized or privatized; government posts were offered to leading figures of 'civil' society – ostensibly without a political affiliation; their reputation owed much to their media skills.

In 1997, the structure of the French economy remains marked by tensions and forces of the past. France has a mixed economy. Neo-liberal advocates and free-market economics appear to have triumphed: few, if any, national political leaders challenge assumptions that underline their cause. Some observers claim indeed that the French economy has benefited both from the radical shot-in-the-arm applied by left-wing governments, and from the corrective measures subsequently taken by conservative governments. This continual process throughout the 1980s of 'action' and 'reaction' was particularly in evidence in the area of new communication technologies.

In 1981, the Left argued that the new technologies were a means of escaping from the economic crisis that was then common to many advanced industrial economies. The government launched a two-pronged action programme: the nationalization of key companies in the communications equipment sector (Matra, Thomson, CGE), and a comprehensive industrial policy for the 'electronics sector' or '*filière*' – a term used in the Farnoux report of March 1982. This policy straddled the entire Research and

Development process, from basic component chips to a wide range of technologies, products and services (fibreoptics, digitalization of telecommunications etc.). This policy was gradually abandoned. It failed to have the desired impact in combating unemployment; the attempt to encompass all the links in the electronics chain foundered; the contrasting positions of the various nationalized companies in their respective markets made the implementation of a coherent collective policy impossible. Furthermore, the government of the Left was forced to adapt its policy from 1982–3 on to the underlying trend towards the privatization of industrial production; the state adopted a lower profile in the management of the economy. Thus the policy of the Chirac government from 1986 merely accentuated a trend that had begun, albeit discreetly (around 1985), with the privatization of companies nationalized by the Left in the early 1980s, and the privatization of other industrial groups. In the communications media sector, the privatization of France's leading (and oldest) public service TV channel, TF1, in 1986–7, was strongly criticized; yet, in acting thus, the Chirac government was 'building on' a policy that appeared during the socialist (Fabius) government of 1984–6, with the emergence of private sector TV channels (La Cinq and TV6).

From the mid-1970s, beginning with the Giscard d'Estaing presidency, successive governments sought to transform the French telecoms system from one of the most backward of advanced industrial societies to one of the most modern of the industrialized world. D.G.T-France Télécom also symbolized government determination to modernize French industry. French companies were obliged to be more attentive to the international environment and market possibilities, and were afforded assistance in facing the challenge of the emerging world leaders in communications technologies.

Within France, the decentralization policy of the Mauroy (1981–4) government proved sufficiently far-reaching that no subsequent government dared call it into question (even on the Right). The transfer of various powers to the regions was seen as an integral part of the reshaping of the public sphere. In the communications sector, new media outlets and new operators emerged; it was realized both that the local context might be influenced by the national and international strategies of the actors or operators present at the local level, and that established actors might call on greater resources than newly emerging local actors.

For at least 25 years – beginning with the events of May–June 1968 – the audiovisual issue was a central feature of national politics: the status and nature of the broadcasting regulatory body featured in the platform on which François Mitterrand was re-elected President in 1988. In 1995, for the first time during a campaign to elect a president of the Fifth Republic, audiovisual policy was not an issue. Following the election of Jacques Chirac as President (May 1995), the government headed by Alain Juppé did not even have a minister with responsibility for communication policy. The state continued to focus the political agenda on privatization and deregulation, and on the resulting reduction in the role of the state (as employer, provision of social security benefits etc.). The period of fundamental policy debates appeared to have ended. Likewise, the main thrust of deregulation and industrial reorganization came to a close as European market factors and international capital flows replaced all talk of 'national champions'.

Development of the press and broadcasting since 1945

There are at least two possible interpretations of the development of the press and broadcasting (or more generally, of print media and the audio-visual sector) during the past 50 years. Broadcasting and the press developed separately, and insofar as there was contact, the new broadcasting media undermined the print media. According to this interpretation, the trend towards the concentration of ownership of newspaper publishing companies is endogenous, whereas the subsequent diversification of many media companies is due to the growing interdependence of the audiovisual and print media; this interdependence called into question the state control of broadcasting that dates from 1945.

The other interpretation involves a radically different approach. Communication technologies, rather than the media themselves, are the key factor. This approach highlights the perceived convergence between telecommunications and computing. Regulatory texts and policy have rarely, if at all, run counter to the main economic and technological trends of communications development. In recent years, laws, rules and regulations have attempted, rather, to provide a very loose framework for a sector that is in considerable flux. New actors have emerged and others disappeared; new media outlets have come on-stream and long-established media have been revitalized.

The press

The number of newspaper titles has declined since 1945: there were 11 general interest (i.e. non-specialist) Parisian dailies and 65 provincial dailies in 1988. Many partisan and committed, politically or otherwise, daily 'newspapers' folded, whereas ostensibly middle of the road or apolitical titles fared better. The regional daily newspaper (as opposed to the 'departmental' or 'county' title) has expanded over the past two to three decades, often at the expense of the provincial markets of Parisian dailies.

The 1944 ordinance aimed to protect the press from capitalist forces and from foreign influences: the full financial details of newspaper publishing company accounts were to be published; the same entity (an individual or a company) was not to control or manage more than one daily newspaper. This rule was repeatedly violated. On the one hand, the state did little to offset the market trend towards the concentration of ownership; on the other, it subsidized the newspaper industry. A complex system of direct and, above all, indirect subsidies helped newspaper publishers modernize their plant and presses and thus indirectly helped them acquire other newspaper titles. In

1982–4, the left-wing government headed by Pierre Mauroy attempted to update this text and the Léotard law of 1986 modified the context in which newspaper publishing groups sought to expand their multi-media interests. From the vantage point of 1990, it appears that it is indeed print-based multi-media groups that have emerged triumphant from the trend towards the concentration of ownership and towards diversification. These groups were precisely those that proved the most skilful in playing a system of fiscal aids and political connections: companies such as Hachette and Hersant thus emerged in the 1980s as leading actors in the new version of 'the French media landscape'. In the early 1990s, groups that were not overly and ostensibly politicized (ownership of national, Paris-based newspaper titles) and that diversified abroad and in multi-media interests (such as Hachette) were in better shape than groups like Hersant or others suffering from declining sales and advertising revenues of a dwindling newspaper market.

Concentration of press ownership

In France, the concentration of the ownership of print media occurred in two ways: expansion from a given title's original catchment area and chain ownership of newspapers established across the country. Regional newspaper publishing groups (such as Ouest-France) belong to the first category; the Hersant and Hachette groups to the second. In both cases, a merger or the acquisition of majority control came about as a result of a process in which the company that was ultimately taken over was initially the aggressor. In both cases, likewise, a merger leads the successful company to threaten yet another group. 'Frontier disputes' between rival groups led them to agreements intended to avoid 'newspaper wars' with compromises over who should distribute which title where.

The (shared) control of the advertising revenue of newspaper titles which pool their advertising space effectively dissuades any potential new market entrants. But such pooling of advertising revenue strengthens the hand of the advertising middlemen who have more say over the news/editorial content because they 'control' the advertising columns. There are 17 such pooled advertising newspaper groups. Nearly every individual newspaper title has 'surrendered' (at least in part) the control of its advertising columns to bulk ad space vendors: the latter are sometimes subsidiaries of advertising groups like Publicis or Havas; others are an integral part of a press group, such as Hersant's Publiprint.

Broadcasting

The Ordinance of 23 March 1945 formalized the state monopoly of broadcasting: this was assigned to Radiodiffusion de France (which later became Radiodiffusion-Télévision de France (RTF)). Television, like radio before it, developed very slowly at first. The earliest experimental broadcasts dated from the late 1930s: the three state channels only enjoyed full nationwide coverage by the early 1970s. Successive broadcasting reforms often complicated the resolution of technical problems.

Initially established as a public company accountable to the Ministry of Information, RTF in June 1964, became an 'Office' (ORTF), closely supervised by the government. In 1969, Prime Minister Jacques Chaban Delmas, seeking to liberalize the medium in the aftermath of the 'events' of May 1968, abolished the Ministry of Information. Three years later, the Act of 3 July 1972 confirmed the basic principles of the public service broadcasting monopoly.

When Valéry Giscard d'Estaing became President of the Republic in 1974, a purge occurred at the Maison Ronde (Broadcasting House) and a new Act (July 1974) substantially changed the situation. The 'Office' was split up into seven public companies (*établissements* and *sociétés*) that together formed public service broadcasting: TF1, Antenne 2, FR3, Radio France, TDF, SFP, INA. Only in 1982 did the Act – of 29 July – at last end the state monopoly of television programme channels; the 1982 law encouraged a diversity of channels. But in the new context, PSB no longer had a clearly defined place, and the transition from a state to a public service broadcasting ethos proved an on-going process lasting a decade or more.

Technological progress, on the one hand, fostered the free radio movement – *les radios libres* – and, on the other, encouraged those in charge of the broadcasting and telecommunications transmission monopolies to profit from the new opportunities. The DGT, for instance, became involved in the provision of value-added services and encountered the competition of private sector actors in satellites and telematics.

One of the overall aims of the 1982 Audiovisual Communications Act was to open up the media field to new actors and to allow traditional actors new opportunities. The provisions of the law were so couched as to allow subsequent decrees (*décrets d'application*) to fill in specific points. The process of deregulation proved even more extensive than that originally envisaged by the proponents of the law.

The law allowed for the development of a private audiovisual sector. Independent or 'free' radio stations as well as videotex fell within its remit. The law distinguished between the media and their content. It recognized that it would be increasingly difficult to maintain the existing separation between 'private correspondence' (the telephone network) and public broadcasting (TDF transmission equipment). The Act distinguished between media that were 'rare' or 'abundant'. For instance, the state might concede a 'public service' to a private concern, in the case of a severe scarcity of transmission facilities (terrestrial television channels, satellite transponders).

The Act established an independent broadcasting regulatory body, the Haute Autorité de la Communication Audiovisuelle (HA). The HA was to ensure the independence of public service broadcasting (PSB). The HA appointed the chief executives (PDG) of the national and regional public broadcasting companies and issued operating licences to local radio stations and cable TV operators. Members of the HA were appointed for nine years, according to a procedure similar to that used to appoint members of the Constitutional Council. The HA was to act as a buffer between public service broadcasting bodies and the government. Tension later arose between an Haute Autorité trying to assert its powers and a government seeking to preserve its ability to influence developments (and appointments) in the broadcasting sector.

While providing a formal structure for PSB, the 1982 law said little or nothing about how this was to be funded: the government, for example, continued to determine the TV licence fee, the major component in the funding of PSB companies. The government and the regulatory body alike had to respond to the demands and pressures of often contradictory forces. Paradoxically, a government committed to a system that gave pride of place to PSB, experienced growing pressures to develop private sector broadcasting.

In 1986, the new right-wing parliamentary majority voted in the communications law piloted through parliament by Communication Minister François Léotard. This both signalled the end of the Fillioud law of 1982 and opened the path to deregulation, overseen by a new regulatory body that replaced the HA – the Commission Nationale de la Communication et des Libertés (CNCL). In May 1988, the new left-of-centre government of Michel Rocard secured parliamentary support for the establishment of yet another regulatory body, the Conseil Supérieur de l'Audiovisuel, in place of the discredited (argued President Mitterrand and the Left) CNCL. Between 1982 and 1989, the issue of the broadcasting regulatory body replaced that of the status of broadcasting programme channels as the most contentious issue for communication policy-makers.

During the second presidency of the socialist François Mitterrand, the appointment of first left-wing (1988) and then right-wing (1993) governments did not lead to major changes in audiovisual policy. The role and resources of public service broadcasting, however, continued to remain a contentious issue. The Tasca (1989) and Lang (1990) legislation led to the pooling of resources, a common management structure and the definition of complementary strategies for the two main public service channels; thus Antenne 2 and FR3 underwent a change – France 2, France 3 – in the process of becoming the two constituent parts of a holding company – France-Television – run by a single Director-General. In February 1994 the Carignon law – named after the Communication Minister of the Balladur government (1993–5) – updated minor aspects of the existing broadcasting legislation and facilitated the launch in December 1994 of the education channel (La Cinquième) for which the Parisian intelligentsia had been lobbying for over a decade. La Cinquième shared a frequency (and transmission time) with the cultural channel 'La Sept'; this frequency was previously used to transmit the programmes of the insolvent and now defunct private channel 'La Cinq'.

The press

The 1980s saw several pieces of legislation intended to preserve the pluralism of newspaper titles, the diversity of press ownership and to ensure the transparency of the accounts of newspaper publishing companies. The law of 23 October 1984 set up a 'press transparency and pluralism commission': newspaper publishers such as Robert Hersant ignored the commission and a subsequent law, promulgated in August 1986, abolished it. The 1984 law was enacted under the socialists (the Mauroy–Fabius administrations of 1981–6); the 1986 law under the conservative–liberal Chirac administration. Press policy in the 1980s, like broadcasting policy, was a political ping-pong game. With the advent of the democratic socialist left-of-centre Rocard administration (May 1988) the reform of the press no longer figured on the political agenda.

France is the EU country which, with Italy, has the most complete and varied system of direct and indirect press subsidies: the figure involved represents some 12–15% of the total turnover of the French press. The principle of such aid dates from the Liberation (even if the press enjoyed certain advantages, such as preferential postal tariffs, long before). Parliament examines these 'aids' every year when it debates the government's budget proposals. A state fund operates to favour financially weak political daily newspapers: in 1988 beneficiaries included the Catholic *La Croix – L'Evénement*, the Communist party's *L'Humanité*, the right-wing *Présent* and the left-of-centre *Libération*.

The trend towards the concentration of ownership is less advanced in France than in other EU countries. In 1986, the ten leading newspaper and magazine publishing groups accounted for half of the total turnover of the press, and the top 30 for three-quarters. (In the UK, four companies accounted for 80% of the turnover of the companies publishing national dailies.) Yet the issue of mergers and takeovers involving newspaper titles is politically acutely sensitive.

Occupying the first or second rank in classifications of French press publishing companies, the Hersant 'group' was the bane of the French socialists, especially in the early and mid-1980s. Hersant epitomized the failure of such anti-concentration measures in France. The 1944 ordinance stipulated that no one *personne* (an individual, or a company) should publish, directly or through an intermediary, more than one daily: in 1976 dailies published by the Hersant group included the regional daily *Paris-Normandie* and three Parisian dailies with national pretensions – the conservative *Le Figaro*, the popular (in style and content) *France-Soir* and (the moribund) *L'Aurore*. Tainted with a collaborationist past (in Pétain's France, 1940–4), and known for his outspoken anti-communism and contempt for (some of) the journalists who worked for him, Hersant was the *bête noire* of socialists and journalist trade unions. The 1983 press bill was largely seen as directed specifically against him. Yet, heavily amended, the 1984 press law fixed limits on the concentration of ownership that, in effect, did not force the Hersant – or any other – group to divest itself of any of its titles: no group was to control titles whose combined circulation exceeded 15% that of national dailies, or 15% that of regional dailies, or 10% of the total circulation of both.

The 1984 law was not retroactive – and Hersant rode roughshod over it. In January 1986 he acquired the company publishing *Le Progrès*, the major regional daily published in Lyons, France's second biggest city, and various satellite titles – irrespective of protests of government ministers and of the press transparency and pluralism commission. Hersant stated: 'I am merely anticipating the next law.' So it proved: after the parliamentary elections of March 1986, and the appointment of the Chirac government, a new press law was promulgated in August and completed following the 'observations' of the Constitutional Council on 27 November. It abolished the commission and reduced the requirements intended to ensure the transparency of the accounts of communications companies. Above all, the 1986 communications legislation imposed limits on the concentration of ownership by companies with multi-media interests – in the press, radio and in terrestrial, cable and satellite television. These limits were, however, relatively generous. For example, a group may control up to 30% of the circulation of the daily press, provided that it does not control other media; if it has substantial interests in the broadcasting media, it may control up to 10% of the circulation of the daily press. The law did not take into account the ownership of weekly or other non-daily titles. The Hersant group, once again, did not have to divest itself of any titles; and, in February 1987, the CNCL, the regulatory body set up by the 1986 law, awarded the franchise to operate the fifth terrestrial TV channel in France to a consortium in which a Hersant company, TVES, was the lead operator, with a 25% stake.

Ownership and finance

The horizontal and vertical integration of leading communications groups increased during the 1980s: print media groups diversified into other media; companies or conglomerates diversified into the hardware or software of the communications sector from which they had previously been absent; leading French print media groups pursued their expansion in Europe and abroad; and foreign groups acquired or launched titles in the French daily newspaper and magazine press. French press groups were not authorized to diversify into radio and television until the mid-1980s; previously, their expansion was mainly confined to publishing and advertising. During the 1980s, the structure of the French media market became more similar to that of other European countries; the struggle for the control of French press groups, often considered previously primarily in terms of political influence, increasingly has been decided by strictly financial considerations.

None the less, when considered in a European context, the French press has continued to present three major weaknesses: the readership of daily newspapers is ageing and declining; advertising revenue is relatively limited (both in absolute terms, and in terms of the decline of the press's share of total advertising expenditure); French press companies are under-capitalized and profit margins are low.

These factors accentuated during the 1980s the trend towards the concentration of ownership discernible since the early 1950s, especially in the daily newspaper market. The increase in the sales price of a daily has been substantially greater than the rise of the cost of living: expressed in constant francs, a paper that sold for 4.50 francs in 1988 cost the reader 1.10 francs in 1947. Titles disappeared or else merged and shared advertising revenue. From the mid-1960s, the modernization of printing technologies and plant, and the advent of commercial television (advertising was authorized on PSB TV channels from 1968), led to a perceived shortfall in press revenues that accentuated the trend to the concentration of ownership. These factors were again significant in the 1980s, with the advent of electronic publishing, offset printing and photocomposition, on the one hand, and, on the other, the passage between 1983 and 1986 from three public service TV channels (whose advertising was limited to 25% of total revenue) to six channels that all carry advertising and where, in the main, the 'commercial logic' prevails.

According to France's leading economic news magazine, *L'Expansion* – itself the flagship of France's 12th biggest press group – 14 groups had a turnover exceeding Ffr1 bn in 1988. The five leading groups were Hachette-Presse, Hersant Group, Editions Mondiales, Ouest-France and CEP Communications.

Hachette-Presse exemplifies the difficulty of analysing the ownership structure and conglomerate interests of French communications groups. Hachette-Presse is a division of Hachette: with a total group turnover in 1988 of Ffr24.4 bn (29.05 bn in 1989), the latter was the 28th biggest French industrial company. Its president, Jean-Luc Lagardère, also heads the electronics (civilian and military communications) group Matra, ranked number 35 among French industrial companies; Lagardère's right-hand man, and indeed his associate in the acquisition of Hachette in 1981, is Daniel Filipacchi of Publications Filipacchi – the publisher of titles such as *Paris-Match* – ranked number 8 among the print media groups.

During the past decade, the Hachette group, like that of Robert Hersant, tested the provisions of French common law and communications law concerning 'the dominant position' acquired in certain market sectors by the emerging multi-media conglomerates. In late 1990 (September–October) Hachette obtained the authorization of the broadcasting regulatory authority, the CSA, to replace the Hersant group as the lead operator in the consortium holding the franchise for La Cinq.

The attempt in 1990 by France's leading multi-media group to acquire control of France's second main private sector TV channel (estimated share of the TV viewing public: 12%) posed a series of issues relating to pluralism and the concentration of ownership. These specifically concerned: the treatment of La Cinq by *Télé 7 Jours* (Hachette-owned), France's leading

TV programme listings magazine; the control of the advertising budgets and airtime of La Cinq; the possibility of vertical integration with production companies that were already, in effect, Hachette subsidiaries; and, in sound radio, the links between Europe 1, Europe 2 (a purveyor of programmes, not a radio network) and Skyrock (an FM radio network of the Filipacchi group, whose advertising revenues and airtime are run by Europe 1).

Structure and organization

French newspapers are generally divided into Paris-based titles (with 'national' pretensions) and provincial (regional and 'departmental' or county) daily newspapers. Some titles published in Paris are genuinely national: they are to be found on sale in many of the 50 000 newspaper sales-points across France (*Le Monde*, *Le Figaro*, for instance). But other Parisian titles, such as *Le Quotidien de Paris*, while they may count politically as part of the 'national' press, have low circulations (well under 50 000 copies, for example); they are on sale primarily in Paris and other major cities, and through subscription (*La Croix–L'Evénement* is primarily distributed via subscription).

In 1988, there were 11 general interest (i.e. non-specialist) French daily newspapers published in Paris. There were 65 provincial dailies. The provincial titles accounted for 70.8% of the total circulation of the French daily newspaper press. In many regions of France there is one dominant title, published in the major city of the region. From the 1950s to the 1980s, there long existed tacit agreements between the leading titles of neighbouring regions not to engage in a 'newspaper war' and compete for sales and – even more important – advertising revenue in 'border' areas.

Between 1952 and 1988, the total circulation of the French daily press rose from 9.6 million to 13.05 million copies: but given the growth of the French population, newspaper readership overall is declining.

The relatively poor performance of French daily newspapers (compared to their British and German counterparts) is partly offset by the strength of the magazine and 'periodical' press.

Three groups dominate the 'periodical' press sector: Hachette (publisher of *Télé 7 Jours*), Editions mondiales (with *Télé Poche* and *Modes et Travaux*) and Prisma Presse (with *Femme Actuelle*, *Prima* and *Télé Loisirs*). Prisma Presse is a subsidiary of the German group Gruner & Jahr, whilst the British group EMAP is becoming a significant player in the French magazine press.

In 1995, the state of the French daily newspaper market could best be described as 'sluggish': Paris-based daily national titles were in a more critical state than the regional and provincial dailies. Some Parisian titles succeeded in relaunching, with a new appeal (format, circulation, advertising revenue). *Le Monde* did so in 1995, while the attempted relaunch of *Libération* was less successful. Some Parisian titles folded (*Le Quotidien de Paris*); but – despite the many Cassandras – some new titles succeeded in identifying and targetting a market (such as the low-price, tabloid format *Information*, owned in 1995 by a company headed by André Rousselet, formerly President Mitterrand's media policy adviser and the 'creator' of Canal Plus).

Electronic media

The situation in 1995 had largely been shaped by the Léotard communications law of September 1986 (which the Lang-Tasca laws of 1989, 1990 partly modified) and by the Carignon law of February 1994. The left-of-centre government in office from May 1988 decided not to repeat 'the errors' of previous governments, which had repealed the audiovisual legislation of their predecessors. A central issue of the period between 1982 and 1989 was the status, functions and powers of an independent regulatory body for the audiovisual sector. The controversy surrounding the creation of the three successive bodies – Haute Autorité, Commission Nationale de la Communication et des Libertés, Conseil Supérieur de l'Audiovisuel – highlighted the issue of their membership and mode of appointment: on each occasion, the opposition suspected that the body would be indirectly controlled by the government; they saw each major decision of the regulatory body as proof of this self-fulfilling prophecy.

By 1990, it appeared that the heated and impassioned climate surrounding previous broadcasting reforms was a thing of the past. The CSA was entrusted with the preservation of pluralism of the means of expression (and their ownership); the issues of advertising and sponsorship in broadcasting fell within its remit; it appointed the chief executives of public service broadcasting organizations; it issued licences to run radio stations and to operate private television channels (either terrestrial or relayed by satellite) and the licences to operate cable networks.

Television

Meanwhile, the complexity of the television industry grew throughout the 1980s. This was due largely to the increase in the number of channels and their different legal status and funding. By 1990, there were channels with local, national and European programmes, audiences and ambitions. Some television channels were terrestrial, others were relayed by cable and/or satellite; some satellite TV channels were relayed Direct-to-Home (DTH), like TDF1, while others used telecommunications satellites, such as Télécom 1–2.

The Tasca law of 1990 created a 'super-president' or overlord for the two public service channels, Antenne 2 (A2) and France Régions 3 (FR3), launched respectively in 1964 and 1972. Their 1990 budget was respectively Ffr3.3 bn and Ffr3.4 bn.

The super-president was to marshall the joint resources of these PBS channels and ensure that they complemented one another in the competition against private sector channels and secured 40% of the total audience. FR3 chafed against the obligation – in principle, temporary – to surrender transmission time and broadcast (on Saturdays) programmes of the new public service channel beamed via TDF1 (from April 1989). Because it could otherwise only be received by satellite (and because less than 100 000 households had satellite receiver equipment), this channel, the SEPT (Société d'Editions de Programmes de Télévision), appeared in dire need of the publicity or 'window of opportunity' conferred by the use of FR3 transmission time.

Defined 'as a cultural channel with a European vocation', the SEPT is owned by various public service broadcasting organizations: FR3 has 45%, l'Institut National de l'Audiovisuel 15%, Radio France 15% and the state 25%. In September 1992 Arte began relaying 'La SEPT' via the terrestrial channel previously occupied by (now defunct) 'La Cinq'. From December 1994 they shared the frequency with the new educational channel 'La Cinquième'.

The public service television channels are: FR2 (national channel), FR3 (national and regional channel – it has 12 regional stations), SEPT/Arte (European channel), TV 5-Europe (European channel launched in November 1983, transmits programmes broadcast by various French-speaking countries, by satellite), and R.F.O. (transmits radio and TV programmes to French overseas territories and possessions). Arte and La Cinquième have a special public statute.

Private television channels

Canal Plus was the first private sector channel to be launched (November 1984). This subscriber channel is owned by a company holding a public service operating licence (issued in December 1983). The company's shareholders include Havas, CGE, CDC, Société générale, CCF and the l'Oréal group; company personnel and the general public own some 25% of the stock. After severe initial difficulties (the number of subscribers failed to meet anticipated target figures), Canal Plus has created, during the past few years, a host of subsidiary companies, and acquired minority interests in others, notably in the fields of audiovisual production, telematics and home shopping (by TV). It has also sited subscription TV companies in Belgium, Spain and elsewhere, and has interests in newspaper publishing, satellite and TV reception equipment companies. Canal Plus has more than 2.8 million subscribers and shows substantial profits. It was France's 29th service company in 1988, with a turnover of Ffr4.3 bn (TF1, France's premier TV channel, ranked 33rd, with a turnover of Ffr3.4 bn). It expects a steady growth in the number of subscribers in France and abroad, and is well placed to profit from the development of cable and satellite television.

TF1 (Télévision Française 1) was the first channel to be launched in France (8 December 1935). It was the first to carry commercial advertising (1968); from 1975, it broadcast in colour; and it was the first and only public service channel to be privatized (in 1987). The general public holds 33.8% of the stock and company employees 10%; 56.2% of shares are owned by a group of shareholders, the most important of which is the Bouygues construction company, in effect the 'owner-operator' of TF1, with 25% of the stock. The other major shareholders of this group include Pergamon, Maxwell, Maxwell Media SA, Editions mondiales, Bernard Tapie, Société générale and three other banks. In the period after 1989 Berlusconi acquired stock and Maxwell announced he wanted to sell out.

In February 1987, the CNCL awarded the licence to operate the fifth channel, La Cinq, to the Hersant and Berlusconi groups (which each had 25% of the stock of the operating company) for ten years. This licence superseded that awarded in 1985 (under the socialists) to a consortium of the Berlusconi, Seydoux and Riboud groups, which the Chirac government rescinded. M6 (Métropole télévision) is in a similar position. The Chirac government rescinded the operating licence issued under the socialists in 1985–6 for a TV music channel, TV6 (promoted by a consortium of advertising, cinema and radio companies – Publicis, Gaumont and NRJ), and the CNCL, in March 1987, awarded a licence to operate a new general channel, M6, owned by a consortium led by the CLT and the Lyonnaise des Eaux group.

The central issue in 1990 was no longer that of government interference but the ability of the advertising market to finance five general interest channels. Total advertising spend in 1989 was in the order of Ffr11.5 bn. The growth in the size of the overall advertising 'cake' slowed down, from 15.5% in 1988 and 12.9% in 1989 to an anticipated 9% in 1990 (source: IREP – l'Institut de recherche de d'études publicitaires). While the size of the TV 'share' of the cake had increased substantially in the 1980s, there were growing fears both that companies were preferring to advertise via non-media outlets (direct marketing, sales promotions etc.) and that the TV advertising market did not generate revenue sufficient to fund five general interest channels. Junior Communications Minister Catherine Tasca stated that there was one general interest channel too many. La Cinq had an audience share of 12% and a deficit of Ffr2.5 bn; M6 had an audience share of 8% and losses of Ffr1.2 bn. TF1 emerged triumphant during the 1986–1990 period in the competition for TV advertising revenues, a competition waged against both private sector and public service channels. In 1989, A2 failed to attract its target advertising revenues and had losses of Ffr321 m; it responded by preparing a 1991 budget in which anticipated revenue from licence fees exceed that from advertising. To help offset their continued losses, La Cinq and M6 battled to acquire full nationwide reception and, following the success of Hachette in replacing Hersant as the lead operator of La Cinq, there was (again) talk of some form of alliance between La Cinq and M6, aimed primarily against TF1.

TF1 and Canal Plus are profit-making: in 1989, their net profits were Ffr220 m and 740 m respectively. But TF1 represented a very heavy initial investment (Ffr6 bn in 1987 to acquire the licence to operate the channel for ten years); its profits, on a turnover of 5.3 bn, were relatively modest. La Cinq and M6, in their programme schedules (which contained many low-quality American programmes), contributed to the inflation in the cost of acquiring programme transmission rights, while failing to contribute to the production of French quality programmes; they occupied TV broadcasting frequencies that others dearly sought. In short, the increase in the number of channels did not lead to a corresponding increase in the quality of programmes on offer, and programme schedules, indeed, tended to a certain uniformity.

Programme schedules of existing, terrestrial channels, are continually modified – partly in response to the proliferation of 'thematic' channels transmitted by cable or satellite.

Local television

As with 'national' TV channels, at local level it is also necessary to distinguish between terrestrial and cable TV channels. In 1990, there were three local terrestrial TV channels: Télé-Toulouse, 8 Mont-Blanc and Télé 30 Lyon Métropole. They all carry local programmes and relay Euromusique or CNN programmes, and they are all loss-making.

Fifteen cable network TV channels form the other category of local TV channels. They are located in towns which have a cable network and which has assigned one channel to a local TV company. In the Cable Plan of 1982 (see below), local cable TV networks were assigned a major and vital role; in 1997, this was no longer the case.

Cable

In November 1982, the Mauroy government announced the cable plan, advocating the large-scale systematic cabling of the country. The minister presented cable as 'a massive, consistent and orderly solution to satisfy multiple communication needs'. But it was not before May 1984 that the government announced how the plan was to be implemented. The two-year interval was taken up with discussion by all the parties concerned as to how to achieve the initial objective, namely connecting 1.5 million homes in three years and the bulk of the population within about 15 years. In 1984, some 2% of households were cabled. The decision taken in the spring of 1984 represented a compromise between several sets of projects and strategies and an attempt to fulfil the main industrial objective, namely developing optical fibre technology. The cable plan rapidly encountered opposition from several parties. Local authorities had recently gained in power as a result of decentralization legislation; for electoral (and other) reasons they were little attracted by the massive investment cable required. The decision to assign to a state organization (the DGT) the overall control of the implementation of the new technology antagonized the manufacturers of cable equipment, who proved unable to produce what was required within the agreed price and time.

Following the Léotard communications law of 1986, the government officially abandoned the cable plan. The public operator, WT, was no longer in sole control of the implementation of the plan; likewise, the decision to use only optical fibre (and therefore maximize the interactivity potential of videocommunications) was abandoned. The result was that France would be cabled in a piecemeal fashion. Fifty-four local authorities had signed agreements with WT prior to the abandonment of the cable plan; another 49 undertook to be cabled, but on an ad hoc basis.

In 1990, some 2.4 million cable connections had been laid down; there were about 386 000 individual or collective subscribers. The penetration rate was about 16%. It was anticipated that by the end of 1990, there would be 500 000 subscribers for 3.3 million connections, and, by 1992, 1.3 million subscribers for 6 million connections.

The cabling of France therefore, entered by the late 1980s a more realistic phase. The industrial dimension remains present; but this is no longer piloted by public operators, the WT and TDF, but by private operators. The latter build the networks and have gone into audiovisual production; they promise to be the carrier for technical and commercial integration at the local, national and transnational levels and in multimedia activities.

By 1997, as a result of substantial investment by both state and private operators (SLEE, CGE, Bouygues, Havas etc.) many cable networks had been laid down; the take-up rate has remained low, with only 1.2 million households connected out of the more than 20 million.

Satellite

The decision to build a joint Franco-German satellite – taken by Valéry Giscard d'Estaing and Helmut Schmidt in 1979 – was never rescinded. But, with the passage of time, it appeared that the technology initially chosen was obsolete and unreliable. Successive governments were tempted to abandon a costly project (Ffr4 bn), but they yielded to the arguments of the industrial groups manufacturing the satellites and TV reception equipment. At stake was the future of the European TV industry (and what was left of the European electronics industry). The goal was HDT (High Definition Television) and the imposition of the European standard, the D2MAC Packet. In October 1990, it seemed that the TDF1–2 satellites, launched during the previous year, were unable to provide more than a minimal service: they could transmit the signals of only three channels. Both before and after their launch and entry into service, however, these satellites (or rather access to one of their transponders) were considered by various multi-media groups vital to their development.

Between 1988 and 1990, the CSA awarded the operating licence for use of the five channels that could be beamed via the TDF transponder to one

German-language channel and three (and a half) subscriber TV channels. The companies applying for a place on the French 'hot bird' planned to dovetail satellite with their cable or terrestrial transmissions. Commercial considerations were, at most, a secondary concern for the various satellite operators, especially the SEPT. The aim, rather, was to have access to the maximum possible means of transmitting programmes and thereby facilitate expansion. Thus, a general interest terrestrial channel like TF1 wanted to gain access to scrambled or encoded transmission (as is the case with some cable and satellite technologies); the CSA, however, rejected its application. The same general aim lies behind Canal Plus' strategy in its dealings with cable operators and behind the latter's strategy in diversifying into a range of media.

The TDF series of satellites never operated properly and is still not functioning. France Telecom's DBS proved successful but is currently challenged by Astra (Canal Plus, for example, chose to sign a contract with the Luxembourg operator to transmit its range – 'bouquet' – of programmes) and by Eutelsat (thus Arte is currently devising another 'bouquet' of public programme channels to be transmitted by Eutelsat).

Telematics

TDF's teletext system, Antiope, has been in decline whereas Minitel has gained an increasing number of subscribers (especially for professional, as opposed to domestic, usage). Seven years after it was launched as a commercial proposition, the Minitel videotex service could be accessed from 4.7 million terminals, most of them distributed free by PTT-France Télécom. The videotex industry employed 10 000 people and had a turnover of Ffr2 bn.

In 1995, France Television was experimenting with various multi-media technologies; it planned to join the 'electronic highway' 'bandwagon' symbolized by Internet, via improvements to the technologies that led to the Minitel.

Radio

In this sphere also, the political and professional agenda altered rapidly. The issue of pirate radio stations has been one of the key factors in bringing about the changes in the regulation of the audiovisual sector in the early 1980s. In the late 1970s, the threat to the state broadcasting monopoly posed by pirate radio stations led to their repression; but the socialist candidate François Mitterrand in the presidential election of 1981 came out in their support.

Private radio stations gradually gained in legality. 'Associations' were allowed to operate radio stations in a 1981 law; from 1984, private stations were authorized to carry advertising; in 1986 they were allowed to progress from a purely local dimension and form networks operating on a national scale. This seemingly haphazard process had many consequences: FM radio was the scene of considerable inventiveness, with the trying out of new programme formats and content, but it also saw the death of attempts at convivial (and amateur) sound broadcasting; newspaper publishing groups diversified into radio, and some municipal authorities tried to create their own (propaganda) stations. The main victors to emerge from this turbulent scene were new professional broadcasters (such as NRJ), who dominated the growing number of networks (and their affiliates).

Radio 'turbulence' has now ended. The actors who traditionally dominated sound broadcasting in France have emerged triumphant and reinvigorated from the severe (FM) competition. The long-established 'peripheral' radio stations (RTL, RMC, Europe 1) are now established on the FM wavelength (in addition to their traditional medium wave frequencies). The public service national radio station, Radio France, diversified into local broadcasting; in 1990 Radio France boasted a wider range of stations – France Inter, France Musique, France Culture, but also (the distinct and autonomous) Radio France International and several successful innovations of the 1980s, the 'round the clock' news service, France Infos, and 47 local radio stations – at town, district or departmental (county) level.

In addition to the public service radio stations which are still doing well (the success of France Info, the mixed results of the local radio station network), some of the new commercial radio stations (Skyrock, Fun radio – associated with RTL – etc.) played the provocative card, with talk-shows aimed at the young (and which, on occasion, provoked controversy and the intervention of the broadcasting regulatory body, the CSA).

Policies for the press and broadcasting

It has been said that France is a country of great geographical and cultural diversity, counterbalanced by a heavy-handed central government. The resultant underlying tension periodically explodes, in the form of political crises and national traumas, with Frenchmen divided into radically opposing camps. The present mood of relative calm, and of quiescence between the Left and the Right, may well be due less to the development of consensus politics than to the inability of political ideologies to apprehend and analyse the forces making for social change.

Broadcasting has long been highly politicized in France. Criticisms levelled at 'audiovisual' policy-makers and managers include 'government interference', excessive bureaucracy and the promotion of a 'homogenous culture'. As a symbol of Parisian centralism, state broadcasting was a target for various regional movements (Basque, Breton, Alsatian, Corsican and Occitan) that strive for recognition of their cultural identity and press for local self-government. The broadcasting reforms of the past decade, therefore, have to be seen in this general context. The reforms (of many sectors of public life) implemented after 1981 by the first non-conservative government for 23 years – the 'Government of the Left' appointed by François Mitterrand after his (first) election as President – reversed, or tried to break, century-old trends. Undertaken at a time of economic crisis, they disturbed established social and political attitudes and forces. Media policy issues in the 1990s have so far proved less contentious.

Policy trends

In the late 1990s issues remaining on the policy agenda include:

- the telecoms operator, the public utility France Telecom, has moved gingerly towards a more competitive environment, strategic alliances with its chosen European ally – Deutsche Telekom – and a form of privatization, despite the resistance of the unions representing most of its employees,
- France has championed the defence of the French language, of European culture and the French audiovisual industry – exemplified by the 'war against Hollywood' and the updating of the 'television without frontiers' EC Directive;
- the utopian rhetoric associated with the creation of an electronic agora and interactive democracy has lost its resonance in a society preoccupied by 'the social divide' in an urbanized, pluricultural society in crisis. At the same time, educational and other (non-commercial and non-entertainment) applications of new technologies (CD ROM, Internet etc.) remain a policy concern.

Statistics

1 ECU = 6.45 French francs, Ffr

Population (1995)

Inhabitants	58.3 million
Geographical size	549 000 km^2
Population density	102 per km^2

The press

Print media: top circulation (1995–6)

Télé 7 Jours	Wkly TV mag	2 789 818
Télé Z	Wkly TV mag	2 117 651
Télé Star	Wkly TV mag	1 853 347
Femme Actuelle	Wkly women's mag	1 768 519
Télé Loisirs	Wkly TV mag	1 574 899
Télé Poche	Wkly TV mag	1 349 419
Prima	Mthly women's mag	1 119 542
Notre Temps	Sr citizens' mthly mag	1 062 361
Reader's Digest	Gen. interest mthly mag	812 255
Ouest-France	Regional daily paper	769 001

Source: Diffusion Contrôle

Broadcasting (1995)

National television channels	
PBS	5
FR2, FR3, SEPT/Arte, TV5-Europe, R.F.O.	
Private	4
Canal Plus, TF1, La Cinq, M6	
Number of national radio channels	7
Local TV channels	
Terrestrial	3
Télé Toulouse, 8 Mont Blanc, Télé Lyon Métropole	
Cable network	15

Market shares of terrestrial over-the-air channels

	1993	1990
TF1	38.2	41
FR2	26.1	22
FR3	16.6	12
Canal Plus	4.7	4.7
Arte	1	(La Cinq) 11
M6	10.7	8.5
Others	2.6	

Source: Mediamat Médiamétrie

PSB financing

	Advertising	Licence fees	Sponsorship	Other
FR2	54.5%	40%	1.2%	4.3%
FR3	20.0%	80%		

Cable penetration

	1988	1990	1992	1993
No. of households linked to network	900 000	2 800 000	4 700 000	5 100 000
No. of subscribers	100 000	500 000	1 000 000	1 230 000

Cable network operating companies
Market shares

	No. of households linked to network	% share
France Telecom Câble	606 000	12.2
Lyonnaise Communication	1 275 000	25.3
Communication Developpement	1 011 000	20.1
Générales des Eaux	1 654 000	32.8
Others	484 000	9.6

Take-up rate

	No. of subscribers
France Telecom Câble	107 000
Lyonnaise Communication	208 000
Communication Developpement	807 000
Générale des Eaux	360 000
Others	172 000

6
Federal Republic of Germany (FRG)

Hans J. Kleinsteuber

National profile

Describing the national characteristics of Germany at this time is far from easy. The country was divided as a result of the Second World War and two separate political entities existed for 45 years. For the first four years after the war these were occupation zones, but in 1949 two states were established. In the field of mass media, two totally different systems emerged that very much resembled the models of their respective political 'camps', led by the United States and the Soviet Union.

As a consequence of the fast-developing unification process since October 1989, almost all indicators have changed or are changing, or more precisely, the system of the West has been adopted by the East with some modifications. On the historic side, the overview presented here concentrates on West Germany. But we also briefly describe the 'socialist' system of the former German Democratic Republic (GDR) and analyse the emerging framework for a common media system in a unified Germany. The term Federal Republic of Germany (FRG) means the Western part of the divided Germany, after 3 October 1990 it refers to the unified German state.

The (former) FRG made up the greater part of Germany, its territory – including West Berlin – covered 248 621 km^2, with a population of 62.7 million (1989). It had among the highest densities of population (ca. 250 inhabitants per km^2) in the world. It was concentrated in heavily industrialized regions of the country like the Ruhr and Rhine Valley, West Berlin, Munich, Stuttgart and Hamburg.

The territory of the former GDR covered 108 333 km^2. The population was around 16.4 million, mostly clustered in East Berlin and the South of the country (Leipzig, Dresden).

As the political system was shaped according to that of the Soviet Union, decision-making, including the media, was under control of the ruling communist party, the SED. After the fall of the wall that had divided both countries until November 1989, the East German system virtually collapsed. In March 1990 a freely elected and non-communist government took over and later the East German parliament decided to join the Federal Republic. Since 3 October 1990, both Germanies have been united, consisting now of

16 federal states (*Länder*) in the Federal Republic. Now the territories are combined, being home to about 81.1 million people.

High incomes and economic wealth ensure high expenditures for advertising and media consumption. The figure for total advertising expenditure for main media in all of Germany in 1994 was DM34.0 bn and showed rates of growth (from 1993, +8.6%) which were clearly above GNP growth rates.

Development of the press and broadcasting since 1945

The beginnings of the German press

Newspapers in the modern meaning of that word started in the then German-speaking part of the world in 1609 (in Wolfenbüttel and Strasburg). Comparable to other industrialized states in Western Europe, the history of the mass media (i.e. the press) in Germany goes back to the seventeenth century and is closely linked to the emerging capitalist state and its industrial economy. Up to the beginning of the twentieth century, and during the Weimar Republic, a mass press had grown up, with a commercial character and already highly concentrated (owned by publishers like Rudolf Mosse, Leopold Ullstein and August Scherl). Also a strong party press had developed – the Social Democratic Party (SPD) was one of the large publishers. During the First World War the ultra-conservative industrialist Alfred Hugenberg started to build up a 'media empire', that supported the political extreme Right and helped Hitler into power.

In the Third Reich a process of '*Gleichschaltung*' (making equal = elimination of opposition) affected all mass media. Publications of the Social Democrats, the Communists and the trade unions were banned, their property taken over by the National Socialist Party and integrated into their propaganda machine. Jewish publishers and journalists were thrown out of their positions, exiled or prosecuted. All media were placed under the control of the Reichsministerium für Volksaufklärung und Propaganda (Josef Goebbels' Ministry for Popular Enlightenment and Propaganda), that gave out detailed daily guidelines for the reporting of the news. Even though an increasing part of the press was owned by the Nazi Party itself, quite a number of local publishers could survive, going along politically because private property was somehow respected in the Third Reich.

The creation of the present system

After the unconditional surrender in 1945 the Allies introduced a completely new media system in East and West Germany. As a result, the mass media are almost solely the product of the post-war years. The press was to be reintroduced under a system of licences and all former newspaper owners (prior to 1945) had to be excluded from press activities.

In the Soviet zone, the occupying power immediately started to favour the Communist Party and its 'transmission' organizations, and made survival increasingly difficult for publications of other parties. After forming the SED

(Socialist Unity Party of Germany) in 1946, the media system was brought in line with official SED policy. *Neues Deutschland* – the central party paper, resembling the Soviet *Pravda* – became the leading newspaper. Radio and later television were also closely controlled by the SED.

Newspapers in the FRG

The Western allies clearly decided in favour of a gradual rebuilding of a private and commercial press. The new owners had to be individuals with an anti-Fascist and pro-democratic background, but even so, quite a few former Nazis made their way into the post-war media. From July to September 1945, in total 169 papers were licensed: 71 in the British sector, 58 in the American, 20 in the French and 20 jointly in West Berlin. In the course of this licensing process nearly all the former publishers were excluded.

With the founding of the Federal Republic in 1949 and the enaction of the Basic Law as its Constitution, the practice of compulsory licensing ended. Responsibility for press policy was handed over to German authorities and the market opened for all kinds of interest. Immediately the pre-war publishers tried to get into business again and a wave of new papers entered the market. Within half a year the number of publications rose by around 400 to a total of 568.

But the following years proved that the 'licensed press' had established itself firmly; since 1945 in fact, nearly all of the present-day internationally known German publications, like *Der Spiegel*, *Die Zeit*, *Der Stern* or *Die Welt*, were licensed in the post-war years. Only a few of the old newspaper publishers were able to survive, mainly on the local level or with specialist magazines. In the 1950s the distinction between licensed press and former publishers became more and more meaningless. In 1954 the publishers founded their umbrella organization Bundesverband Deutscher Zeitungsverleger (BDZV). In 1956 a body was founded for self-regulation, the Press Council (Deutscher Presserat). It is modelled on the British Press Council, comprising publishers and journalists.

The years after 1950 brought the conflicts typical for such a press system, namely conflicts of competition between broadcasting and press, tensions over the relationship of the press and political power, issues of press concentration and introduction of new technologies. One of the continuities is that the print publishers have attempted, since the 1950s, to gain access to broadcasting. Therefore, one of the first conflicts was advertising in public service broadcasting, which was attacked by the publishers as they feared heavy competition for advertising revenue. However reports of independent commissions (like the Michel Report of 1967) as well as court rulings established the right of public service broadcasters to advertise, as long as this did not endanger the financial health (i.e. the diversity) of the press.

Another controversy influencing the German press system was linked to discussions on state security in the 1960s. The leading news magazine *Der Spiegel* was accused of having published defence secrets, its publisher and the responsible journalist were jailed and the premises searched. This 'Spiegel Affair' (1962) ended with a clear victory for press freedom: the publisher was acquitted and the instigator of the action, Minister of Defence F.J. Strauss, was forced to resign. As part of the Cold War, amendments to the Basic Law were discussed for the eventuality of a national emergency and some media control was proposed. But when the articles were passed in 1968, the freedom of the press, as laid down in art. 5 of the Basic Law, remained unchanged. Both the Spiegel Affair and the discussions over state security consolidated and strengthened the freedom of the press in Germany.

As in other Western countries, the main internal danger for the press is its high degree of concentration. Although the German press is at first sight diverse, with an exceptional high share of local and regional papers, the figures show a clear process of concentration since the 1950s, accompanied by an increase in cross-ownership. The number of 'independent editorial units' (i.e. units that produce a complete newspaper with all sections) has fallen constantly, mainly for economic reasons. The greatest steps in the concentration process followed the general recessions in 1966/7 and 1973/4.

Historical development of broadcasting

As in other parts of Europe, the history of civilian radio usage began after the First World War. The war had left a relatively strong electronics industry and many people were trained in the new technology. Some revolutionary radio operators took an active part in the November Revolution of 1918 that finished the monarchy in Germany. The start of civic radio broadcasting came in 1923, based on a close relationship between the national postal administration (the Post) and the already established electronics industry. For example: the person responsible for most of the decisions about early German radio was Hans Bredow, who had been a director of the leading company – AEG-Telefunken – before he occupied managing positions within the Post. During the early years of the Weimar Republic, radio programmes were produced by private companies (financed by fees and very little commercial advertising), which were later in the 1920s taken over by the Post. In those years, the Post, together with the national and *Länder* governments, had a leading influence on the programmes. Parties of the political Left, demanding access to the media with a proletarian Workers Radio Movement, remained unsuccessful.

When the Nazi movement seized power in 1933, radio broadcasting, which had already been subjugated to far-reaching political control during the years of the depression, was immediately turned into the leading Fascist propaganda instrument. New pro-Hitler personnel, associated with and directed by Goebbels' Ministry of Propaganda, produced programmes that influenced German minds much more than any other media. The electronics industry's contribution to this development was the mass production of a cheap radio, the People's Wireless (the so-called Goebbels' lip). It was constructed to receive Hitler's speeches even at the far end of the country, but listening to foreign programmes was technically impossible (and also banned).

TV was tested as far back as 1936, when the Olympic Games in Berlin could be seen on screens in public halls in Berlin and Hamburg, but the construction plants were later converted to military purposes. Considering this early broadcasting history, it was only too clear that, in 1945, the occupation forces insisted on media having to start from scratch.

The British established one unified radio organization located in Hamburg, covering almost the entire North and West of Germany (except the US-occupied port of Bremen, which still has its own small broadcasting corporation). The radio station in Hamburg (NWDR) was set up on the lines of the centralized BBC structure, and its first director, Sir Hugh Greene, later became Director-General of the BBC. In later years, the NWDR was split into NDR Hamburg, WDR Cologne and SFB Berlin.

The Americans left a more regionalized broadcasting structure in their occupation zone, based on *Länder* borders, and therefore similar to their own, rather decentralized system. The Americans planned to establish a commercial system (like they did in occupied Japan) but were forced to drop these plans on account of British resistance.

The French occupation zone covered two independent territories along the French border, i.e. two German *Länder* of that time. 'Their' radio organization is still in existence today (SWF Baden-Baden) and serves two regions with – by today's standards – rather artificial borders.

During the late 1940s broadcasting was handed back to German management. The structure created by the allies was firmly established and widely accepted at that time and changed amazingly little in the following years. It was mainly adapted to the needs of the German federal system.

Historical development of the media system in the former GDR

Until the end of 1989 the media system of the GDR was under the tight control of the SED. With the help of the Soviets, the SED had established a centralized information system between 1945 and 1959, in which the mass media were supposed to function as 'instruments of the worker and peasant power'. They were instructed to serve as 'propagandist, agitator and organizer' of the masses.

The structure of the national and regional daily press did not change much after 1952. Thirty-nine daily newspapers were published, of which the SED directly edited 16. The others were owned by the parties of the so-called Democratic Block (CDU, LDPN, NDPD, DBP) or mass organizations like the unions and Socialist Youth. The SED press dominated, with a circulation of 6.6 million.

The SED had founded four main institutions to control the media: the Press Office of the Ministerial President, the Department for Agitation and

Propaganda under the Central Committee of the SED, the state owned news agency Allgemeine Deutsche Nachrichtenagentur (ADN) and the Office for Paper Distribution. Formal political censorship was not practised, but the SED gave out detailed guidelines on how to report the news. The education of journalists was monopolized under party supervision (in Leipzig) and journalists who did not go along were threatened with expulsion. The result of this 'guided' system of news management was a highly homogenous and dull press; access to foreign, especially West German, publications was barred.

The radio and television system was also directly influenced and organized by the political leaders and the SED. Radio started as early as 1945 under Soviet control and reached full supply of the population in the mid-1950s. The first television programme was transmitted in December 1952, actually on Stalin's birthday. Due to problems in the industrial production of TV sets, television supply reached its peak only very late in the 1960s.

Much of the population of East Germany could always receive Western television, exceptions being the southeast around Dresden (therefore called the 'valley of the unsuspecting') and the northeast around Greifswald. Western radio was freely available everywhere. Until the 1970s the SED leadership tried to ban Western reception, but afterwards it was tolerated. Even cable systems carried Western channels and TV sets were provided with the Western colour specification (West Germany transmits in PAL, the East in SECAM). West German television had ratings up to 40 and 60% during prime time; Eastern news programmes in particular were rarely watched and often only reacted and responded to the Western message (for instance the notorious 'Black Channel' presented by Karl Eduard von Schnitzler). During the last years of GDR's existence, entertainment shows and Western films were on the increase, in order to draw viewers away from watching Western programmes.

The press

Policy framework

The present media system is based on a rather short article of the Basic Law. It says:

> Everybody has the right to free expression and publication of his opinion in word, writing and picture and the right to obtain information without hindrance from sources generally accessible. The freedom of the press and of reporting by broadcasting and film is guaranteed. There must be no censorship. (art. 5 (1))

Apart from these general guidelines, which are part of the human rights section of the constitution, the Basic Law offers little further reference to the media framework of the country. The reason is simple: after the Second World War and Germany's unconditional surrender, the system of the press and broadcasting was only gradually handed over to German management.

Those who had been working on the constitution had only a limited mandate to decide upon the future structure of the German media.

Traditionally press laws were put out by the federal government (the first press law stems from 1874). The Basic Law stipulates (in art. 70) that law-making for the press rests now with the individual *Länder*, but the federal government may put out a common frame of regulations (art. 75). All *Länder* have put out press laws that define what 'press' actually means and regulate its obligations and privileges. The *Länder* press laws, although varying in detail and formulation, follow the normative content of the Basic Law and ensure a democratic press. They set as key principles the freedom from dependency on registration or licensing, and they describe central functions of the press, like the dissemination of information, participation in opinion-forming etc. The laws contain an obligation of accuracy for the press and the right of reply.

In the 1970s the social-liberal government tried to introduce the federal press law (as demanded in art. 75) as a general framework for the more specific regulations of the *Länder*. It included paragraphs on editorial statutes (meaning journalist co-determination) and freedom of opinion for journalists, as was demanded by the journalism unions. The publisher organizations fought fiercely against this bill and won: there is still no federal press law.

The press regulations mentioned impose only a few material restrictions on the press; in fact, the freedom of the press turns out to be very much the freedom of the proprietors of newspapers and magazines. This fact is especially reflected in the legally protected right of the publisher to define the general political line of the publication ('*Tendenzschutz*'); therefore the extensive German co-determination (Mitbestimmung) law is much restricted for publishing companies.

A special regulation for the press was included in the Federal Cartel Law in 1976. The critical definition of market dominance was more strictly put forward for the press than for other products. The level for notification to the Cartel Office was lowered to DM25 m DM in the case of mergers between press companies. Since 1976 the Federal Cartel Office has intervened several times against attempts to merge press companies, e.g. it stopped Burda from buying into the Springer company in 1981. But its policy approach is generally not hard-line.

Structure and organization

The structure of the West German press is characterized by:

- a high number of titles;
- many strong local newspapers;
- only a few national papers;
- a great number of magazines;
- a weak position of the party press;

- a dependency on advertising income;
- a high degree of economic concentration.

At the end of 1994 the number of 'independent editorial units' (meaning full publishing entities that produce all parts of a paper) for daily newspapers was 136, the number of newspapers was 383 and the total number of titles (including local variations) 1597. This reflects a situation where the press appears to be highly diversified and local, but in fact much is contributed by more centrally located offices. The circulation figures show that the local and regional press is very important in Germany: total circulation is 32.9 million, of these 18.2 million are classified as local and regional subscription papers, only 1.5 million see themselves as national and may be bought everywhere in the country. Because of this situation, more than 90% of the subscription press claims to be local. Another 5.6 million papers were 'sold in the street', another word for the tabloid press, often referred to in Germany as the 'boulevard press'. Most of the tabloid press (like *BILD*) is published in regionalized editions, meaning most content is central, some is added by journalists in the region. But – as already mentioned – the '*Heimatpresse*' (home press) is in many cases only partially independent. Because of concentration processes and for financial reasons these papers closely work together with larger newspapers or other local and regional papers.

Compared to the time before the Second World War only a few national papers exist. The national papers cover mainly a liberal and conservative spectrum. Apart from the *Tageszeitung* (*taz*), which started in 1979 as an 'alternative' paper but is quite established now, there is no left-wing daily. All major newspapers claim to be independent or non-party-political, but in fact a large number are highly sympathetic to the conservative Christian Democratic Party (CDU, in Bavaria CSU). The phenomenon *BILD Zeitung* (that is, Picture Paper) deserves a special mention in describing the West German Press. This daily newspaper, with its extraordinarily high circulation (4.3 million), uses the tabloid format and questionable reporting standards and shows traditionally a strong right-wing orientation.

All in all, in 1992 703 general magazines (with 124.6 million copies) and 964 specialized periodicals (with 16.9 million copies) were being published. A new type of newspaper, which became much stronger after 1945, is the weekly, looking like a newspaper but published once a week. It presents less actual news and more analysis and background information. Altogether 2.1 million are sold every week. Very successful and important is *Die Zeit* (circulation ca. 500 000), a liberal and independent paper. The protestant church edits the *Deutsche Allgemeine Sonntagsblatt* (ca. 90 000) and the Catholic church the *Rheinischer Merkur* (ca. 111 000).

A news magazine, modelled after the American *Time* magazine and for a long time with a virtual monopoly in its market is *Der Spiegel* (circulation ca. 1 million). With its investigative style of journalism, it has made quite a number of scandals public and is counted as the most influential political publication in the FRG. Recently a newly established magazine, *Focus* (circulation 500 000) is competing directly with *Der Spiegel*, being more colourful, more flashy and more conservative. The market for general interest magazines is still quite alive, *Der Stern* by Gruner & Jahr (controlled by Bertelsmann) being the most successful and the best known, with a liberal and investigative format.

Ownership and finance

The West German market for daily newspapers is dominated by a few groups of publishers. The largest market share is controlled by the Axel Springer Group with ca. 23% in 1993 (*BILD*, *Welt*, *Hamburger Abendblatt*, *Berliner Morgenpost* etc.) Second position is taken by the WAZ group with nearly 5.6% (*Westdeutsche Allgemeine Zeitung* etc.) which is more a regional publisher. Third place is taken by Verlagsgruppe Stuttgarter Zeitung (5.2%) and DuMont Schauberg, Cologne (4.5%). A rather recent competitor is Gruner & Jahr, mainly controlled by Bertelsmann which controls 3.8%.

The largest ten publishing groups represent 55.6% of the total circulation in 1993 (54.8% in West Germany 1989). Their ranking and market share has changed little after unification as the major Western publishers were all allowed to buy newspapers in East Germany. Advertising ensures 60–70% of all revenues in newspaper business. Newspapers take a share of about 26% of all advertising expenditures, magazines about 30% in 1993 (1980: 47%). Commercial broadcasting is gradually taking up larger shares – television 34% (in 1980: 17%), radio 7%.

The Springer group as a whole (which controls more than 70% of the daily market in the two largest cities, Berlin and Hamburg), is well known for its conservative attitude, reflecting the views of Axel Springer himself. He was influenced by experiences of the Cold War, considered himself a militant anti-Communist and used his papers to propagate his views. Before he died, he changed his 'press empire' to a joint stock company, with especially selected conservative shareholders (among them his widow and Leo Kirch).

Although Axel Springer Verlag ranks as the largest newspaper publishing group in Europe, it is only the second largest media group in Germany. The multi-media conglomerate Bertelsmann, being active on all major German markets as well as world-wide, produced a turnover in 1989 that was three times higher.

The press in the GDR until November 1989

A unique feature of the GDR was the high per capita consumption of newspapers. With a total circulation of 9.7 million, 583 copies of newspapers were sold per 1000 inhabitants. But the reason for this impressive figure was mainly political: low prices and a general tendency to subscribe to the *Neues Deutschland* besides the local paper. The SED party press played a dominant role and directly controlled two-thirds of the daily circulation. On the other hand, magazines (for instance TV guides) were produced at a limited number only and were therefore scarce; new subscriptions were only accepted if old ones were cancelled.

Although paper scarcity prevented any innovations in the press system after the late 1970s, the supply was still diversified (if measured only by the number of titles): 1812 titles existed, with 39 daily newspapers with a circulation of 9.7 million in total, 30 weekly and monthly papers (9.5 million circulation), 667 papers published for businesses by the SED (2 million), 508 magazines of general and special interest and a great number of regional and local information papers.

The press after unification

With the political liberalization of the GDR, control over the press collapsed and the journalists gained a very high degree of independence. But immediately after the opening of the border, Western publications flooded into East Germany and competed with the old publications. Western magazines and the tabloid press in particular gained large market shares (papers like *BILD* started to produce regional editions for East Germany). Many of the old publications died. In the early days of the 'non-violent revolution' quite a number of new publications, often with an 'alternative' concept, appeared, but hardly any survived.

The only type of publication that seems to have been little harmed by the change is the local dailies, based on subscription (regardless of whether they had a communist past). There were 15 districts (*Bezirke*) in the former GDR, each with a communist paper dominating the market. The largest publisher of the country, the SED-owned Berliner Verlag, was purchased by a consortium in 1990, consisting of Bertelsmann and Maxwell, later being taken over by Bertelsmann alone. Their paper *Berliner Zeitung* is quite successful in East Berlin, as such challenging the dominant position of Springer on the Berlin market. In terms of readership Berlin is still very much divided: people in West and East read mostly different papers with different styles and a different focus on the world.

All other district papers of the communist party also survived and proved to be stable even after unification. They were all sold by the *Treuhand*, the trustee for enterprises in East Germany, to the leading publishers of West Germany, sometimes 100%, in other cases joint ownership was established; for example, Springer bought the leading papers of Leipzig (50%) and Rostock (75%), Bertelsmann purchased besides the above-mentioned Berlin paper also the Dresden paper (60%). The result is that practically all East German publishing rests in West German hands and the concentration rate is higher than in the West. A few magazines have been especially created for the Eastern market: one is the tabloid *Super Illu*. The central paper of the communist party, *Neues Deutschland*, is still published on a much smaller scale, being close to the PDS, the left-leaning party that grew out of the SED. In terms of what Germans read, the country is still partially divided.

Also, with the survival of the district press the old communist system of districts lives on, whereas on the political side, *Länder* have been introduced in the meantime.

Electronic media

Legal framework

As was described above, the Basic Law stipulates that the sole responsibility for broadcasting rests with the states (*Länder*) of the Federal Republic as part of their 'cultural sovereignty'. An exception is that radio and TV corporations whose main function is to provide foreign countries with information are based on federal legislation – *Deutsche Welle* (DW). The organizational and legal structure of all other broadcasting corporations is defined in *Länder* laws and, if more than one state is involved, in agreements between several *Länder* (e.g. ZDF). The result is a uniquely decentralized broadcasting system, with production centres in every region of the country. Central political influence is exercised at the *Länder* level; the Bonn government mainly uses the PTT as a political tool.

Another crucial legal actor in broadcasting policy was and still is the Federal Constitutional Court, stating its opinion in leading decisions, namely in 1961, 1971, 1981, 1986 and 1992. Whereas the Court defended the public service system in earlier decisions (especially in 1961 when it banned a commercial television venture by the federal government), its ruling in 1986 argued that commercial broadcasting is protected by the constitution, provided that some basic principles are guarded, like secured financing and public service being able to take care of what they called a basic supply of programmes.

With the advent of new electronic technologies (cable and satellite) all *Länder* drafted media laws in the 1980s that specifically regulate the electronic media outside the conventional public corporations, mainly by handing out commercial radio and television licences and deciding what programmes may be fed into cable systems. For this purpose new supervisory bodies (*Landesmedienanstalten*) were created, each with a council, that resembles those of the public broadcasters. A national framework of regulations is laid down in agreement between all *Länder* (*Medienstaatsvertrag*). In 1990 this federal structure was also introduced in the newly established *Länder* of the East, thereby marking the end of the old GDR's centralized TV broadcaster DFF. The final structure was laid down in a *Medienstaatsvertrag* of 1991 that was to last until the end of 1996. Also European television regulations were transformed into German law by this agreement. In 1997 a new agreement was accepted between all *Länder* to update and extend that agreement for the years to come.

The German PTT, Deutsche Telekom, is a partly privatized institution, based on federal law and supervised by the Postal Ministry in Bonn. The Telekom enjoys a relatively strong position in conventional broadcasting (including ownership of most of the transmitters) as well as in cable and satellite technology (managing nearly all cable systems and claiming to be the largest owner of cable systems in the world; it also owns considerable shares in the DBS system Astra).

Structure and organization

The traditional public service broadcaster is an independent and non-commercial organization, financed primarily by fees and resembling to a certain extent the British BBC. It is referred to as an *Anstalt*. The typical *Anstalt* provides public service radio and television programmes to a region, which in many cases means a *Land* (like WDR in North Rhine–Westphalia or BR in Bavaria). But NDR is the joint corporation for the Northern *Länder* (Schleswig Holstein, Hamburg, Lower Saxony and, after unification, Mecklenburg–Vorpommern). All regional corporations together founded the ARD (Arbeitsgemeinschaft der Rundfunkanstalten Deutschlands) and contribute according to their size to the first TV channel (see table in Statistics section). In addition, they independently organize a regional Third Programme that offers regional news and a more culturally and educationally oriented content. Many of these Third Programmes are transmitted via satellite and may be seen on cable in other parts of the country.

Under ARD coordination about 40% of all programmes are fed in centrally, such as national news, weather, sports and movies. Programming on the first (ARD) channel is nationwide, except at short breaks during early evening, when a regional (in the city *Länder* like Berlin and Hamburg local) programme is offered.

The second German channel (ZDF, Zweites Deutsches Fernsehen) is based on an agreement of all *Länder* (*ZDF-Staatsvertrag*) and located in Mainz. ZDF offers one national and undivided television programme, but maintains offices in the different parts of the country.

During the process of unification several models were discussed but finally the Western model was exported into the East. The GDR had itself reorganized in five new *Länder* and East Berlin joined West Berlin. Three *Länder* (Saxonia, Thuringia, Saxonia-Anhalt) established the new corporation Mitteldeutscher Rundfunk (MDR), Brandenburg set up the Ostdeutsche Rundfunk Brandenburg (ORB), Mecklenburg-Vorpommern joined the Western NDR and East Berlin, the Western SFB. They were all integrated into the existing ARD. The East German *Länder* also entered the existing ZDF structure. Politicization played a dominant role in all this: the MDR area included *Länder* governed by the CDU, Brandenburg was held by the SPD. Nearly all of the leading personnel of the new East German corporations came from the West, usually with the right party connections; unemployment among journalists became a problem, as all Eastern broadcasting institutions were abolished.

All *Länder* broadcasters offer between three and five radio programmes in their respective region, some of them regionalized or localized. Usually one channel offers the popular music format with advertisements, other channels specialize in more conservative music, classical music or talk programmes. Former national radio channels from East and West that served primarily propaganda purposes were transformed in 1993 into Deutschlandradio, again based on two *Staatsverträge*. Jointly managed by ARD and ZDF, two radio programmes are offered, one specializing in cultural, the other in news content.

All broadcasting corporations are governed by an independent broadcasting council (*Rundfunkrat*), whose representatives are supposed – according to the Federal Constitutional Court's ruling – to reflect the 'socially relevant groups' of society. These delegates are either elected in parliament or they are selected and sent from groups such as political parties, business and labour organizations, churches, farmers, sports bodies and representatives of women, culture etc. Even though in theory only a few or none have been sent directly from the major political parties, the councils are heavily influenced by party interests. The reason is that German parties are relatively strong in all segments of the political and social system and penetrate practically all of the 'socially relevant groups'.

The head of the *Anstalt* is an elected Director-General (*Intendant*), usually a rather powerful position. The Director, the Director's representative and all heads of departments (and often the regular journalists as well) are usually selected along party lines; proportional representation by the major parties – CDU and SPD – is the rule.

The public broadcasters ARD and ZDF also offer a minor cable channel, 3Sat (together with ORF and SRG), showing mainly cultural programming, often reruns from the main channels. In 1992 Arte began transmission, a joint German–French project for cultural programming. On the German side the responsibility rests with ARD and ZDF and the seat is in Baden-Baden, also home of SWF. In Germany Arte is only available on cable and satellite. In 1997 ARD and ZDF started new special interest channels for children, and for coverage of events (parliamentary debates, conferences etc.).

In the mid-1980s commercial competition started to challenge the public system and what is called today a 'dual system' was established. Two commercial TV channels began operation, one at the beginning emanating from Luxembourg (RTL), the other around a cable pilot project in Ludwigshafen (Sat1). They proved successful and soon more programmes were available. By 1997 more than a dozen TV programmes were available, with even more being announced.

Today German commercial television is controlled by two groups of owners who call themselves 'sender families'. One, the strongest, is lead by Leo Kirch and consists of Sat1, Pro7, DSF, Kabel 1; the other is headed by Bertelsmann and the Luxembourg-based CLT, including RTL, RTL2 and Vox. The pay-TV company Premiere is jointly owned by Bertelsmann, Kirch and the French Canal Plus. Among the many programmes now offered is a German news channel n-tv (with CNN being one of the owners) and Viva1/Viva2, two music channels in direct competition to MTV, owned by the music industry. Initially transmission of new commercial programmes was via cable, but the conservative government of CDU/FDP ensured that Telekom opened new terrestrial channels in at least parts of the country and for the major broadcasters. Today the 'technical reach' of the leading channels RTL and Sat1 is above 90%. Some of the last terrestrial frequencies were reserved for local/regional television; such stations operate now in Berlin (Berlin 1A, a German–American venture), Hamburg, Munich and elsewhere, often in network agreements with national broadcasters.

In several cases the licensing authorities (the *Landesmedienanstalten*) had problems finding out who actually owned the companies applying for a TV licence. The old regulations demanded that no company should control more than one general programme (like RTL) and one specialized programme (like DSF). Obviously the authorities did not look into detail, and accepted questionable statements: for example, Pro7, a general channel, was licensed to the son of Leo Kirch, it being seemingly apparent this was just an addition to the Kirch empire. The CDU argued in favour of less regulation, the SPD demanded stricter controls. The outcome of the ongoing negotiations has been incorporated in the updated version of the Staatsvertrag, which became effective at the beginning of 1997. It relaxes the rules for programmers in television, stipulating that each media conglomerate should not control a market share higher than 30% of all household ratings. This general limit is set so high that it is not reached by any broadcaster, including Kirch and Bertelsmann. The loosening of regulations has led to a merger of the broadcasting activities of Bertelsmann/Ufa and CLT/RTL in one single company, Ufa/CLT now being the most extensive TV actor in Europe, controlling 19 TV and 23 radio broadcasters. It has also renewed the power struggles over German TV broadcasters, especially between Kirch and Springer over Sat1 and between Bertelsmann and Kirch over Premiere.

Programme policies

The two public national channels, ARD and ZDF, and also the regional channels, are required by law to offer a comprehensive and integrated programme that is politically balanced. There is direct competition between ARD and ZDF, but also limited coordination, especially in coverage of sports or politics events that require a joint effort. The Federal Constitutional Court demanded that the public broadcasters provide the country with a 'basic supply' of programmes, whereas the commercial competitors are much freer to adapt to audience choice.

Based on these incongruencies, the commercial broadcasters have started a battle for ever-larger market shares that is reflected in rating figures. In 1994 the average German watched television for 178 minutes a day (radio 168 minutes); East Germans watching more TV than West Germans. In 1994 the national market shares of the two main public channels were roughly equal to those of the two leading commercial channels, RTL and

Sat1. The combined share of the Third Programmes was about as high as that of Pro7. It is evident that people now view more commercial than public programmes, with RTL being the clear leader, Sat1 finding itself on a level with ARD and ZDF, and Pro7 having high growth rates. The share of commercial viewing is especially high in Eastern Germany.

Ownership and financing

As public service broadcasters, the *Anstalten* are mainly financed by a monthly licence fee (combined fee for radio and television raised to DM28.25 per month in 1997). In addition, considerable revenue is derived from 20 minutes of advertising each weekday, but its importance is going down due to the stiff competition for advertising money that public broadcasters are clearly losing. Whenever the question of a licence fee increase comes up, the public broadcasters prove to be extremely vulnerable to political pressure, the more so as all *Länder* parliaments have to agree on a common fee. A system of financial support by the large broadcasters (like WDR) to the very small ones (like RB) takes care of some financial balancing. The commercial broadcasters earn all their money from advertising of course.

The commercial television broadcasters in Germany are mainly owned by the leading national media companies, but some non-media and foreign ownership may be found. The main owners of Sat1 are Europe's most influential film distributor Leo Kirch and the Springer publishing company (in which Kirch again holds a significant share). RTL is controlled by Ufa/Bertelsmann and the Luxembourg CLT, which merged their activities recently. Pro7 has as dominating owner, Leo Kirch's son Thomas and the REWE supermarket company. It will go public as a stock company during 1997.

The main pay-TV company Premiere started in 1991 and has the following shareholders: Ufa/Bertelsmann (37.5%), Canal Plus (37.5%), Kirch (25%). Quite a number of foreign investors are active on the German market besides the already mentioned CLT; among these are Berlusconi (shares in DSF), Murdoch (shares in Vox), Time–Warner, CNN, Sony and others.

Foreign media availability

West Germany, being a middle-sized country in the heart of Europe with many neighbouring countries, traditionally receives a large number of programmes from the outside: RTL Radio was quite influential already in the 1950s. Spillover was especially strong from German-speaking neighbouring countries (GDR, Austria, Switzerland). On cable systems today up to about one-third of the channels come from other countries. But because of wide availability of German language TV on cable and satellite, interest in non-German programmes is very limited. An exception is the rather large community of Turks living in Germany; for them the state TV channel TRT is transmitted via cable and several commercial programmes are to be reached via satellite.

The situation in the Eastern part of Germany is outlined in the section on the historical development of the media system in the former GDR.

Local TV and radio

In the decentralized system of the FRG, regional (mostly *Länder*-wide) broadcasting is offered on the ARD channels, rarely on commercial TV. Local public broadcasting is offered in some large cities, where city *Anstalten* are located, especially in Berlin, Hamburg and Bremen. In a few places, including Berlin and Hamburg, national commercial channels are required to offer some local broadcasting as a prerequisite of their licence. Also, in a few cities local/regional TV stations have been licensed, as described above.

Public radio is rarely national, mostly regional and again sometimes local. Commercial radio is local in large cities and in some *Länder*, like Bavaria, Baden-Württemberg and North Rhine–Westphalia; in other places it is organized as a *Land*-wide network. There is no national commercial radio except on cable and satellite.

New electronic mass media

Among the countries of Europe with large populations, Germany has the highest percentage of cabled households; it also has more households cabled than any other European state – more than 40% of the 33 million households. In the 1970s cabling was heavily disputed between the major parties and especially the SPD was accused of holding back this new technology to protect the public broadcasting system. After the Bonn government changed to the CDU in 1982, the PTT (Telekom) started to invest tremendous funds in the cable infrastructure; much of all cabling is done by Telekom. The main interest behind this policy was to support commercial competition and to weaken the public system. Furthermore, the Telekom administration was ordered to search for additional terrestrial frequencies. As a result, RTL and Sat1 found the opportunity in quite a number of larger cities for conventional transmission.

The Federal Republic, being a highly industrialized country, started to invest in national direct broadcasting satellite (DBS) systems from the 1970s (Sat1 and 2), but the first of the satellites launched never worked while the second one met little interest among broadcasters. Seeing the success of Astra, which also carries nearly all German language channels, the Telekom developed and launched a specification of smaller satellites (DFS/Kopernikus 1 and 2) with little success. Telekom now is one of the major shareholders of the Astra company SES. In 1994 about 8 million households, more than half of them in Eastern Germany, had installed an Astra antenna to receive television via DBS satellite.

In the early 1980s new telematic technologies were introduced, very much like in other parts of Europe. Teletext (the German specification called *Videotext*) reached in 1994 46% of all households. About 52% of all households owned a VCR in 1994. Videotex (called *Bildschirmtext* or *Btx* in Germany) had a very slow start. In 1995 it was changed into an on-line service of the Telekom, named T-Online, with more than 1 million subscribers in 1997.

In 1994 the large broadcasters started drawing up plans to move into digital television. This would involve the use of digital technology to provide the consumer with more TV programmes, including pay-per-view and near-video-on-demand, via the Astra satellite and/or cable systems. The leading actor in this was Leo Kirch, starting his version as DF1 (Digitales Fernsehen 1) in July 1996, offering more than 20 programmes, most of them out of Kirch's large film library. Some premium films and sports events required extra payment. This venture had a difficult start: Kirch planned to have 200 000 subscribers at the end of 1996, but had found 20 000 at the most. Other actors, like Bertelsmann and RTL, planning on moving into digital TV, pulled back after realizing the demand was poor. In 1997 ARD announced the introduction of a non-pay version of digital TV, and also the pay-TV company Premiere started Premiere Digital, mainly with time-shifted programming.

Policies for press and broadcasting

Main actors and interests

The central actors in German media policy are the political parties, especially the *Länder* organizations of the two large parties CDU and SPD that control much of the public broadcasting sector. During the 1980s they initiated new broadcasting laws for the commercial sector and assigned themselves central positions in the newly founded supervising bodies. The federal government generally exerts little influence, its main tool being the Deutsche Telekom. But during the peak months of unification it used the unclear situation to determine much of the process of broadcast integration.

The most influential business actors are the large media companies (like Bertelsmann and Springer) that have dominated publishing for a long time and successfully started to demand licensing of commercial broadcasting. They now occupy leading positions in radio and television in addition to the print media, thereby causing new problems of media concentration. Most of them (Springer, Bauer, Burda) tend towards the CDU and find in this party a ready ally for more commercialization. The Bertelsmann company behaves in a more independent manner and is sometimes seen closer to the SPD. Foreign actors do exist, but their influence is limited (RTL, Berlusconi).

Strangely enough, the strong influence of the two leading parties upon public service broadcasting is now clearly repeated in the field of commercial television and radio. Smaller parties like the liberal FDP and the environment-oriented Greens are without much power, as smaller media companies see themselves excluded from the 'sender family' system.

Main issues

Until the beginning of the unification process in late 1989, the central theme of the 1980s had been the introduction of commercial broadcasting. The CDU favoured this policy direction and started to license such broadcasters in *Länder* where it had a majority. The SPD tried to oppose this policy but found that it could not stop the new course and finally jumped on the bandwagon. After years of strong polarization, media policy is now again based on a broad consensus between the *Länder*. In 1986 and in 1992 the Federal Constitutional Court sanctioned the commercialization process, but cautioned against double monopolies (including press and broadcasting) and demanded the protection of the bases of the public system.

Policy trends

The 1980s, especially the second half, brought tremendous change for the German media system, especially in broadcasting. The most important event was, of course, the fall of the East German regime and its disappearance in just one year (1989/90). This process was accompanied by the virtual vanishing of the communist-inspired media system of the GDR and the near total takeover by the Western press system, with the adoption of Western public service broadcasting. Introduction of commercial programmes in the East came a little later.

The second important change was the introduction of commercial broadcasting on a large scale. Up to 1984 there was a public service monopoly for television (as well as for radio); in 1995 clearly more than half of all programming hours and more than half of all consumed television came from commercial providers.

The third change is that the old polarization between the major parties (CDU vs. SPD) and to a lesser extent important social groups (business vs. labour) over media policy and the introduction of commercial TV and radio has very much disappeared. All *Länder* began to allow commercial broadcasting and established respective licensing and supervising bodies. In public statements CDU and SPD *Länder* might still differ somewhat, but in practice they cooperate, as it has been the rule in this largely consensual political system. As the media strategies of the two large parties are mostly similar, two 'sender families' were established, each one operating close to one of the two major parties.

A fourth development has also to be mentioned. In the middle of the 1990s major broadcasting activities are grouped around two 'sender families', one being controlled by Leo Kirch and being close to the CDU/

CSU parties and based in conservative Bavaria. Kirch does not only own large shares in a number of TV programmes like Sat1 and Pro 7 but also influences the largest European publishing house, Springer: his position is so strong that he is now labelled as by far the most influential 'media mogul' of Germany. The other 'family' is headed by Bertelsmann, and includes RTL channels (that Bertelsmann shares with CLT), Vox, Premiere and the influential Gruner & Jahr publishing house; most of its activities are located in North Rhine–Westphalia and Hamburg, which are both centres of the SPD party.

The fifth result is that the future of the public broadcasting system looks rather gloomy. The unification process was very much carried through by public service broadcasters, feeling responsible for the integration of all Germans as part of their public service responsibility. In 1995 public broadcasting is continuously losing viewers and political support and at the same time has to cope with serious financial difficulties. Increase of the licence fee will be very difficult to arrange, as all 16 *Länder* parliaments (increased from 11 since unification) have to agree and act jointly.

Finally, regulation of commercial broadcasting has proved to be mostly unsuccessful as the authority of the *Länder* regulatory bodies has remained weak. Commercial broadcasters threaten to move to another *Land* if they do not get what they expect. The attempt to limit media concentration in the *Staatsvertrag* of 1991 mostly failed, making possible the establishment of the two 'sender families'. This process was further strengthened by the new Staatsvertrag of 1997.

Degree of policy integration

As was described before, Germany is a rather decentralized country in terms of political decision-making. PTT Deutsche Telekom policy rests with the Bonn government, newspaper regulation with both Federal and *Länder* governments, broadcasting with the *Länder*. Conflicts may arise, but are usually solved as a compromise between all actors. (Sometimes conflicts may only be solved on a constitutional basis: the *Länder* attacked the Bonn government for signing the EU television directive of 1989, claiming that matters of broadcasting were their exclusive domain. The Federal Constitutional Court decided that the *Länder* have to be included in shaping European media policy.) This decentralized structure made the integration of the new East German *Länder* into the Federal Republic relatively easy. But this integration, in fact, meant the introduction of the Western system in the East. This process of 'colonization' is highlighted by the situation that nearly all press and broadcasting production centres will remain in the West, the East being just a welcomed market extension.

As was described above, a federal press policy does not exist at present, since the SPD's attempt in the 1970s failed miserably. The large publishing companies expanded into electronic media in the 1980s and a system of broadcast regulation was established. But the relatively large and highly politicized regulatory bureaucracy is proving ineffective. It rarely limits commercial behaviour and has been unable to cope with cross-ownership problems. As it showed little resistance to commercial interests, it did very little to strengthen non-commercial broadcasting in Germany. Radio stations, working on a private, non-profit basis are still the exception; in some *Länder* none exists at all.

Since the end of 1989 the large print and broadcasting companies have extended their influence into East Germany. A policy concept to cope with these market expansions and to check the power of the large media companies is not in sight.

Statistics

(1 ECU = c.1.84 Deutsch Mark, DM)

Population (1993)

Number of inhabitants	81.1 million
Geographical size	356 954 km²
Population density	232 per km²
Number of households	33 420 900

Broadcasting

Public broadcasting	
Number of radio licences (1996)	36.5 million
Number of TV licences (1996)	32.6 million
Cost of licence fee (since Jan. 1992: increase scheduled 1997)	
Radio and television	DM28.25

Public television (1997)	
Terrestrial networks	3
ARD, ZDF, (regional) Third Programmes	
Programmes on satellite and cable	4
3Sat, Arte, Kinderkanal (children), Phönix (events)	

Commercial television and owner consortia (1997)
RTL (Bertelsmann, CLT, WAZ)
Sat1 (Kirch, Springer)
RTL2 (Bertelsmann, CLT, Bauer, Tele München)
Vox
Pro7 (Kirch [Thomas], REWE)
Kabel 1 (Kirch [Thomas], REWE)
Super RTL (CLT, Disney)
Premiere (Canal Plus, Bertelsmann, Kirch)
n-tv (CNN, Time–Warner)
Deutsches Sportfernsehen (Kirch, Berlusconi, Ringier, Springer)
Viva1 (Sony, Warner, Thorn EMI, Philips, Otto)
Viva2 (Sony, Warner, Thorn EMI, Philips, Otto)
VH-1 (Viacom)
TM3 (Bauer, Tele München)

Foreign programmes on cable (1996)
Euronews
Eurosport
MTV
NBC Super
CNN International
TV5
TRT (Turkish)
BBC World et al.

Number of minutes, public television (1995)	
ARD	332 801 min
ZDF	341 744 min
ARD, regional programmes	375 651 min
ARD + ZDF, morning TV	130 062 min
3Sat	397 682 min
ARD/ZDF for Arte	52 259 min

ARD contributing broadcasting corporations and respective *Länder* and their share in national ARD programming in 1993	
Bayerischer Rundfunk BR (Bayern)	14.5%
Hessischer Rundfunk HR (Hessen)	7.0%
Norddeutscher Rundfunk NDR (Schleswig Holstein, Hamberg, Lower Saxony, Mecklenburg Vorpommern)	16.25%
Radio Bremen RB (Bremen)	2.5%
Saarländischer Rundfunk SR (Saarland)	2.5%
Sender Freies Berlin SFB (Berlin)	6.0%
Süddeutscher Rundfunk SDR (northern part of Baden-Württemberg)	7.75%
Südwestfunk SWF (Rheinland Pfalz, southern part of Baden-Württemberg)	9.75%
Westdeutscher Rundfunk WDR (North Rhine–Westphalia)	22.0%
Mitteldeutscher Rundfunk MDR (Saxonia, Thuringia, Saxonia-Anhalt)	9.75%
Ostdeutscher Rundfunk Brandenburg ORB (Brandenburg)	2.0%

New electronic media

VCR penetration (1996)	61.5%
Teletext (*Videotext*) (1996)	59.9% of all sets
Videotex (*Bildschirmtext, Telekom Online*) (1996)	1 195 000 users
Households passed by cable (1996)	24.7 million (= 66% of all households)
Households subscribing to cable (1996)	16.3 million (= 43.8% of all households)

The press

Newspapers in West Germany (1994)	
Number of newspapers (total)	1597
Independent editorial units	136
Number of daily newspapers	367
local and regional	383
National	7
Sunday papers	9
Weekly papers	31

Circulation	
Per 1000 inhabitants (data for 1994; all actually sold)	24
Total circulation	7.7 million

Daily newspapers	5.8 million
Subscription, local and regional	18.2 million
Subscription, national	1.5 million
Street sale	1 million
Sunday papers	9 million
Weekly papers	1 million

National newspapers (1993/4)

	Circulation	Political profile
BILD	4 300 000	Conservative
Süddeutsche Zeitung	407 000	Liberal
FAZ	391 000	Conservative/liberal
Welt	215 000	Conservative
Frankfurter Rundschau	188 000	Social democrat/liberal
Tageszeitung	60 000	Green/left

Market share and concentration in newspapers (1993)

	Circulation	Market
1. Axel Springer Verlag, Hamburg	5 891 859	22.8%
2. Zeitungsgruppe WAZ, Essen	1 449 023	5.6%
3. Verlagsgruppe Stuttgarter Zeitung	1 331 988	5.2%
4. Verlagsgruppe M. DuMont Schauberg, Köln	1 173 767	4.5%
5. Gruner & Jahr, AG & Co. KG, Hamburg	981 928	3.8%
6. Verlagsgruppe Süddeutscher Verlag	861 848	3.3%
7. Frankfurter Allgemeine Zeitung GMBH	807 277	3.1%
8. Verlagsgruppe Münchner Zeitungsverlag	682 573	2.7%
9. Georg von Holtzbrinck GMBH & Co. KG, Stgt	647 711	2.5%
10. Verlagsgruppe Madsack/Gerstenberg	642 394	2.1%

Media companies: ranking and turnover (1994)

1. Bertelsmann AG	DM18.4 bn
2. Springer AG	DM3.9 bn
3. Gruner & Jahr	DM3.8 bn
4. Heinrich Bauer	DM2.8 bn
5. WAZ Gruppe	DM2.5 bn
6. Holtzbrinck	DM2.3 bn
7. Medien-Union	DM1.8 bn
8. Burda	DM1.5 bn
9. Süddeutscher Verlag	DM1.1 bn
10. Sebaldus	DM0.97 bn

Division of advertising revenues between media (1994)

Newspapers	3.5%
Magazines	8.5%
Television	8.4%
Radio	6.7%
Billboards etc.	2.9%
Cinemas	1.0%

References

ARD Yearbook (annual since 1969) Cologne: ARD.

Bausch, H. (ed.) (1980) *Rundfunk in Deutschland* (5 vols). Munich: Deutscher Taschenbuch Verlag.

BDZV (annual) *Zeitungen* (Yearbook of the Publisher's Organization). Bonn: BDZV.
Braunschweig, S., Kleinsteuber, H.J., Wiesner, V. and Wilke, P. (1990) *Radio und Fernsehen in der Bundesrepublik*. Cologne: Bund.
DLM Yearbook (biennial, since 1988) Yearbook of the Landesmedienanstalten. Munich.
Geserick, R. (1989) *40 Jahre Presse, Rundfunk und Kommunikationspolitik in der DDR*. Munich: Minerva.
Holzweissig, G. (1989) *Massenmedien in der DDR*. Berlin: Holzapfel.
Humphreys, P.J. (1994) *Media and Media Policy in West Germany. The Press and Broadcasting since 1945*, rev. edn. London: Berg.
Kleinsteuber, H.J. (1982) *Rundfunkpolitik. Der Kampf um die Macht über Hörfunk und Fernsehen*. Opladen: Leske.
Media Perspektiven (annual) *Daten zur Mediensituation in der Bundesrepublik*. Frankfurt.
Meyn, H. (1994) *Massenmedien in der Bundesrepublik Deutschland*. Berlin: Colloquium.
Pürer, H. and Raabe, J. (1994) *Medien in Deutschland: Presse* (vol. 1). Munich: Ölschläger.
Tonnemacher, J. (1996) *Kommunikations politik in Deutschland*. Konstanz: UVK medien.
Williams, A. (1976) *Broadcasting and Democracy in West Germany*. Bradford University Press and London: Crosby Lockwood Staples.
ZDF Yearbook (annual, since 1962). Mainz: ZDF.

Periodicals: *Media Perspektiven, Rundfunk und Fernsehen, Publizistik, Medium.*

7

Greece

Panayote Elias Dimitras

National profile

Greece is one of the smaller European countries, located on the southern part of the Balkan peninsula, at the south-eastern end of the continent. Its 132 000 km^2 are inhabited by some ten million people. This relatively small density (76 per km^2) is due to the landscape of the country (a large part of continental Greece is mountainous) and to the consecutive waves of emigration (an estimated 2 million Greeks emigrated during the past 100 years, of which less than 500 000 eventually returned to Greece). The low density figure, though, hides a significant discrepancy: one-third of the total population (some 3.5 million) live in the 427 km^2 metropolitan area of the country's capital, Athens (a density of some 8 200 per km^2 as opposed to 55 per km^2 in the rest of continental Greece).

Greece has an apparently homogeneous population: some 98% of its citizens primarily speak the same, Greek, language and at least nominally identify with the same, Orthodox Christian, religion; however, for more than half a million Greek citizens the mother tongue is not Greek but Arvanite (akin to Albanian), Vlach (akin to Romanian) and Macedonian, but the state neither recognizes nor teaches these languages.

Except for the communist Left (the orthodox communist KKE and the modernist Progressive Left Coalition), the country's two-and-a-half party system is notorious for the absence of organized, principled parties. Instead, parties depend on the personality of their leader. Both major political parties that have ruled Greece since the restoration of democracy in 1974, the conservative New Democracy (ND, 1974–81 and 1990–3) and the Panhellenic Socialist Movement (PASOK, 1981–9 and since 1993), as well as the new nationalist splinter of ND, Political Spring, share this characteristic. The average citizen feels a profound mistrust of the state: this civic behaviour was inherited from the period of the four-centuries-long Ottoman occupation and was perpetuated by the dysfunctioning of the centralized, Napoleonic administration imposed upon Greeks after independence: the predominantly traditionalist politicians have consciously opted for the dysfunctioning of a state whose imported structure they never liked.

Development of the press and broadcasting since 1945

A country with a dysfunctioning administrative, political and economic system could only have a dysfunctioning media. The first Greek government after the Second World War forbade the publication of the wartime newspapers; but, after the December 1944 communist uprising, the ban was lifted. The ensuing civil war, that lasted through 1949, prevented any effort to cleanse Greece from the collaborationist elements, generally as well as in the press. In the first 20 years of the post-war period the circulation of the dailies more than doubled, from an average of 320 000 in the early and mid-1950s to over 700 000 in the mid-1960s: at the same time, the internal synthesis of the circulation changed, as the morning papers' lead over the afternoon ones in the early 1950s gave way to an uncontested lead of the latter ever since. On the other hand, some two-thirds of the circulation was concentrated in Greater Athens, which had at the time about one-quarter of the total population.

Immediately after the military coup in 1967, six newspapers chose or were forced to close down: during the seven-year dictatorship, only nine newspapers (four morning and five afternoon ones) circulated, heavily censored in the beginning, less so towards the end; their circulation oscillated around 600 000. The restoration of democracy in 1974 led to an understandable blossoming of the press: with three of the six newspapers shut down in 1967, and the official communist one outlawed in 1946, reappearing to bring the number of newspapers to 12 (usually seven morning and five afternoon ones through to 1979). Circulation rose by 50% to exceed 900 000 copies in 1974–5. As the Right settled in (through 1981), circulation fell to as low as 750 000 by the end of the decade. Again, political change (a socialist government between 1981 and 1989) led to more newspapers being published, an average of 16, and to a substantial boost in circulation which reached an average of nearly one million copies between 1984 and 1989. This rise came almost exclusively from the copies sold outside Greater Athens, which accounted thenceforth for nearly half the total circulation; in the same period, the morning papers' circulation fell to less than 10% of the total. Moreover, the 1980s saw the entry in the print media business of outside businessmen who, in 1995, controlled seven of the 16 dailies.

A constitutional act in 1945 gave birth to the National Radio Foundation (EIR). However, mainly because of the civil war, it took eight years for the government to give EIR a legal framework. With Law 2312/1953, EIR became a Legal Entity of Public Law and acquired the monopoly over all electronic media. Radio broadcasting in Greece was regulated by that 1953 law until 1975, with only minor alterations.

Television first appeared in 1960 at Salonica's International Fair (an annual September event), in order to advertise the fair's exhibited products. This private, limited, television station operated legally under licence until 1968, and illegally for a further year after that. The first effort to broadcast a regular television programme was not made until 1966. When that programme proceeded from the experimental stage, a new law (745/1970) was introduced: it changed the title of the state broadcasting authority to National Radio and Television Foundation (EIRT) and provided the framework for the operation of the first television station. In 1975, finally, EIRT was changed into a state-controlled joint stock company, ERT (Greek Radio & Television).

The state monopoly, however, was, since the beginning, violated by the armed forces. Indeed, as early as 1951 a bill allowed them 'to install radio or television stations . . . for the information, the education, the entertainment and the general improvement of the cultural level of the Armed Forces; furthermore, in times of war, to strengthen the spirit of the fighting Nation'. The armed forces' dominant role in the post-civil war, strongly anti-Communist Greek state, led to an unchecked expansion of that radio network into a fully equipped service, antagonistic to EIR (and later EIRT). The 1970 legislation recognized that reality and provided a legal framework to the Armed Forces' Information Service (YENED), which had also installed an initially primitive television station in 1965. This unique situation of a nationwide armed forces network ended in 1982, when YENED was transformed into a civilian, state-owned broadcasting service, ERT2. ERT and ERT2 merged into one company (ERT) in 1987.

Until the 1980s, the Greek media scene was a 'paradise', in the initial, Persian meaning of walled gardens. The printed media were in the hands of traditional publishers, while a state monopoly controlled broadcast media. The 1990s brought the 'fall from paradise', as the calm 'walled gardens' were substituted by fierce competition: in the print media, between traditional publishers and wealthy businessmen who have also acquired or published newspapers; in broadcasting, between state and private media.

The press

Article 14 of the Constitution guarantees the freedom of speech and of the press, forbidding 'censorship and any other preventive measure'. Seizure of newspapers or of any other print medium is forbidden, except with court order in the cases of an offense against Christian and any other 'known religion', or against the President of the Republic, the publication of information on sensitive defense matters or which could threaten the territorial integrity of the country, and the publication of obscene material. Three condemnations after such seizures led to temporary or permanent closing down of the newspapers. The Constitution also calls for laws to define the right to reply, as well as the conditions and qualifications for the profession of journalist, and it allows for a law to mandate that the financing of the newspapers and magazines be made publicly known. Finally, it specifies that press-related crimes be tried expediently, like crimes caught in the act (*en flagrant délit*).

The press law dates from 1938, though it has been amended many times since. It provides for the right to reply and for criminal and civil suits for libel; the former, though, have short prescription periods which practically guarantee impunity in the slow Greek judicial system, despite the swift procedure mandated by the Constitution. A minimum sale price for the daily and weekly newspapers is set by the government. Since 1988, the owners must be publicly known, which means that even press-related joint stock companies (*sociétés anonymes*) ought to have personalized stocks for their shareholders.

By the end of 1995, 16 national dailies were published in Athens (for circulation figures of the ten largest, see the Statistics section): the morning *Avgi* ('Dawn', pro-Coalition), *Kathimerini* ('Daily', Centre–Right), *Logos* ('Speech', Centre–Left), *Rizospastis* ('Radical', official KKE daily); the afternoon *Adesmeftos Typos* ('Non-aligned Press', Centre–Right), *Apogevmatini* ('Afternoon', Centre–Right), *Avriani* ('Tomorrow', Centre–Left), *Eleftheri Ora* ('Free Time', extreme Right), *Eleftheros* ('Free', Centre–Right), *Eleftheros Typos* ('Free Press', Centre–Right), *Eleftherotypia* ('Freedom of the Press', Centre–Left), *Estia* ('Focus', extreme Right), *Ethnos* ('Nation', Centre–Left), *Nea* ('News', Centre–Left), *Niki* ('Victory', Centre–Left), *Onoma* ('Name', Centre–Right). Two dailies in Salonica, the morning *Makedonia* ('Macedonia', Centre–Right) and the afternoon *Thessaloniki* ('Salonica', Centre–Left), had a regional circulation in Northern Greece, while there existed scores of local dailies, most with no more than four pages. Moreover, there were four national financial and five national sports newspapers.

Newspaper ownership brings the publishers considerable influence (many dramatic events – revolutions, government changes, etc. – were initiated or heavily influenced by the most powerful publishers), name recognition and respect across the political spectrum. A number of businessmen from the shipping industry or other sectors which frequently deal with the government (public contractors, arms dealers etc.) entered the field and slowly displaced the traditional publishers. In 1995, only one of the pre-1974 publishers was still in business: Lambrakis, the heir to the most powerful press group from the inter-war period (with the daily *Nea*, three weeklies, one fortnightly, two monthlies, one yearly, one radio station and a 20% share in the most successful private television station, Mega) and still the country's biggest, both in terms of turnover and of profits. The recently successful but traditional publisher George Kouris owned one national daily (*Avriani*), along with one sports daily, one radio station and two television stations (one only partly); the daily *Eleftherotypia*, a weekly and a 20% share in Mega belonged to another traditional publisher, Tegopoulos. The other traditionally owned papers were the extreme right-wing and communist ones (the latter belonging to political parties), with low circulation except for *Rizospastis*, and two newspapers (*Logos* and *Niki*), again with low circulation, were sold by Kouris to the journalists. On the other hand, the new businessmen owned seven national dailies with more than half the total circulation: three bought traditional titles (*Apogevmatini*, *Ethnos*, *Kathimerini*) while four published new papers (*Adesmeftos Typos*, *Eleftheros*, *Eleftheros Typos*, *Onoma*).

In the early 1980s, newspapers were running large deficits and were therefore very dependent on the state banks' 'soft' loans, and through them on the government. Since the late 1980s, however, almost all major press groups have been making profits due to increases in newspaper sale prices which exceeded average consumer price rises. Also, advertising revenues in newspapers have doubled and advertising in magazines more than quadrupled. Circulation kept going up from 1981 to 1989: but, since 1990, there has been a steady downward trend which brought the corresponding figure to the lowest levels since 1974. Possible explanations for this trend were: the beginning of private television which offered satisfactory news coverage (already, in Greater Athens, circulation had fallen after the advent of non-state-owned radio); the events of 1989 (collapse of communist regimes and formation of a short-lived ecumenical government), which led to major readership losses in the communist and pro-PASOK populist press; the comeback of the Right in power in 1993 (if we recall that circulation was always higher under centrist or socialist than under right-wing governments); and the generalized crisis of confidence in the political system since the beginning of the 1990s.

Traditionally, each newspaper has passionately supported one political party: in the 1980s, the Centre–Right ones favoured New Democracy, the Centre–Left ones PASOK, *Avgi* the Eurocommunists and *Rizospastis* the communists until the two coalesced into the Progressive Left Coalition supported by both newspapers. As a result, more than three-quarters of the readers of each newspaper were voters of the corresponding party. This trend has survived into the 1990s, though less acutely as some Centre-Left papers have become critical of the PASOK leadership and some Centre–Right papers have also become critical of ND.

According to their content, Greek dailies range from extremely populist newspapers that are not only passionately partisan but also violently slanderous to newspapers trying to emulate the authoritative European press (*The Times*, *Le Monde*, etc.). In the 1990s, though, they have all succumbed to the dominant nationalist tendencies in the country. Among populist papers one finds *Avriani*, which 'pioneered' the style, *Eleftheros Typos* and *Adesmeftos Typos*, which is a 'splinter' of the latter. They or their editors have accumulated scores of criminal or civil condemnations for libel; moreover, *Eleftheros Typos* had been the circulation leader most years since 1988. Among the serious papers is *Kathimerini*, the only morning newspaper with a growing circulation in the recent years, and the only paper with a growing circulation in the 1990s, despite the crisis. More generally, nearly all governments have at some point accused the press for 'yellow journalism', a view which many Greeks have shared. On the other hand, they have all attempted to influence the majority of journalists and newspapers, with some 40 million ECUs per annum of subsidies and 'secret funds' (*Kathimerini*, 8

December 1990) or by keeping some 70% of the main journalists on the state payroll, sometimes with 'phony jobs'.

Electronic media

The Constitution excludes broadcast media (along with the cinema and the record industry) from the legal protection offered to the print media. This exception is formulated in art. 15, which also provides for direct state control of radio and television, whose responsibilities should include 'the objective and fair broadcasting of information and news, as well as of products of literature and arts', and 'securing the programming quality required by their social mission and the cultural development of the country'. For a long time, 'direct state control' was interpreted by conservative and socialist governments as tantamount to exclusive state ownership of electronic media.

The extreme pro-government bias of state-owned and government-controlled radio and television led to social pressure for deregulation, led by a group of intellectuals called 'Channel 15', named after the constitutional article. Public opinion's favourable reaction to that pressure made some opposition mayors decide to start radio stations in 1987; in turn, that forced the socialist government to accept the principle of non-state-owned local radio stations in the 1987 law and implement it with a 1988 presidential decree.

Furthermore, the success of those 'free' radio stations prepared the ground for non-state-owned television stations: in late 1988, the socialist government decided that the state company ERT should start over-the-air free retransmission of foreign satellite television programmes (having previously threatened to 'shoot down satellites which overfly Greek air space'); and the opposition mayors of Salonica and Piraeus started local television stations. Finally, the conservative–communist coalition government in 1989 gave in to the intense lobbying of the newspaper publishers and radio station owners and allowed private and municipal local television, including cable, pay-TV and satellite retransmission stations. They also limited ERT's monopoly to national broadcasting and transferred the state's control of the electronic media to a National Radio and Television Council. However, the ensuing conservative government introduced amendments to this law which practically reaffirmed the government's control of the state-owned media. Finally, the socialist government introduced a comprehensive new law on private media in 1995.

Today, therefore, broadcast media in Greece officially function within the framework of laws 1730/1987 (on ERT), 1866/1989 (on the National Radio and Television Council) and 2328/1995, and the ministerial decision 22255/2/1990 of the Minister to the Prime Minister (on the National Radio and Television Council). The state's constitutionally mandated control over them is carried out by the National Radio and Television Council (ESR).

ESR's responsibilities are: to recommend three candidates 'of high reputation and professional competence' per government appointed position on the ERT board, among which the government will select one; to recommend to the government the dismissal of members of the ERT board; to advise the government on granting licences to non-state-owned radio and television stations; to issue codes of ethics for journalists, programmes and advertisements in broadcast media; to oversee the coverage of the activities of parliament and of electoral campaigns by ERT; and to sanction the violations of these codes or of other laws by the stations.

The state company ERT has henceforth the monopoly of only cable and pay-TV broadcasting. ERT is a public company, with the form of a joint stock company (*société anonyme*): its only stockholder is the Greek state.

ERT consists of two national television channels based in Athens (ET1 and ET2), and a third one based in Salonica (ET3), with limited broadcasting range (Athens, Salonica and a few other cities), four national radio stations (ERA1, ERA2, ERA3, ERA-Sport) and 21 regional stations, whose programming partly coincides with that of the national stations. There is also one local radio station in Salonica and a short-wave Voice of Greece servicing most parts of the globe.

In 1991, 65% of ERT's income came from the special mandatory fee that every client of the state-owned Public Power Corporation (DEI), regardless of whether he or she owns a radio or a television, is paying to ERT through the bimonthly electricity bills; 21% came from sales and advertising and 14% from the state budget.

Private and municipal radio stations were allowed in 1988, and television stations in 1989: at first locally, then nationally as well (in fact, national radio stations are merely tolerated, not legally allowed). The government was supposed to grant the appropriate licences on the recommendation of the ESR, which, because of its dysfunctioning, took years to issue such recommendations; and the government has yet to carry out its responsibility. So, in 1995, almost all non-state-owned radio and television stations lacked the required contracts with the state, required to normalize their functioning, though many have been granted licences in principle; in fact, the 1995 law cancelled all old licences.

A renewable, four-year licence to operate only one local FM radio station can be granted by the government, upon the recommendation of the ESR, to a local authority, a company controlled and managed by Greeks or EU citizens, or to a Greek or EU citizen. Networking is allowed only up to five hours a day and after permission of the ESR. Transmitters cannot be used, unless they are unavoidable for the station to cover the whole region (locality is defined in terms of prefecture). The emphasis of the programme should be local.

A renewable, four-year licence to operate only one local, regional or national television station can be granted by the government, upon the recommendation of the ESR, to a local authority or to a company: in the latter, no individual can directly or through his/her relatives own more than

25% of the personalized shares, and foreign, non-EU capital cannot control more than 25% of the total capital. The companies must be reliable, and their members should not have committed any press-related crimes. Local authorities and media-related experience of the shareholders are considered advantages for the granting of licences. No shareholder can have shares in more than one station. Programming must conform to the requirements of the 89/552/EEC directive of 3/10/1989. Presidential decrees should specify the procedure by which 1.5% of the annual gross income (minus taxes and contributions to state agencies) of the state or non-state television companies is invested in Greek feature films also to be shown in theatres; and 0.3% of the annual gross income is donated to two national organizations for the blind.

Advertisements in radio and television cannot exceed 12 minutes per hour, nor 15% of the total daily broadcasting time. Indirect advertising, as well as advertisements of pharmaceutical and tobacco products, and sexual services, are forbidden in all broadcast media. Anyone offended by a radio or television programme has the right to reply, with the ESR acting as the final authority to decide upon these matters.

In 1995, according to Focus data, 99% of the 3 million Greek households had a television set, 96% a colour set, and 52% a VCR. Audience surveys showed strong ratings for the, usually private, local radio stations, well ahead of the national or regional state stations. Moreover, in October 1995, the private channels led the ratings: Mega with a share of 26%, Antenna 24%, Star 16%, Sky 11%, with the state ET1 and ET2 following far behind in fifth and sixth places with a mere 4% and 3% respectively. Other channels had a total 13%, of which less than 1% was for ET3, 1% for satellite channels and 2% for videos.

In 1995 the main national private television stations belonged to shareholders owning other media as well: shareholders in Mega, for example, on the air since November 1989, were the Lambrakis group (the country's biggest private media conglomerate), the Bobolas group (second largest), the Tegopoulos group (fourth largest), the Alafouzos group and the Vardinoyannis group. Antenna, on the air since January 1990, belonged to the Kyriakou group, owning the radio stations with the same name. Star belongs to the Kouris and Vardinoyannis groups and Sky to the Alafouzos group.

Their 8am–2am output was based on the kind of programmes that could attract sizeable audiences, and therefore advertising: series, movies, games, children's shows, music, sports, and news; educational television or documentaries had no place. Their news coverage, initially of better quality than that of the state stations and, especially for Mega, more objective, has lapsed into sensationalism in the mid-1990s. On the other hand, the private channels also had the habit of starting many programmes later or earlier than announced or making unannounced last-minute changes – bad habits of state broadcasting. Nevertheless, their efforts were successful, as, less than one year after their beginning, Mega and Antenna had larger audiences and drew more advertising than the state channels. Overall, only one-third of their programmes were Greek, as compared with more than half for the state channels. Naturally, the private channels' revenue was almost exclusively drawn from advertising.

Since the autumn of 1988, satellite television channels have been available in most parts of the country, through on-the-air retransmission by, in most cases, ERT: in mid-1995, for example, Athenians could watch Euronews, MTV, CNN, RAI Uno, TV5, RIK (Greek Cypriot), besides the three state channels and more than 20 private channels with limited or round-the-clock programmes. Except for a few neighbourhoods in Athens and in Thrace, Greece was not cabled; but in 1994, Filmnet, offering films and sport – especially exclusive coverage of Greek championship football games – signed a contract with ERT and started its pay TV programmes, first in Athens and, by mid-1995, in nearly half the country.

Policies for the press and the broadcasting media have for long been at the centre of political debate in Greece. In the mid-1990s, three different issues were being discussed:

- inadequacy of the legal framework for both the print and the electronic media;
- cross-ownership and media concentration;
- objectivity of news and current affairs programmes in the state-owned broadcast media.

The legal framework existing before 1995 was inadequate and outdated. From its provisions listed above, many were never applied or had repeatedly been violated. Many newspapers and magazines offered gifts or prizes for games (bingo etc.). The dismissals of ERT's boards in the 1990s were not done at the recommendation of the National Radio and Television Council (ESR), and the latter's recommendations for a new board were either legally inappropriate or simply pro-forma. Moreover, all non-state radio and television stations operated without licences as either the ESR or the government had failed to act upon their applications for new licences or for renewals. The rules the ESR issued for the April 1990 campaign were overturned by the State Court.

Many of ERT's institutions were merely ceremonial or not activated. Some media businessmen owned more than one radio or television station. Many 'local' radio stations used transmitters that helped them broadcast far beyond the corresponding prefecture; the emphasis of their programme was not local. Most private television stations were known practically to belong to one owner each, through ways which circumvented the 25% upper limit per individual; among the owners of the two stations which were given licences in the 1990s were the two press groups with an accumulation of many condemnations for press misdemeanours. The 50% European production quota was not observed. The television stations did not invest in Greek movies nor did the private ones contribute to the national organizations for the blind.

Advertisements often ran for more than ten minutes per hour in prime time programmes, and many interrupting them. Sometimes products were advertised for more than the upper limit allowed in radio stations. The new 1995 law was supposed to provide cures for these ills, but once voted, it was hardly activated, so that, by the end of 1995, it was forecast that it would suffer the ill fate of its predecessor.

Whereas in other countries efforts are made and legislation is passed to discourage or forbid the concentration of media, in Greece the laws gave preference to the media companies in granting the licences for private radio and television stations. The result was the creation of a powerful oligopoly around the five shareholders of the most successful private television channel, Mega. The traditional publishers Lambrakis and Tegopoulos, and the new publishers Alafouzos, Bobolas and Vardinoyannis, own four national dailies with nearly half the total circulation; their media groups, which participate in other channels too, gross nearly half the total turnover of the non-state media and make more than half of their total profits. Finally, it has been documented that they have agreed to use the other media they own to promote their television channel. Only marginal political parties and some intellectuals had criticized this arrangement as a threat to real freedom of the press; in vain, since the three main political parties appeared satisfied by it.

The main problem of the state electronic media had been the lack of impartiality in the news and other political broadcasts. Both radio and television 'grew up' in non-democratic periods of Greek history: radio in the Metaxas dictatorship and the German occupation, and television in the Papadopoulos/Ioannidis dictatorship. Hence, these mass media became a propaganda tool of the government, as has been the case in all dictatorships. The democratic governments which succeeded the dictatorships became victims of the temptation to follow the same tactic. Therefore, news coverage was often reminiscent of Third World or non-democratic countries.

A decisive effort to separate the state media from direct government control was made between the summer of 1989 and the spring of 1990. Then, and for the first time since 1952, Greece was governed by coalition governments. The latter created the ESR, with 11 members selected in such a way as to exclude a one-party majority. However, instead of using the opportunity to appoint an independent ERT management, the three parties agreed to distribute among themselves the positions on ERT's board and its various managerial positions, so as to give them to loyal militants. The end result, however, was still the most balanced newscasts state television and radio have ever produced. When a one-party (conservative) government came to power in mid-1990, it quickly did away with the short-lived 'ERT spring': with ministerial decisions, whose doubtful legality was challenged in the courts, the ESR and ERT boards were broadened to 19 and 11 members (the latter from 9 members), in such a way as to give the government unquestionable control over the two bodies; consequently, in all

ERT managerial positions the loyal New Democracy journalists replaced the ones chosen by the ecumenical government, including those who were favourable to the conservative party. When PASOK came back to power in 1993, it merely applied the same practices. Nevertheless, Greek public opinion was less concerned with ERT's partiality in the 1990s than ten years before, as the private channels filled the gap. In fact, it was noticeable that the state media had made no effort to respond to the competition of the private radio stations and television channels, thus quickly losing their predominant position and, consequently, their advertising share. So, since 1990, ERT, still staffed by its 7000-odd personnel (including hundreds of journalists who did not work but received a pay cheque so as to be under control by the government), has been running at huge deficits which the state's budget has had to cover.

Statistics

(1 ECU = 289 drachmas, dr)

Population (1991)	
Number of inhabitants	10 million
Geographical size	132 000 km^2
Population density	76 per km^2
Number of households	3 million

Broadcasting (1995)	
Number of national radio channels	4
Number of national television channels	ca. 10
Number of local television channels	ca. 100
Number of local radio stations	ca. 800
Television penetration	99%
Video penetration	52%
Advertising expenditure (1994, ECUs)	95 m
Television	63 m
Magazines	15 m
Newspapers	11 m
Radio	6 m
Cinema	n.a.
Outdoor	n.a.
Greater Athens and Salonica TV audience share (AGB, October 1995)	
Mega	26%
Antenna	24%
Star	16%
Sky	11%
ET1	4%
ET2	3%
Other Greek channels	13%
Satellite receivers in population	1%
VCR equipment in population	2%

The press

Number of national political daily newspapers		16
Number of regional political daily newspapers		2

Average daily circulation of national political dailies (August 1995)

All dailies		558 495
Morning dailies total		55 354
Kathimerini	centre–Right	40 264
Rizospastis	KKE organ	12 207
Other		2 883
Evening dailies total		503 141
Eleftheros Typos	centre–Right	110 361
Nea	centre–Left	107 705
Eleftherotypia	centre–Left	102 282
Apogevmatini	centre–Right	55 338
Ethnos	centre-Left	50 925
Adesmeftos Typos	centre–Right	40 658
Avriani	centre–Left	13 815
Other		22 057

References

Dimitras, Panayote Elias and Doulkeri, Tessa (1986) 'Greece', in Hans Kleinsteuber, Dennis McQuail and Karen Siune (eds), *Electronic Media and Politics in Western Europe: A Euromedia Research Group Handbook of National Systems*. Frankfurt: Campus Verlag.

Dimitras, Panayote Elias (1992) 'Greece', in Euromedia Research Group (eds), *The Media in Western Europe: The Euromedia Handbook*. London: Sage.

Dimitras, Panayote Elias (1992) 'Greece: unbridled deregulation', in Miquel de Moragas Spa and Carmelo Garitaonandia (eds), *Decentralization in the Global Era: Television in the Regions, Nationalities and Small Countries of the European Union*. London: John Libbey.

Katsoudas, Dimitrios K. (1987) 'The media: the state and broadcasting', in Kevin Featherstone and Dimitrios K. Katsoudas (eds), *Political Change in Greece: Before and After the Colonels*. London: Croom Helm.

Mayer, Kostas (1957–1960) 'History of the Greek press' (in Greek), 3 vols. Athens: Dimopoulos.

8

Ireland

Mary Kelly and Wolfgang Truetzschler

National profile

Situated on the periphery of Europe, in area the Republic of Ireland comprises 70 283 km^2. With 3 621 035 inhabitants (in 1996) it has the second smallest population within the European Union. Following a decline by almost a half in its population since the mid-nineteenth century, first by famine and then mainly through emigration, the population began to increase in the 1960s. Since the late 1970s it has remained relatively stable, despite a return to high emigration among young people during the 1980s.

The country is not densely populated, with 50 inhabitants per km^2, and 43% living in rural areas (i.e. in areas which have fewer than 1500 inhabitants). However, urbanization continues to increase, though slowly. The population is not evenly distributed, with more than half living in the eastern region. The high concentration in Dublin (29% of the population lives in the city and its environment), particularly contributes to this regional imbalance.

There are two official languages in the state, namely Irish and English, but English is the mother tongue for the vast majority of the people. Only 2% of the population live in the Gaeltacht, the native Irish-speaking areas situated mainly on the west coast of Ireland.

According to the 1991 Census results, a third of the population are reported as able to speak Irish, this percentage being particularly high among school-going adolescents, as the teaching of Irish has been compulsory in all schools since the foundation of the state in 1922.

With the rapid increase in educational participation since the 1960s (at present 81% of 17-year-olds attend full-time education), knowledge of Irish has also increased. Thus in the 1991 Census, 55% of 15–19-year-olds are reported as able to speak Irish, but this declines very rapidly to 29% among 25–34-year-olds as Irish is not spoken in everyday life among the great majority of the population.

Although Ireland has traditionally been seen as a predominantly agricultural country, continuing industrialization has changed this. The percentage of the employed labour force in agriculture has declined from 35% in 1961 to just over 11% in 1996. The proportion employed in industry is 27% and in the services sector 62%. The share of women in the workforce in 1996 was 36%. Continued economic growth in the 1990s has reduced the unemployment rate (traditionally one of the highest in Europe) to around 12% of the labour force in 1996. Ireland's industrial development is that of dependent rather than indigenous industrialization, and Ireland's economic structure is similar to that of other peripheral European countries, such as Greece, Spain and Southern Italy (Wickham, 1986). Central to the state's industrial strategy since 1960 has been the attraction of export-oriented foreign companies to invest in Ireland.

Although the Irish economy has achieved a substantial growth in the 1990s, Ireland is still relatively poor in comparison with some other European countries, e.g. in terms of GNP per head of population (cf. Government of Ireland, 1997), due to such factors as late and dependent industrialization, a high birth rate until relatively recently, and high unemployment. Despite this relative poverty, Irish families have been willing to invest quite heavily in buying their own homes and in buying or renting broadcasting equipment. Around 80% of all adults live in owner-occupied homes and of the 1 million households, 96% have a television set, 38% have cabled television and 65% have VCR equipment.

Regarding the political system, the Irish Constitution (1937) declares Ireland to be a sovereign, independent, democratic state. Ireland's political culture has traditionally been predominantly Catholic and rather conservative, especially on family and moral issues such as divorce, contraception and abortion. This is slowly changing with greater tolerance of diversity (Mair, 1992). The economic policies of the two major parties, Fianna Fáil and Fine Gael, tend to be centrist, with a commitment to economic rectitude on the one hand, but also, given Ireland's large dependent population, committed to maintaining welfare policies. All parties, and the great majority of the population, are also committed to membership of the EU. The two more left-wing parties, the Labour Party and the Democratic Left, usually receive around 10–15% of the vote. Both are willing to form coalitions with the centrist parties, and at present (1997) they form a coalition government with Fine Gael.

Traditionally, there is no strong left or agrarian political party as political debate in Ireland has tended to be in nationalist rather than class terms. All parties are committed to promoting industrialization – even dependent industrialization – in the national interest, in particular in the hope of economic regeneration and a consequent reduction in unemployment and emigration. The predominant mode in public policy decisions since the 1960s has emphasized economic and commercial rather than cultural criteria. This has also influenced decisions regarding the development of the new electronic media. Thus while cultural nationalism was the main thrust in the establishment of Irish radio (1926) and television (1961), decisions on the new media in the 1980s and 1990s have been characterized by a strong commercial bias. However, there is also recent evidence of an increasing cultural confidence, both at a grass roots level and as promoted by the state – in this case often linked with the recognition that culture provides jobs.

This can be seen in the implementation of policies establishing the Irish language television service (Teilifís na Gaeilge – TnaG) in 1996, and at a more international level, the promotion (and recent successes) of the Irish film industry and the Irish music industry, which was the fifth highest provider of international hit records in 1995.

Development of the press and broadcasting since 1945

The press

In 1945, the three major national newspapers, as well as the major regional paper and most local papers, were legacies from the nineteenth and early twentieth centuries. The three major dailies were the *Irish Times*, the *Irish Independent*, and the *Irish Press*, while the major regional daily was the *Cork Examiner* (now called *The Examiner* and available nation-wide). When initially established, each was aligned with a particular political tradition and party: the *Irish Times*, established in 1859, represented the Unionist tradition; the *Irish Independent*, established in 1905, represented the constitutional Nationalist tradition and Fine Gael; while the *Irish Press*, established in 1931, represented the Republican and Fianna Fáil traditions.

Over the past 20 years five trends can be identified in the development of the Irish newspaper industry. One trend has been a strong move away from party partisanship in a bid to increase circulation. A second is decline in circulation. While sales of Irish morning newspapers have remained static, sales of evening newspapers have declined by a half and Sundays by a quarter (Competition Authority, 1995). A third trend is increased sales of British daily tabloids. British papers constitute a quarter of the Irish daily newspaper market and a third of the Sunday market. A fourth trend is a clearer differentiation of readers by class and region. While the *Irish Independent* and *Irish Times* continued to serve middle-class readers, the Press group of newspapers continued to serve a more rurally based and declining market. The Independent group, furthermore, developed a group of tabloids for a more downmarket readership. A fifth trend is increased concentration of ownership by Independent Newspapers. These trends contributed significantly to the context within which the second largest press group, Irish Press newspapers, went into liquidation in June 1995.

Public broadcasting services

Broadcasting began in Ireland with the establishment of an Irish radio service in 1926. Radio was under direct state control until the passing of the 1960 Broadcasting Authority Act which established the state-sponsored (public service broadcasting) Radio Telefís Eireann (RTE) Authority. The Act also gave the RTE Authority control over the new Irish television service. Irish broadcasting has since its inception relied both on advertising revenues and licence fees to fund its public service broadcasting. Monopoly state control of broadcasting was abolished in 1989, with the licensing of private commercial broadcasting services.

The 1960 Act brought new life to Irish broadcasting. Not only did Irish television begin, but in 1972 Raidio na Gaeltachta was established transmitting Irish-language programmes; in 1978 a second television channel began transmitting, in the following year a second national radio station, and in 1996 the Irish language television service TnaG commenced broadcasting. Both radio and television, however, faced the problem of fostering Irish culture and home-produced programmes in the context of openness to strong foreign broadcasting competition, especially from Britain. In 1996 just under 70% of all television homes are in multi-channel areas, i.e. ones which can receive British television either off air or via cable.

The founding of a second RTE television channel (RTE2, now known as Network 2) in 1978 was a direct result of demands by single channel areas to equalize the television services being offered in different parts of the country. This decision did not fully satisfy these demands, and after the operation over a period of ten years of illegal deflector systems enabling the reception of British television, the government in 1989 awarded licences to instal and operate a network of multipoint microwave (television re-transmission) distribution systems (MMDS) in those parts of the country in which viewers are currently not able to receive cable television.

As in many other small states, RTE in Ireland has traditionally relied heavily on foreign produced programming. RTE has endeavoured to reduce the proportion of imported programmes to 50% of programming time, and through an increase in the production of cheap but popular home-produced programmes, RTE has managed to achieve a reduction in its reliance on foreign produced software from 65% in 1984 to, according to RTE, 50% since 1994.

Private broadcasting services

Until the end of 1988, Ireland's privately owned broadcasting services traditionally consisted of unlicensed or pirate radio stations (see Mulryan, 1988). At the end of 1988, however, the Irish parliament after many delays, passed the Radio and Television Act 1988. This Act enables the setting up of private commercial broadcasting services. A new regulatory authority for private broadcasters, the 'Independent Radio and Television Commission' (IRTC), was established in October 1988, and several licences for both commercial local radio and for community radio have been awarded by the IRTC since 1989. A licence for a national commercial radio channel was awarded towards the end of 1995.

The franchise for a new national private television service, TV3, was originally awarded in 1989. Due to financial and legal difficulties TV3 has been unable to commence its services. In September 1995 the TV3 consortium was temporarily joined by Ulster Television (UTV), which is based in Northern Ireland and is reported to be the most successful of commercial television companies in the British ITV network. A few months later, however, UTV withdrew from the consortium. In April 1997 Canada's most profitable broadcaster, 'CanWest Global', took a 48% share in TV3 and it is now expected that TV3 will commence broadcasting in 1998.

The press

Legal framework

The press in Ireland, unlike the broadcast media, is not subject to specific legislation, i.e. to a specific press law. The right to freedom of the press is derived from the express right to freedom of expression as enshrined in the Constitution. However, this right is subject to a number of restrictions arising out of considerations of public order and morality, the authority of the state etc., and censorship of publications has had a long and inglorious history since the establishment of the state (Kelly, 1992, 1993). While censorship generally has considerably lessened in recent years, censorship of information on abortion, in particular the names and addresses of abortion clinics in Britain, was rigidly enforced. However, following a number of court cases and considerable conflictual debate, a referendum on the right to such information was carried in 1992. An Act regulating the provision of this information was passed in 1995.

There are also a large number of statutes with implications for press freedom, such as, for example, the Official Secrets Act. Overall, the right to freedom of expression, which encompasses the press, 'is so heavily circumscribed by conditions and limitations as to virtually negate it' (Boyle and McGonagle, 1988: 10). There is neither a press council nor a specific right to reply incorporated in the various statutes that are of relevance to the press. However, some newspapers have voluntarily appointed 'newspaper ombudsmen' as a means of investigating complaints by the readers and of avoiding litigation which may result in the Courts awarding high damages for libel.

Monopoly formation in the press industry is subject to specific cartel legislation. This enables the Minister for Enterprise and Employment to prohibit any changes in the control of newspapers of more than 30% of the shares in the respective newspaper. The Minister may also refer possible anti-competitive activities to the Competition Authority under the Competition Act, 1991. As will be seen below, he has recently done so.

Ownership

Even though Irish law does not explicitly restrict foreign investment in Irish media services, foreign ownership of the press in Ireland is limited. The main attempt was the 1989 acquisition of a controlling 50% share in the loss-making Irish Press Newspapers by the US company Ingersoll Publications. The remainder continued to be owned by the de Valera family. Moreover, the *Sunday Business Post* is 40% owned by German interests. The tabloid newspaper the *Star* is jointly owned by Ireland's Independent Newspapers and Express Newspapers (UK).

A major concern at the present time is concentration of ownership by Independent Newspapers, a company headed by Ireland's only press baron, Dr Tony O'Reilly. This group holds highly profitable newspaper interests in Britain, Australia, New Zealand and South Africa as well as Ireland. The Independent Newspaper Group owns the long-established and successful daily, the *Irish Independent*, also the *Evening Herald* and the *Sunday Independent*.

In the mid-1970s it launched a popular down-market tabloid, the *Sunday World*. In the late 1980s, with Express Newspapers (UK), the Independent Group brought out an Irish edition of the British daily tabloid the *Star*, to compete with the highly popular *Mirror* imported from Britain. In 1990, Independent Newspapers bought a 29.99% holding in the *Sunday Tribune*. Thus, by 1994, it had control of, or a controlling interest in, 65% of the total market for Irish newspapers. Its main competitors among Irish newspaper groups were the publishers of the *Irish Press*, the *Irish Times* and the *Cork Examiner*. The *Irish Times*, under trust ownership, has increased its circulation, and its readers constitute a quarter of the daily Irish newspaper market – predominantly upper and middle class. The circulation of the family-owned *Cork Examiner*'s morning and evening papers constitute a seventh of these markets.

Irish Press was the Independent's main competitor. Radically declining circulation (declining by roughly 60% between 1974 and 1994), as well as major financial and managerial problems, led to its selling half of its shares to the US company Ingersoll Publications in 1989. This proved a highly unsuccessful partnership. The ensuing and prolonged court action led to the breaking up of the partnership and the Supreme Court judgment in May 1995 that Irish Press pay IR£4 m pounds compensation to Ingersoll.

Given the extremely bad financial losses and debts in the Irish Press, Independent Newspapers, in December 1994, moved in and bought a 24.9% share as well as loaning it IR£2 m. None the less, the company collapsed and went into liquidation in June 1995.

Financing

On average, 43% of the revenue from Irish newspapers comes from advertising, and 57% from sales. However, the advertising proportion is much higher in the more upmarket *Irish Times* and *Sunday Business Post*. The prices of Irish papers have increased over the past 20 years at more than twice the rate of inflation and at a faster rate than UK papers. British papers are also cheaper to buy because, unlike the UK, Ireland imposes a 12.5% value-added tax (VAT) on the printing of newspapers. Total UK sales, especially the tabloid *Mirror* and *Sun*, have increased substantially in Ireland in the past 20 years.

In 1994, the Minister for Enterprise and Employment referred the question of UK competition in the Irish newspaper market to the Competition Authority. It judged that no one British newspaper company, including News International, had a dominant position in the Irish market. Murdoch's News International was found to have a 30% share of both the Irish daily tabloid and Sunday tabloid markets. The Competition Authority also advised the Minister that British newspaper companies were not engaged in predatory price policies, attempting to eliminate or weaken competitors, a point vigorously contested by Irish newspapers.

Structure of the press

Traditionally, Ireland has a very high readership and a fairly large number of newspapers for its population: net sales of national newspapers combined total around 4 million copies a week. Since the demise of the Irish Press group, there are now four national or regional morning papers, two evening papers and four Sunday papers. The Irish regional or provincial press consists of approximately 40 newspapers, which tend to be published on a weekly basis.

Electronic media

Legal framework

Broadcasting in Ireland is mainly regulated by three Acts (see Truetzschler, 1991b): the Broadcasting Authority Acts 1960–1993, which regulate the public broadcaster RTE; the Radio and Television Act 1988, which contains the regulations applicable to private commercial broadcasting; and the Broadcasting Act 1990, which, *inter alia*, facilitates the implementation of the EC Directive on Television Broadcasting. The content of foreign satellite television relayed on cable or MMDS is currently not subject to any specific regulations, apart from the fact that the relaying of all television channels requires a licence.

Cable television is governed by the Wireless Telegraphy (Wired Broadcast Relay Licence) Regulations 1974, as amended in 1988; the Multipoint Microwave Distribution System (MMDS), is subject to the Wireless Telegraphy (Television Programme Retransmission) Regulations 1989. Apart from these specific Acts and Regulations, other statutes such as Contempt of Court, Censorship, Defamation, Copyright, Official Secrets Act, Public Order etc. also apply to broadcasting.

The three Acts contain the fairly detailed and explicit regulations for private and public broadcasters. The laws also enable censorship by the government in relation to 'The Troubles' in Northern Ireland, but this section of the law has not been availed of since 1994, the start of the 'peace process' in Northern Ireland. Advertising on RTE is restricted to 10% of total programming time on television (5% on RTE radio); the private broadcasters may broadcast exactly double this amount.

In practice the main difference between private broadcasters and RTE is not so much in the regulations, but more in the monitoring (of the adherence to the regulations) of individual stations by the government and by the IRTC. Thus the public broadcaster has always been subject to fairly close regulation (and even closer scrutinization by politicians). In contrast, the IRTC, whose main function is to ensure the operation of broadcasting services other than those of RTE, has on occasions taken a somewhat more liberal interpretation of the adherence by private broadcasters to the existing regulations.

The most recent piece of broadcasting legislation, the Broadcasting Authority (Amendment) Act 1993, removed the limit on advertising revenue that RTE may earn as stated in the Broadcasting Act 1990. However, the Act also forces RTE to make specific amounts of money available in each financial year for programmes commissioned from the independent television sector. The amounts of money to be made available annually range from IR£5 m in 1994 to 20% of television programme expenditure or IR£12.5 m (whichever is greater) in 1999. Independent television producers are very clearly defined in the Act, thereby ensuring that RTE or any other existing broadcaster is prevented from allocating the money to any subsidiary company.

Recent developments

Towards the end of April 1995 the government published a Green Paper on broadcasting (Government of Ireland, 1995), which discussed in detail the various issues faced by Irish broadcasting as we approach the twenty-first century. The document, one of the first of its kind in the European Union, raised issues on two levels: the philosophical and the practical. On the philosophical level it raised the question of how to organize Irish broadcasting at a time of intense change in Europe where converging technological, economic and political forces threaten the relative autonomy of broadcasting from government and market forces, of how to retain public service broadcasting within the market, of how broadcasting can reflect both local and national culture and how Ireland can ensure its place in a world of broadcasting run by increasingly powerful media magnates/concerns.

On the practical level the Green Paper asked how the public interest in relation to broadcasting can be best served in the future and made a number of suggestions as to how this could possibly be achieved. The suggestions ranged from establishing a 'super authority' responsible for public and private broadcasting services as well as being in charge of transmission facilities, separating RTE radio from RTE television, establishing a news agency to provide an alternative service to that of RTE, new legislation to ensure a reasonable amount of Irish language programming across the whole range of broadcasting services etc. to ensuring that television licence fee revenue constitutes a minimum of 50% of RTE's revenue in order to ensure the independence of RTE from commercial pressures.

The Green Paper did not provide any answers to the various issues raised and suggestions made. The government's aim was to raise the level of public debate and it asked that submissions be made to the government by the end of September 1995. The government received 130 responses to the Green Paper. New legislation on broadcasting rather than a White Paper was to follow in 1996. This did not happen until early 1997, when the Minister presented to government a detailed proposal on new broadcasting legislation. Details of these proposals were not made public at first, although the press did report on some of the contents of the proposed new legislation.

According to newspaper reports, the planned legislation constitutes a radical overhaul of existing broadcasting legislation. It envisages the creation of an Irish Broadcasting Commission, a single regulatory and policy-making body that will oversee the broadcasting sector in Ireland. The public service broadcasting authority would be converted into the board of a national broadcasting corporation to be charged with operating the present RTE services but under the general policy guidance of the Commission. The Commission would also be responsible for the private broadcasting sector (subsequent to the abolition of the IRTC), for the Irish language television station TnaG (currently a subsidiary company of RTE), for the establishment of an Educational Broadcasting Advisory Committee, for the introduction of digital broadcasting services etc. As general elections will have to be held in Ireland during 1997, the government does not have much time for a public discussion of these radical proposals, let alone for the implementation of the new planned legislation.

Structure and organization

RTE operates two national television channels (RTE1 and Network 2) and four national radio services: Radio 1, with a traditional public service programming mix; 2FM, a 24 hour popular music channel; the Irish language Raidio na Gaeltachta; FM3, with its classical music programmes. In 1989 RTE embarked on a joint venture with Radio Luxembourg, namely the operation of a new radio station 'Atlantic 252'. RTE currently holds 20% of the shares in this station. The station is a commercial, wall-to-wall popular music station, financed by British advertising and transmitting its programmes from Ireland to Britain on long wave. Apart from the operation of a local radio station in Cork, the 1988 Act mentioned above excludes RTE from owing local radio stations.

Regarding private commercial broadcasting services, currently there is one national radio station, 'Radio Ireland' (which commenced broadcasting in March 1997), twenty-one local or county radio stations, 13 community radio stations (four of which are community of interest stations). The community stations have been licensed until the end of 1997. There is no local television in Ireland, apart from the local cable television programmes run by the Cork cable TV company.

Cable television relays the Irish and British national television programmes as well as between six and 20 (mainly) English-language satellite television programmes. Pay-TV is provided on cable TV. Annual subscription fees for cable TV/MMDS amount to just under IR£100.

Ownership and economics

The public broadcaster is financed both by licence fees and by advertising, the latter amounting to 64% cent of total revenue in 1996. The new national radio station is owned by Irish accountants and concert promoters, with a minority shareholding held by Scottish Radio Holdings, owners of Scotland's Clyde Radio and Northern Ireland's Downtown Radio. Ownership of private local radio is indeed 'local' and diverse: it includes local business people, teachers, farmers and farming organizations, lawyers, accountants, Irish language groups, former pirate radio operators, former RTE employees – in short people from all 'walks of life'. Some of the new radio stations have received the backing of Irish financial institutions and/or of successful Irish entrepreneurs.

Local newspapers are involved in seven of the 21 local radio stations; shareholdings by the respective local paper are restricted to 25% of the shares in local radio stations. The Churches are minority shareholders in five of the local radio stations. The national press has to date not become active in private radio.

All media in Ireland are commercial in the sense that they all rely on advertising revenue (see statistics below) and local radio is no exception to this. Apart from the two Dublin stations, which broadcast to the most lucrative market in the state, the running of local radio stations cannot be described as 'a licence to print money', as most stations just about break even.

Cable TV in Ireland is provided by 43 cable TV operators, the biggest of which is the firm Cablelink with over 80% of all cable TV subscribers. (Telecom Eireann owns 80% of the shares in Cablelink, the remaining 20% are owned by RTE.) Cable TV in Ireland began in the latter half of the 1970s as a way of relaying British (and Irish) television signals available 'off-air' – it was not the result of any government policy designed to encourage the 'cabling' of the country.

Programming and audiences

The programming on RTE Television is one that is usual for public service broadcasters, i.e. one with a fairly strong emphasis on news and current affairs programmes (see CSO, 1996). RTE's scheduling of programmes is noteworthy in that RTE has always operated in a highly competitive environment and is therefore very skilled in arranging programmes in such a way that its audiences are higher than those of its foreign competitors. Irish language programming on RTE television is currently estimated to amount to only 3% of programming time.

Concerning radio, RTE radio programmes are discussed above. The programming on private commercial radio stations in urban areas is essentially music led, i.e. with the exception of the community radios, these stations broadcast 'wall-to-wall' popular music, interspersed by advertising and by the occasional news bulletin and short, cheaply produced 'current affairs' programmes designed to fulfil the legal requirement that 20% of programming time be devoted to news and current affairs. Rural local radio stations tend to have a higher percentage of talk programmes. There are very few Irish language programmes on private radio.

Concerning listenership to radio, the latest survey data are summarized in the statistics section. The figures show that RTE radio is still the most popular radio station in the state, although local stations have made some inroads into RTE's listenership. The figures for local radio are the national average. The two RTE stations, Raidio na Gaeltachta and FM3, are not included in the usual audience surveys – the national listenership of these stations is estimated to be in the region of only 1–2% of adults (but around 26% in the Gaeltacht for Raidio na Gaeltachta).

Policies for press and broadcasting

Actors and issues

Over the past year, and with the collapse of Irish Press Newspapers, the major actors in the changing newspaper market have included the directors and chief executive of the Irish Press group; the Irish Independent group, who bought 24.9% of the Irish Press; and the Minister for Enterprise and Employment, who referred this share purchase to the Competition Authority on the basis of its possible anti-competitive consequences for the newspaper industry.

When the Press group's market share was added to that of the Independent, the latter's share increased to 64% of all Irish daily papers, 85% of evening papers and 85% of Irish Sunday papers. In the total newspaper market, including Irish and English newspapers, its market share overall was almost 70%.

The Competition Authority thus became another major actor. It concluded that the Independent's action in relation to the Irish Press represented an abuse of its dominant position and was designed to prevent rival newspapers acquiring control of the Irish Press (Interim Report). It thus judged that these actions were very serious breaches of the Competition Act and recommended that the Minister take action.

The Irish Independent, however, robustly maintains that it has not abused its position and that it will challenge in the Courts any Ministerial attempt to insist that it divests itself of its Irish Press shares. It has also stated that it wishes to relaunch at least one of the Irish Press titles – probably the *Sunday Press*. The titles of the three Irish Press newspapers are owned by a separate company, Irish Press Publications, in which the Independent group also has a 24% share, while the Press newspapers were produced by Irish Press Newspapers, now in liquidation. The Minister has stated that he wants these titles placed on the open market so that potential investors can purchase them. No investor has come forward by March 1997, so that it now seems likely that nobody seems prepared to buy the titles.

Journalists as a group proved to have very little power to avert the collapse of the Press group. When management announced its intention to liquidate the company in June 1995, the Irish Press journalists succeeded in having the High Court appoint an Examiner to find possible investors rather than liquidate. The Examiner indicated that the company was capable of survival and possible investors came forward. But objections by Irish Press directors and, it appears, the Irish Independent, thwarted this attempt. Not only have Irish Press journalists had little clout, but politicians and journalists in other non-Independent papers, despite extensive public criticism of the Independent, have in effect delivered nothing to date.

Continuing concern with concentration of media ownership and in particular the dominance of the Independent, and evidence as to the apparent agreement between the Independent and Press to prevent other potential investors from gaining control of the Press, has caused the Minister to appoint a Commission on the Newspaper Industry to examine this issue, among others. The report of this Commission was published in summer 1996. Its main recommendations (see http://www.irlgo.ie/entemp/22ee.htm) are concerned with ways of strengthening the indigenous newspaper industry in relation to UK titles, for example, by calling for the abolition of VAT on the sale of newspapers, by recommending the establishment of a central printing facility, calling for changes in the law of libel and for a ban on below-cost selling of newspapers etc. In the meantime, the major beneficiaries from the shutdown of the Press have been Independent circulation figures and profits.

Three major actors are involved in the formulation of broadcasting policy at present: public broadcasters, the government and private operators. In its submission to the Green Paper, the public broadcaster RTE made a strong case for the continued existence of public service broadcasting and put forward its plans for the future, including ideas for the development of RTE subsequent to the development of digital television. On the other hand the private broadcasters in their submissions were essentially looking for a share in the licence fee income in order to help finance what they see as their public service obligations such as the provision of news and current affairs programmes. However, the Minister's plans for broadcast legislation seem clearly to favour public service broadcasting in the distribution of the licence fee income.

Another quite influential actor is the group of Irish language speakers. Speakers of Ireland's first official language are fairly well served in terms of radio, but the same could not be said for television until the recent establishment of TnaG. Start-up costs for this third national television station were provided from the IR£17 million accumulated surplus in excess of the 'cap' on RTE, which operated until the end of 1993. The running costs are currently provided by a government grant of IR£10 million. Some of the initial programming for the channel is provided by RTE and by independent producers.

Multinational actors, although on the increase over the last few years, are still quite limited in terms of their overall number (see Truetzschler, 1991a). The advent of TV3, with the involvement of a major foreign investor, has changed this to a certain extent (see above). The licences for private radio services are mainly in the hands of Irish companies. In fact, the broadcasting contracts between these companies and the Independent Radio and Television Commission (IRTC) specify that any change in ownership must be referred to the IRTC, whose decisions in turn are subject to approval by the Minister with responsibility for broadcasting.

An actor with great interest in television broadcasting is the Irish film and television programme industry. Other actors include the advertising industry, which is mainly in the hands of the multinational advertising agencies and which was one of the main pressure groups in favour of the introduction of private radio and television services. Political parties and trade union groups are not directly involved in any of the groups which have received local radio licences, although a number of licence holders are known to have connections with political parties.

Policy trends

In terms of broadcasting policy, a certain continuity between the previous and the current government was assured by the 1992 reappointment of Michael D. Higgins as Minister for Arts and Culture (with responsibility for broadcasting) by the current government. A professor of political science, the Minister has been instrumental in shaping the very active broadcasting policies of the current and the previous governments: the non-renewal of the censorship Section 31 of the Broadcasting Authority Acts which enables the government to direct broadcasters to refrain from broadcasting interviews, or reports of interviews, with spokespersons of prohibited organizations, such as the IRA; the publication of the Green Paper outlined above; and the establishment of Teilifís na Gaeilge.

Any broadcasting initiative emanating from Europe is likely to be adopted fairly rapidly in Ireland. Ireland is a staunch member of the EU and generally there is much emphasis on the economic and financial benefits of EU membership for Ireland, although Ireland has fared rather badly within the EU over the past 25 years in comparison to every other EU country in terms of the survival of indigenous manufacturing industry, employment, overall wealth etc. (see NESC, 1989). As has been shown above, the licensing of private broadcasting operations and the regulation of broadcasting in Ireland reflect current European trends, such as abolition of state monopolies, privatization of state enterprises, commercialization of broadcasting, in fact it can be argued that Ireland has simply copied its European partners and has privatized the airwaves, without developing a specifically thought-out policy appropriate to a small state like Ireland. However, this is changing as the current government has begun to develop a cultural and broadcasting policy for Ireland.

Concerning the EU Directive on Television Broadcasting and the Council of Europe Convention on Transfrontier Television, existing Irish media law is broadly in line with these. Furthermore, RTE programming is in accordance with the quotas of made-in-Europe non-news programmes and of independent productions.

Convergence

In terms of the introduction of new technologies, some cable operators are currently undertaking a number of trials of video-on-demand (VOD) and digitally compressed television in different parts of Ireland. As well as that, it seems that Telecom Eireann (TE) is studying the provision of VOD over its telephone network and an announcement on this is expected in the near future. It also seems likely that major developments in this area can be expected once TE loses its monopoly in the provision of voice telephony (in the year 2000 at the latest).

Concerning the development of the 'infobahn' or 'information superhighway', there are no clear figures concerning the number of Irish people connected to the Internet. Estimates in early 1997 put the figure at around a rapidly increasing 100 000–150 000.

Statistics

(1 ECU = IR£0.74)

Population (1996)

Number of inhabitants	3.6 m
Geographical size	70 283 km^2
Population density	50 per km^2
Number of households	1.1 m

Broadcasting

Television household penetration (estimated)	97%
Cost of licence fee (1996)	
Black and white	IR£52
Colour	IR£70
National television channels	
Public (RTE 1, Network 2, TnaG)	3
Private (TV3 planned for 1998)	(1)
Number of hours of television broadcast (1995)	10 500
National radio channels	
Public (Radio 1, Network 2, FM3, Raidio na Gaeltachta)	4
Private (Radio Ireland)	1

Market shares of television channels in Ireland	
RTE 1 and Network 2	59%
BBC 1 and 2	15%
UTV/Channel 4	16%
Satellite channels	10%

Source: AC Nielson RTE, December 1996

Local radio stations	
Public	1
Private	21
Community	13
Reach of national/local 'Yesterday Listenership' in % weekdays	
Any Radio	89
RTE Radio 1	35
RTE 2FM	29
Home local station	48
Any local station	54

Source: JNLR, 1996

New electronic media

TV households with:	
VCR	65%
Teletext	39%
Cable television	38%

The press

Circulation* of the 10 largest newspapers (1996)	
National/regional dailies	
Irish Independent	160 032
Irish Times	102 460
Evening Herald	113 024
Star	85 979
Examiner (formerly *Cork Examiner*)	55 983
Evening Echo	25 491
National Sundays	
Sunday Independent	342 153
Sunday World	232 139
Sunday Tribune	76 454
Sunday Business Post	37 785

* Sales in the Republic of Ireland, excluding Northern Ireland, Britain and other sales

Source: Audit Bureau of Circulation, 1997

Media economics

(Ireland's media revenue, 1996, IR£ m)	
Print media	154
TV	95
Radio	27
Cinema	3
Outdoor	20
Direct marketing/mail	98
Total	397

Source: The second author's own research and IAPI, 1997

References

AGB TAM/RTE (1994) *A Report on Television Trends in Ireland 1990–1994*. Dublin: RTE.

Boyle, K. and McGonagle, M. (1988) *Press Freedom and Libel*. Dublin: National Newspapers of Ireland.

Competition Authority (1995) Interim Report. Dublin: Department of Enterprise and Employment.

CSO (Central Statistics Office) (1996) *Statistical Abstract 1996*. Dublin: The Stationery Office.

CSO (Central Statistics Office) (1997) *1996 Labour Force Survey*. Dublin: The Stationery Office.

Curtin Dorgan Associates (1990) *The Irish Film and TV Programme Production Industry*. Dublin: Curtin Dorgan Associates.

Government of Ireland (1995) *Active or Passive? Broadcasting in the Future Tense*. Dublin: The Stationery Office.

Government of Ireland (1997) Economic Background to the Budget 1997. http://www.irlgov.ie/budget/economic.html.

IAPI (Institute of Advertising Practitioners in Ireland) (1997) *Newsletter*, February/March.

JNLR (Joint National Listenership Research) (1996) Dublin: Market Research Bureau of Ireland.

Kelly, M. (1992) 'The media and national identity in Ireland', in P. Clancy et al. (eds), *Ireland and Poland, Comparative Perspectives*. Department of Sociology, University College, Dublin.

Kelly, M. (1993) 'Censorship and the media', in A. Connelly (ed.), *Gender and the Law in Ireland*. Dublin: Oak Tree Press.

Mair, Peter (1992) 'Explaining the absence of class politics in Ireland', in J.H. Goldthorpe and C.T. Whelan (eds), *The Development of Industrial Society in Ireland*. Oxford: Oxford University Press.

Mulryan, P. (1988) *Radio, Radio: The Story of Independent, Local, Community and Pirate Radio*. Dublin: Borderline Publications.

NESC (National Social and Economic Council) (1989) *Ireland in the European Community: Performance, Prospect and Strategy*. Dublin: NESC.

Truetzschler, W. (1991a) 'Foreign investment in the media in Ireland', *Irish Communications Review*, 1(1): 1–3.

Truetzschler, W. (1991b) 'Broadcasting law and broadcasting policy in Ireland', *Irish Communications Review*, 1(1): 24–7.

Wickham, J. (1986) 'Industrialization, work and unemployment', in P. Clancy et al. (eds), *Ireland: A Sociological Profile*. Dublin: Institute of Public Administration.

9

Italy

Gianpietro Mazzoleni

National profile

Of the larger countries of Europe, Italy is one of the most heavily populated. In 1993 the number of inhabitants was about 57.9 million over an area of 301 280 km^2 – a density of 191 inhabitants per km^2. About 30% of the population live in 49 towns with more than 100 000 inhabitants. Four metropolitan cities (Rome, Milan, Naples, Turin) have populations of over 1 million.

The natural population growth is steadily declining – 2.2 per thousand in 1990, compared to the 7.4 of 1951. The structure of the population is characterized by a high percentage of people in the middle and upper age groups. The increase in the elderly age group is common to other European countries.

Living around the country's borders are French, German and Slovenian minorities, with a total of less than half a million people. Despite their limited numbers, these language minorities enjoy privileges such as special radio and TV broadcasts, besides newspapers and schools in their own languages.

Geographically, Italy is surrounded in the north by the Alps and in the centre and south by the Mediterranean Sea. The reception of foreign TV broadcasts only recently overcame these natural obstacles. The mountainous character of large areas (one-third of domestic territory) and the long distances (more than 1500 km from Milan to Palermo) have had an impact on the development policies of the mass media in the country.

From the late 1940s until 1992, Italy was governed by coalition governments, mostly led by the Christian Democratic Party (DC), the Centre-moderate biggest party. The opposition never succeeded in gaining executive power. The long-lasting dominance of the same parties favoured their penetration into almost all sectors of the life of the nation, and especially in the economic sectors (banks, finance, industry) and the communication industry (newspapers, radio and TV, culture). A typical feature of that political season was the *lottizzazione*, i.e. the partitioning of power among all parties, opposition included. The most striking example was the public broadcasting company (Rai), where the parties had placed their yes-men from the governing body down to the television channels and news services. The parties' influence was (and to a certain extent still is) extensive in press organizations, even if not as formally as in the public broadcasting company.

The investigations of the public prosecutors of the parties' corrupt practices broke apart the old establishment and Italy's political system is now undergoing a deep institutional and moral mutation that has been defined as a 'passage from the First to the Second Republic'.

The victory in the 1994 general elections of a media tycoon, Silvio Berlusconi, opened an array of unprecedented issues on the mixture of private and public interests in the information domains, with possible risks for democracy.

Italy's economic system has been characterized for decades by an extensive state participation ranging from banking and finance to agriculture. New government policies, however, lean in the direction of a gradual pull-out from all sectors by means of privatization of public estates and shares. In the field of media and electronic communications, the state no longer holds a radio and television monopoly; this was rescinded in the 1990 Broadcasting Act (law no. 223). The liberalization of the telecommunications services is soon to be enacted, following EU policy.

The running of the public broadcasting channels is contracted to Rai and the telephones to Telecom Italia. The postal service is still directly managed by the Ministry of PTT. The press sector as a whole is independent of state participation and works in a competitive environment. Following a long economic crisis of the press in the early 1980s, negotiations between the government and the publishers led to parliament passing the Press Law (no. 416/1981), which opened the way for special financial help by the state. For the first time in Italian press history, the same law prohibited concentration of ownership. Beside these special subsidies, all daily newspapers, weeklies and periodical magazines are subsidized indirectly by low VAT, low postal distribution rates and the like. Later legislation has since modified the conditions and the subsidies introduced by the 1991 bill.

Development of the press and broadcasting since 1945

The press

The post-war history of the Italian press can be divided in five periods.

The decade immediately following the Second World War (1945–1954) was a period of rebirth and normalization of the entire media system. The main dailies (*Il Corriere della Sera, La Stampa, La Nazione, Il Resto del Carlino, Il Messaggero, Il Mattino*) consolidated their traditional leadership. During this decade the daily press upheld dominant social values. This endured for another decade, with certain exceptions.

The years from 1954 to 1979 were years of great internal migration, of the so-called 'economic boom' and of the race towards the affluent society. It was a stagnant period for the press, with regard to ownership patterns and circulation figures. The two most notable exceptions were the launching of the progressive (and aggressive) news magazine *L'Espresso*, and of the daily *Il Giorno*, both breaking new ground in the news-making domains. The daily circulation remained stable at around the 5 million copies that had been a constant pattern for decades. In contrast, the weekly press registered high penetration peaks, reaching in the mid-1960s the highest European figure.

From 1970 to 1985 the media went through an 'ordeal by fire', as witnessed by rapid changes in customs, technology and political outlooks. The daily press in particular showed signs of awakening and was in fact in the vanguard of the country's political and cultural evolution. The old dailies inaugurated a brand of journalism more keen on monitoring the social dynamics. New, prestigious newspapers were established (*Il Giornale Nuovo*, *La Repubblica*). This is also the period, however, of financial difficulties for the whole press sector, which opened the way for powerful interest groups to seize control of the major newspapers. The Press Law in 1981 attempted to rescue the ailing press and introduced legal barriers to the concentration of ownership in the hands of industrial trusts. While the financial subsidies worked, helping the publishers to get over the crisis, the antitrust measures were unable to uphold the cherished pluralism: a group of industrialists led by Fiat established the RCS Rizzoli-Corriere della Sera trust, a giant with assets in all publishing areas (books, periodicals, dailies).

During the late 1980s the Italian press sector did well. The crisis of the previous years was fully overcome. The marriage between marketing and advertising and the news industry became very strong. The expansion of advertising investments, thanks mostly to the revolution in the television domain, also drew a large amount of financial resources to the press, easing the process of transition to the new technologies and opening the way to sales promotion operations. By resorting to bingo, gadgets, prizes, folders, etc. in order to increase the entertainment value of the news, the daily press circulation reached a peak of 7 million copies in 1989. The sporting dailies and the small, local newspapers registered the highest growth rates.

The 'political revolution' that started in 1992 and led to the dismissal of the old political class had an impact also in the press precincts. Italy's journalism, traditionally subservient to the political parties, began to break free from the political line and to take sides with the critics and with public opinion in the country, infuriated with the old parties and leaders. The print media were distinguished in the 1994 campaign and in the Berlusconi government months for their fierce resistance to the tycoon's political words and deeds. From the industrial and financial perspectives, these years appear to be fairly stagnant, registering crises for a number of dailies, a decrease in circulation rates, diminished profits of the biggest papers and a less lively marketing aggressiveness.

Radio and television

Rai was created after the war in 1946. In 1947 parliament appointed a committee to control the objectivity and political independence of radio broadcasts. The three national radio programmes were initiated in 1950.

Regular television broadcasts began in January 1954, with a coverage of 36% of the national territory. In November 1961, Rai inaugurated the second television channel, covering 52% of Italy. The diffusion of television in Italy, as in other countries, has been very rapid. In 1960 there were 2 million subscribers, in 1971 10 million and in 1984, 14 million.

A regular colour television service (PAL system) began in 1975. In the same year parliament approved an important reform bill (Law no. 103) that conferred exclusive broadcasting rights on Rai and reorganized the entire sector, allowing for the establishment of private cable TV. The pressure by private interests was so strong that they succeeded in attaining a ruling from the Constitutional Court (no. 202/1976) that acknowledged their right to broadcast in limited areas.

From that moment on, about 600 local television stations and more than 2500 radio stations were set up all over the country, a phenomenon that literally changed the traditional electronic mass media scene in Italy.

In 1979 Rai, in an extreme attempt to counteract the explosion of local private broadcasting, inaugurated its third television channel, a network of regionally based production centres.

In 1981–2 four nationwide commercial networks were established by private entrepreneurs (businessmen such as Silvio Berlusconi, and publishers like Rizzoli, Mondadori and Rusconi). Due to financial difficulties, the Italia Uno and Rete 4 networks, owned by the publishers, were sold to the Berlusconi trust in 1983–84.

Since 1976 the radio–TV situation in Italy has been so chaotic that it has been compared to the Wild West, with unregulated competition, births and deaths of hundreds of broadcasting enterprises, rocketing programme costs and, above all, the consolidation of a private broadcasting industry, monopolized by a single trust.

The policy-makers appeared unable (or unwilling) for more than a decade to approve a bill that would put some order in the broadcasting sector. Finally, in August 1990, Parliament passed the long-waited Broadcasting Act that, even if critics saw it as a 'legalization of the status quo', introduced a series of measures that imposed transparency in the media industry.

The electoral success in 1994 of the tycoon-politician Silvio Berlusconi raised the questions about the validity of those 'rules of the game'. A harsh political debate accompanied the tycoon's conquest of power, focusing on the demand for new warranties against concentration of television channels and against the conflict of interests, in defence of public television.

The press

Policy framework

Several laws and codes were enacted in the years following the end of the Second World War relating to information conveyed by the print media.

Of course, the Constitution guarantees 'freedom of expression' to all citizens (art. 21), but the legislation foresees a series of conditions (and restrictions) to be met in order to exercise that freedom. The old Press Law, law no. 47 of 1948, is the principal body of legislation regulating this complex matter. It has undergone obvious and continuous updating. This law provides basic norms dealing with the journalists' profession: it regulates the right to secrecy, safeguards moral standards, the right to reply, defamation and libel, the penal responsibility of the editors and reporters and the like.

The new Press Law of 1981 (with updates in 1984 and 1987) contains more detailed legislation aimed at regulating the information industry. It introduced a series of subsidies that helped Italy's press out of financial and structural crisis. Beside the subsidies chapter, the Law represented a true turning point both in policy-making and in the development of the entire sector.

The most significant innovations it inaugurated refer to:

- The transparency of ownership of publishing companies (ownership must be made public and owners may not be active outside the publishing field).
- The Guarantor (a sort of high authority of publishing with several enforcing powers and supervising tasks).
- The National Press Register (all daily newspapers, periodicals, press agencies and companies selling advertising to the press must register in order to be operational).
- The transfer of shares (should be communicated to the Guarantor).
- The concentration of the daily press (the acquisition of newspapers leading to a dominant position in the market is blocked by a series of detailed norms).
- The establishment of cooperatives of journalists (in case of cessation of publication of a newspaper by the former owner).
- The price of newspaper copies (formerly fixed by government, liberalized in January 1988).

Not all the new norms have worked in the implementation process, especially those concerning the concentration of daily newspapers. The binding legal devices could not block the birth of a huge trust such as the one commanded by Fiat, which (directly) controls the daily *La Stampa*, one of the top national newspapers, and (indirectly – that is through a financial branch) the publishing giant Rizzoli-Corriere della Sera. The Guarantor took the case to court and parliament tried to tighten the norms in 1987, but unsuccessfully. The Supreme Court ruled (against the Guarantor's thesis) the formal non-existence of a Fiat trust, and (against parliament's action) declared null the retroactive effect of the 1987 new legal measures.

Ownership and finance

In Italy in 1994 there were 94 daily newspapers, most of them owned or controlled by a small number of publishing trusts including the following.

The CIR of Olivetti's chairman Carlo de Benedetti owns *La Repubblica* (daily circulation in 1993: 624 353 copies) and 12 provincial newspapers, controlling 12.27% of the copies printed in the country.

The RCS, controlled by Gemina SpA, a financial trust gathering several interests but with Fiat in a leading position, owns the major Italian daily *Il Corriere della Sera* (circulation in 1993: 647 630), and *La Gazzetta dello Sport* (circulation in 1993: 410 411). It controls 15.41% of the total printing.

The Fiat group directly owns *La Stampa* (circulation in 1993: 428 530), with a 5.94% share of the total printing.

The Monti-Riffeser family publishes *Il Resto del Carlino* (circulation in 1993: 231 970), *La Nazione* (circulation: 204 868) and *Il Tempo* (circulation: 89 509), controlling 6.60% of the total printing.

The Ferfin (Ferruzzi) owns Rome's daily *Il Messaggero* (circulation in 1993: 296 170, a share of 4.47%).

There is also a series of minor groups publishing other dailies. The oil public company ENI owns *Il Giorno*, a national newspaper (circulation in 1993: 153 606); the ex-communist party controls the daily *L'Unità* (circulation in 1993: 126 646); the Industrialists' Association prints the top economic paper, *Il Sole–24 Ore* (circulation in 1993: 334 888).

The traditional publishing houses that made their money out of printing activities (Mondadori, Rizzoli) have in recent years given in to the pressure of financial capital coming from non-publishing operations. So, Berlusconi (a tycoon who made his fortunes in real estate), Agnelli (the automobile mogul), Ferruzzi (the food and chemical giant), De Benedetti (an industrialist and financier) and other less famous private entrepreneurs all manifested concrete interest in the old and new media fields, seizing relevant blocks of shares in those publishing corporations. The main reason for their inroads into the media business is financial: unlike in the early 1980s, the sector is a gold mine (thanks also to the connection with the booming advertising industry). A further reason, at times even stronger than the financial one, is the wish to influence public opinion and the political arena. In this latter case the buying and selling of dailies by private interests often takes on the character of 'give and take' with the political powers, which are traditionally sensitive to the information issue.

Characterization of the newspapers

Italy's daily press is usually defined in terms of two parameters: geographic coverage and content. Table 1 shows the typology of the press in 1995.

Table 1 *Italian press by geographical coverage and content*

Type	Circulation share (%)
National	36.13
Supra-regional	15.66
Regional	14.68
Provincial	10.10
Sports	12.04
Other (economic, political)	11.39

Italy does not have typical yellow-press newspapers. The few attempts, in 1981 (with *L'Occhio*) and 1995 (with the *Telegiornale*), to launch a tabloid imitating the UK's *Sun* or Germany's *BILD* failed within weeks. This is mainly due to the existence of a successful weekly press of genuine popular character. The daily press is instead, in the collective imagery of Italians, synonymous with an elite information product. The real popular dailies in Italy are undoubtedly the sporting papers, as against the remaining types which are more like the so-called 'quality' papers.

As far as political allegiance is concerned, it is quite difficult to pinpoint exactly the position of Italian newspapers in relation to different sub-cultural areas. The majority of dailies consider themselves 'independent'. An average reader can easily tell if a paper is 'progressive', 'moderate' or 'conservative' but it is not feasible to list here the 94 dailies accordingly.

In 1980, 56.2% of the Italian population read a newspaper at least once a week; the figure reached 65.7% in 1992. Despite the significant increase, still a little less than half of the population ever takes a newspaper in their hands.

The profile of the average reader is 'male, employed, less than 45 years old, with a higher education, belonging to middle–high social status, living in urban areas of North–Central Italy'. The most preferred topics by readers are (data for 1992): current events (81.9%), political events (31.8%), sports (34.6%), entertainment (27.9%), health and medicine (27.0%), cultural topics (25.3%), economy (13.9%).

Among the complex historical and cultural reasons that explain the low readership of newspapers in Italy is the singular constraint of the distribution network. Italy has Europe's highest percentage of daily newspapers distributed through the news-stands: 93% vs. 91% for Spain, 69.7% for France, 50% for the UK, 34.5% for Germany (FIEJ figures, 1993). The monopoly of the news-stands has been attacked several times by Italy's Publishers' Association (FIEG), which blames such a distribution bottleneck for the country's poor newspaper consumption. Parliament, however, has repeatedly voted against the liberalization of distribution channels.

Electronic media

Legal framework

Italy's broadcasting sector is regulated by two major bodies of law, no. 103 of 1975 and no. 223 of 1990 (the Broadcasting Act). The former, with some updating introduced in 1990 and 1993, is still enforced and regulates public broadcasting. For more than a decade this law provided the only legal framework of the broadcasting field. One of its key features was the ban on any private initiative in radio and television activities. It was clearly unfit to handle the tremendous pressures that led to the rise of commercial television. The situation of non-regulation favoured chaotic development of the sector, eventually stabilized in the partition of the field between Rai, the public company, and Berlusconi's Fininvest. The road to this duopoly is strewn with tens (hundreds, counting radio) of casualties, victims of the 'law of the market place', otherwise called the 'television war' between cumbersome giants.

The 1990 Broadcasting Act to a certain extent froze this situation, basically acknowledging the territorial conquests of Rai and Berlusconi, each commanding three channels. However, the law stipulates the following important regulatory measures:

- Broadcasting is no longer a state monopoly, private enterprises can apply for licences to run stations.
- Private companies may broadcast live, nationwide, by means of technical link-ups.
- The Guarantor for Broadcasting and Publishing is established as the high authority over both fields.
- Programmes may have advertisement breaks, with a number of limitations, according to EU Directive no. 89/552.
- Advertising should not exceed 15% of the daily transmission time and an hourly quota of 18%.
- Contents and programme schedules may not be influenced by sponsors.
- The norms in the 1947 Press Law regulating the right of reply apply also to broadcasting.
- A National Register of Broadcasting Organizations is established.
- Cross-ownership of media must meet the following conditions:
  anyone controlling over 16% of the total daily newspaper circulation may not hold any licence to run a national television network;
  anyone controlling 8–16% of the daily circulation may hold only one licence;
  anyone controlling less than 8% of the daily circulation may hold two licences;
  anyone with no shares in the daily press publishing companies may hold up to three licences.

- Private licensees broadcasting nationwide are obliged to transmit a daily news service.
- Forty per cent of the yearly transmission time has to be covered by programmes produced in Europe in the first three years following the granting of the licence, 51% in the following years; no less than 50% of these has to be of Italian production.
- The household licence fee is maintained in favour of the public broadcasting company (Rai).
- A Board of Viewers is appointed as a consultative body to the Guarantor.

As far as cable television is concerned, law no. 103 of 1975 actually suffocated it by limiting it to a one-channel option and restricting its diffusion to small local markets. Those constraints provoked the private entrepreneurs' attack on the radio and television monopoly that led to the Constitutional Court's ruling of 1976 which opened broadcasting to private companies. The 1990 Broadcasting Act briefly deals with cable television, stating that it may be multi-channel and that it is regulated by similar norms to broadcasting. In 1996 no cable television channel existed in Italy, although there were plans to introduce it on experimental basis in certain metropolitan areas (such as Milan).

Pay-TV, even though not mentioned in the Broadcasting Act of 1990, has been later (in 1992) assimilated to broadcast television and therefore subject to the existing norms dealing with this. In fact, out of the 12 licences for nationwide networks foreseen in the Broadcasting Act, three have been reserved by the Ministry of PTT to encrypted broadcast channels. They still use terrestrial frequencies but gradually will have to pass on to Direct Broadcasting Satellite (DBS) channels.

The market for home video, VCRs and recorded cassettes has expanded rapidly in the early 1990s, reaching the consumption rates of other major European countries. The sector, however, is not the object of any specific legislation. The few norms regarding the field (indirectly) are those concerning the protection of copyright.

The 'mass telematics' sector, videotex, audiotex and teletext, enjoys more attention from policy-makers. The videotex (Videotel) and audiotex (Audiotel) run by the public telephone company Telecom Italia in particular have been targets of several ministerial decrees (on technical standards, service regulations, tariffs, restrictions of content, safeguards of minor users, and the like).

As with the DBS television, the existing policies deal rather with technological and financial aspects of a future Italian-made satellite (Sarit). There is no real national service of this kind, even if Rai beams two of its national channels also through satellite. People can get easy access to satellites such as Astra and Eutelsat but consumption of DBS television in Italy has a strong competitor in the wide and cheap availability of traditional broadcast television.

Map of the system

There has been no planned policy design behind the change of Italy's radio and television system from a monopolized structure to a mixed system. The spontaneous and uncontrolled 'revolution' of the mid-1970s imposed commercial broadcasting and forced public radio and television to give up its traditional monopoly. The 1990 Broadcasting Act gave only political ratification to this de facto situation.

Besides those that obtained an official licence from the Ministry of PTT (see Statistical section), there are also a number of other commercial networks which are actually 'syndications' or associations of local stations that maintain a fairly large autonomy in programme schedules, advertising collection and financial structure. In addition, there exist about 1000 small and medium-size independent private local television stations.

The radio sector has a structure analogous to that of television. The public broadcasting company, Rai, runs three AM/FM nationwide channels.

Altogether the Rai channels had 13 million listeners in 1995. There are about 14 commercial networks holding a licence and they reach 25 million listeners in an average day. These commercial radio networks, as well as the 1700 or so local stations that applied in 1993 for a ministerial licence, depending exclusively on advertising, offer mostly music, heavily packed with spot advertisements, and very little news.

Other features that complete the overall map of Italy's broadcasting system regard the areas of advertising, programme production and audience monitoring.

Advertising was in Rai's monopoly years a secondary source of income, the main source being the household licence fees. Since the arrival of private radio and television channels advertising has become 'the' resource par excellence of the domestic broadcasting market. The tumultuous growth of television and its enormous ability to grab substantial slices of available resources blew up the traditional balances that privileged the press, thus provoking dramatic shock waves in the entire mass media system. The main 'villain' of this uprising was Silvio Berlusconi, who inaugurated defiant techniques that disconcerted the traditional market leaders.

In 1975 61.9% of the total advertising spend went to the press, only 15.4% to television (Rai); in 1988 the press got 43.4% while television took 47.8%, in 1994 the press' quota dropped to 38.1% and that of television reached 53.5%. The marriage between advertising and commercial television, unavoidable since the private channels live only on advertising revenues, has also brought deep changes in the traditional patterns of programme output and in the development of this medium. Rai programmes were never 'sliced' with spot ads: advertising was concentrated in few slots before and after. The commercial stations imported the American pattern with an excessive number of breaks that annoyed the viewers. The number of spot ads shown in 1981 was 260 000 but reached 1 million in 1992!

The explosion in the number of commercial stations has increased the total daily transmitting time immensely. This led broadcasters to buy programmes on foreign markets. With 71% of the total offer made of imported programming, Italy was in the mid-1980s the country airing the highest proportion of foreign television programmes. The keen competition between public and private networks and between big and small stations in the international marketplaces led to soaring prices, even for the low quality material. In the past few years the situation has changed somewhat, as the major networks increased their home production quotas. All imported programmes are regularly dubbed on Italian television.

The issue of audience monitoring inflamed the television field for almost a decade. Before the rise of commercial broadcasting Rai monitored its audience by means of diaries. The new stations contracted the monitoring of their audiences to a number of pollsters. The data often clashed and aroused endless quarrels between public and private channels. Finally, in 1986 a new, independent organization (Auditel) was established to measure the audience for the entire television system, based on meter technology (a national sample of 2420 households). A similar organization was established in 1988, to monitor the audience rates for the radio sector (Audiradio).

Organization of the two major broadcasting groups

Rai is a publicly owned company, governed by a board appointed by the presidents of the Chamber of Deputies and of the Senate. It enjoys the financial privilege of getting its income from both the household licence fee (in 1992 51%) and advertising (31%). Sales of programmes and other commercial activities account for the remaining 18%. Besides broadcasting, through a number of subsidiary companies, Rai undertakes a series of related activities: publishing, records, advertising, programme sales. Rai employs 12 255 people, and transmits 32 315 hours of nationwide and 6330 hours of regional and minority television broadcasts, and a total of 52 646 hours of radio programmes (1995).

The content of the public company's transmissions is detailed below in Table 2.

As far as the production figures of television programmes are concerned, Rai has consistently had very high levels of home production, in contrast to the commercial channels that have been heavy importers of foreign material. The situation changed in the 1980s, when the public broadcasting company, in order to counteract the fierce competition from the private networks, increased its import rates. In the early 1990s things have again changed in the direction of a larger home production quota by both Rai and the commercial channels. In 1994, the Rai quota was 65.2%, while the Fininvest's was 47.7%.

Rai does not have regular satellite broadcasts because this service is not included in the agreement between the state and the public company. A revision of the agreement in 1995 opens the way to satellite television: it is

Table 2 *Structure of Rai transmissions (1994)*

Programme type	% of total
News	12.8
Information and culture	24.1
Sports	8.6
Film	19.7
TV fiction	12.0
Children's	4.4
Entertainment	9.6
Talk show	7.3
Drama/serious music	1.6
TOTAL	100.0

Source: Annuario Rai, 1994

Rai's intention to inaugurate in the near future eight 'thematic channels', that is pay-TV channels, beamed from Eutelsat satellites.

The Berlusconi broadcasting empire epitomizes the deep change undergone in the past 20 years by Italy's television system. When speaking of the commercial networks, one automatically thinks of Berlusconi's channels. Of course, there exist many other private enterprises, but their influence is marginal. Berlusconi's Fininvest, together with Rai controls 90% of the domestic television market, justifying the term 'duopoly'.

The 1995 turnover of Mediaset (the Fininvest's holding for television and advertising) was 2954 bn lire. In 1995 Berlusconi sold 20% of the shares in his television empire to Leo Kirch (10%), the Saudi Prince Al-Waleed (4.5%) and the South African financier Johan Rupert (5.5%). Less than 2500 employees work in the television divisions. The Fininvest-owned channels aired a total of 26 280 hours in 1995. Their home production quota was 44% in 1995. Table 3 analyses the range of programming on the three Berlusconi channels.

Compared to the variety of the programming of the public channels, the offer of the commercial ones appears quite biased towards entertainment and

Table 3 *Content of programmes offered by Fininvest (1994)*

Programme type	% of total
News	13.7
Information and culture	10.7
Sports	3.2
Film	14.5
TV fiction	33.3
Children's	7.6
Entertainment	7.4
Talk-show	9.4
Drama/serious music	0.2
TOTAL	100.0

Source: Annuario Rai, 1994

Table 4 *Prime time audience ratings (%) from 1992 to 1995*

	1992	1993	1994	1995
Rai	47.3	48.0	48.3	49.0
Fininvest	43.4	43.8	43.5	43.4
Other networks	9.3	8.2	8.2	7.6

Source: Auditel

advertising, and private television is perceived as such by the viewers. In January 1991, however, the three commercial channels inaugurated a regular daily news service, thus presenting themselves as key information outlets, in competition with the previous monopoly of public television.

The competition between the two oligopolies is carried at all levels, but especially on audience share. Table 4 depicts the trend in prime time ratings from 1992 to 1995.

The stepping of Berlusconi into the political arena in 1994, as leader of a political party (Forza Italia), and then as Prime Minister, raised the issue of the compatibility between his business activities and interests and political and institutional responsibilities. The opportunity to introduce into the country's legislation a warranty measure such as the US 'blind trust', obliging Berlusconi to give up his business, has had a difficult journey in parliament.

The 'new media'

The abundance of programme content made available by dozens of nationwide networks and hundreds of local stations restrained the demand for different outlets for more than a decade. This accounts for the limited growth of the 'new media' and the 'telematic media', compared with other countries.

The first casualty of the channel surplus was cable television. It simply does not exist in Italy, not even on a small scale. Telecom Italia has recently started its planned cabling of the country, connecting 10 million households by 1998. This will eventually permit the establishment of cable television stations. At the same time, the public telephone company invested 1800 bn lire to launch video-on-demand (VoD) services by 1997

Satellite television in the mid-1990s is not yet a familiar feature of audiovisual consumption, even if antenna-dishes increasingly appear on the roofs of many buildings in the cities as well as in the villages. Unofficial estimates indicate that 2% of households possessed satellite receivers in 1995. The programmes that consumers get are only offered by channels beaming from foreign satellites (Astra, Eutelsat), as there is no regular DBS service offered by Rai and Fininvest.

The Rai teletext service, called Televideo, became operational in 1985, employing the UK Teletext, Level 1 standard. More than 50% of television sets are equipped to receive the service. It offers a daily average of 1600 pages of information, the most popular ones being those carrying the latest news, the weather forecasts, soccer results and the TV programme guide. Televideo also provides subtitling in English, French and German to the Italian programmes beamed from RaiSat. Rai plans to 'regionalize' the information provision, offering a segmented service in all regions by 1997. The Teletext service is also offered by commercial channels and a few local stations.

The videotex service Videotel is operated by the public telephone company Telecom Italia. Following a long period of testing (from 1982 to 1986), the service became operational in 1986, based on the CEPT standard, level 3. To boost the consumer take-up, the company set low tariffs, rented the terminals at a cheap rate and established link-ups with the French Minitel. After a few years of growth, the service never really took off. The turnover of 93 bn lire in 1992 fell to 40 bn in 1994. Several factors worked against the service: delays in government regulation of the tariffs and the technical and functional features of the service, several cases of piracy that discouraged the users, and the diffusion of Internet. The introduction of the 'kiosk' system in 1996 was Telecom Italia's attempt at relaunching Videotel.

By contrast the phone service Audiotel, also operated by Telecom, has shown a rapid diffusion since its start in 1993, especially due to its easy access. In 1994 400 information providers offered 1900 different services. Several abuses in the chat lines and messageries stirred criticism from consumers, forcing the carrier to tighten the norms regulating the medium.

Pay-TV is offered in Italy over the terrestrial frequencies, as no cable TV exists. The three channels, TELEPIU' 1, TELEPIU' 2, TELEPIU' 3, are owned by groups of different shareholders, behind whom allegedly is also Silvio Berlusconi (banned from overt ownership of further channels by the Broadcasting Act). Each channel has a different viewer profile and scheduling: the first channel features recent films, the second is a sport channel, the third offers a mix of culture, information and education.

Finally, the home video sector is buoyant in the mid-1990s. In just a few years this sector has scored a very high growth rate, following a poor start due to the proliferation of broadcast outlets. In 1990 26% of Italian households owned a VCR, increasing to 47% in 1994.

Policies for press and broadcasting

After more than a decade of delays and tottering steps by government and political forces in the fields of broadcasting and new electronic media, the policy-makers have come to life in the 1990s. New laws have been passed and new government actions have led to a less 'sloppy' handling of the domestic electronic media world; a 'high authority' has been established for the communication sector and in a word, the system seems finally to have plugged in with the mainstream of Europe's media policy.

The rationale behind Italy's eccentric conduct in the media domain lies in its unique political environment. Economy, media and politics have always been closely associated in Italy. On one side, most fortunes and misfortunes of domestic industrialists can be interpreted in terms of the intensity of their connections with political circles. Moreover the domestic media are connected with the political establishment and the parties have always been extremely sensitive on communication issues. Domestic tycoons must blandish some political party, even one not in power, in order to do business.

The political parties worked out at least three modes of conditioning mass communication: running their own media, influencing the editors and editorial boards of the press and broadcast media, and using the reform bill proposals as pressure tools. In recent years this interaction pattern showed some cracks, due to the shifting of traditional political balances and to the greater independence of the economic actors. Politics has gradually lost the previous central and 'necessary' character it possessed in the country's life.

In the field of mass communication this new wave is characterized by 'market logic'. Between industrialists, parties and communication institutions new balances are being established. The basic model is, however, still that of 'imperfect exchange', but now the politician is losing primacy to the economic entrepreneur, and the media see their role revalued. This transition is not painless. The perception by the political establishment of losing control of communications has pushed parties and governments to take contradictory actions. They immobilized themselves in a policy stalemate and, fearing also to lose the citadels still under their influence, majority and opposition forces clung to them by partitioning Rai between themselves. The wild 'deregulation' in broadcasting that characterized the late 1970s and the 1980s exposed the sector to political blackmail.

The mostly defensive strategies adopted by political parties *vis-à-vis* the developments in the media marketplace did not appear to be gaining the upper hand. Their inability to work out positive regulations weakened their political dominance: tycoons and trusts met only weak legal opposition when they moved into electronic mass media. They gained enormous influence, and were practically beyond any political control. The 1990 Broadcasting Act itself showed this political acceptance of the market-originated revolution.

The disappearance of the old political establishment in 1992–4 also sent shock waves through the mass media system. The transition governments of those years as well as the Berlusconi cabinet attempted with some success to dismantle the domination of the former parties over the Rai governing body and channels. At the same time, the Berlusconis' monopoly of commercial television channels came under fire from the opposition forces, which also strongly pushed toward a reform of the Broadcasting Act. They accused the legitimized Rai–Fininvest duopoly of killing any real pluralism. In fact, in 1994 the Constitutional Court declared one of the anti-trust measures of that law (art. 15 §4) unconstitutional, because it actually allowed a single enterprise to own three private networks, thus impeding pluralism. Parliament at the end of 1995, after a more than one-year-long heated tug-of-war had not succeeded in finding a viable agreement on new legislation on anti-trust nor on the entire radio–television system. The three referenda promoted in the spring of 1995 by a few political movements to bypass the parliamentary stalemate and to introduce some drastic anti-concentration measures missed the target, as the majority of citizens voted against the proposed prohibition to own more than one television channel (referendum no. 1), against the ban on commercial breaks in broadcast movies (referendum no. 2), in favour of a partial privatization of Rai (referendum no. 3).

In 1996 the new Prodi cabinet, backed by a coalition of Centre–Left parties, presented a legislation proposal regarding the electronic media and telecommunication sectors. The Bill had a difficult journey through parliament. When and if approved, the new law is likely to introduce profound changes in Italy's media domain.

Statistics

(1 ECU = 2080 lire)

Population (1995)

Number of inhabitants	57.2 million
Geographical size	301 280 km^2
Population density	191 per km^2
Number of households (1990)	20.3 million

Broadcasting

Public broadcasting (1995)	
Number of household licence fees	16 091 000
Cost of household licence fee	158 000 lire
Number of television channels	3
Number of broadcast hours	32 315
Number of radio listeners to national channels (average day)	
Radio1	8.2 million
Radio2	6.1 million
Radio3	1.7 million
Number of broadcast hours	52 646

Commercial broadcasting (1995)	
Number of TV networks	6
Number of pay-TV channels	3
Number of pay-TV subscribers (1995)	850 000
Number of local TV stations	793
Number of radio networks	17
Number of local radio stations	1261

Television audience (prime time) (1995)	
Public television	49.0
Rai Uno	23.8
Rai Due	14.3
Rai Tre	10.9

Commercial networks	
(Major)	43.4
Canale 5	22.3
Italia 1	12.3
Rete4	8.8
(Minor – TeleMonteCarlo, Videomusic)	7.6
Pay-TV channels	
TELEPIU' 1, TELEPIU' 2, TELEPIU' 3	3

New electronic media

VCR penetration (1995)	50%
Teletext (only Rai) penetration	46%
Daily average of pages offered	1600
Percentage of households with satellite receivers	2%
Audiotex (1995)	
Number of information providers	400
Number of services offered	1900
Videotex (1994)	
Number of information providers	720
Number of users	172 000

The press

Daily press	
Circulation (1995)	6 283 000
Price per copy (1995)	1500 lire
Readers on an average day (1996)	20 686 000
Weekly press	
Circulation (1993)	15 307 000
Readers (1996)	29 119 000

Advertising investments (1995)

	%	bn lire
Press		
Daily	15.4	
Periodical	16.8	
Total	32.2	2597
Television		
Public	18.2	
Commercial networks	[illegible]	
Other	3.2	
Total	68.6	4893
Radio		
Public	1.6	
Commercial	1.5	
Total	3.1	263
Cinema	0.4	30
Outdoor	3.7	236
TOTAL	100.0	8069

Statistical sources: Rai, Annuario 1994; Relazione Semestrale Garante Editoria, 1994; UPA, 1995; Auditel, 1996; Audiradio, 1996; Audipress, 1996; FIEG, 1995; ISTAT, 1996

References

AEC (1995) *Rapporto sull'economia della cultura in Italia 1980–1990*. Rome and Bologna: AEC.

Castronovo, Valerio and Tranfaglia, Nicola (eds) (1994) *La stampa italiana nell'età della TV, 1975–1994*. Bari: Laterza.

Dorfles, Piero (ed.) (1993) *Atlante della radio e della televisione*. Rome: Nuova ERI.

Institute of Media Economics (1993) *Media Industry in Europe*. London: John Libbey.

Institute of Media Economics (1996) *L'industria della communicazione in Italia*. Milan: Guerini.

Mazzoleni, Gianpietro (1995) 'Towards a Videocracy? Italian political communication at turning point', *European Journal of Communication*, 10(3): 291–319.

Menduni, Enrico (1994) *La radio nell'era della TV*. Bologna: II Mulino.

10

Luxembourg

Mario Hirsch

National profile

In a tiny area of 2586 km^2, some 406 600 people live in Luxembourg, two-thirds of them concentrated in and around Luxembourg City and the southern part.

Thirty-one per cent of the total population (124 500 residents) are of foreign origin, mostly Portuguese and Italian. Furthermore, more than 50 000 people from the neighbouring regions of France, Belgium and Germany commute daily to work in Luxembourg. Foreigners (both resident immigrants and cross-border commuters) account for 52% of the working population. The Luxembourg economy has undergone dramatic structural changes over the past decades, with the rapid decline of the steel industry (in 1970 close to 30 000 people were employed in that sector, barely 4000 were left at the end of 1996) and agriculture. The services sector expanded considerably and continues to do so. Over 20 000 people are employed in the banking and insurance sector. GNP was in excess of 10 bn ECU in 1995.

Officially Luxembourg is a trilingual country (Luxembourgish, French, German). While French is the administrative language, German is the language of the media, both for the printed press and as indicated by the viewing preferences of TV and radio audiences.

Development of the press and broadcasting since 1945

Media activities have always been almost exclusively the domain of private initiative. This holds true not only for the press but also for audiovisual media. With the exception of videotex and satellite developments, the public sector has never had any real stake in media developments. It has however been instrumental in providing a 'liberal' environment for entrepreneurial developments in the field, encouraging Luxembourg's role as a platform for international operators.

In contrast to broadcasting (where CLT/RTL enjoyed a de facto monopoly until 1991), the Luxembourg press situation has always been astonishingly diversified. No less than five dailies with a total circulation of over 100 000 copies are published, alongside five weeklies and a large number of periodical publications. The Luxembourg press presents the peculiarity that it is closely linked to the main political parties. Because most publications could not subsist on their own, they benefit, since 1976, from considerable public subsidies, both direct and indirect.

Broadcasting in Luxembourg started at the end of the 1920s when French financial and industrial interests (Havas, Paribas, CSF etc.) founded Compagnie Luxembourgeoise de Radiodiffusion (CLR), renamed Compagnie Luxembourgeoise de Télédiffusion (CLT) after the war. Luxembourg was discovered as a convenient operating base for commercial broadcasting when, in France and elsewhere, broadcasting became either nationalized or subject to all kinds of restrictions. In comparison, Luxembourg offered the advantage of a very liberal broadcasting law (the law of 1929) and no intention by the government to become involved in broadcasting except for the granting of authorizations to private entrepreneurs. In 1930 the government granted CLR a de facto monopoly. This monopoly is not written into the law, but is mentioned only in the franchise agreement between the government and CLR. CLR (and later CLT) was to use this privileged position to start multilingual programme activities aimed at neighbouring countries and beyond.

The drawback of this very special approach was (and is to some extent until today, despite the liberalization that took place in 1991) that broadcasting aimed specifically at Luxembourg audiences, which also falls under CLT's monopoly according to the company's reading of the franchise agreement, was never a top priority and remained underdeveloped both as far as radio and television are concerned for the obvious reason that it did not make commercial sense to devote specific programming to a native audience of only some 270 000 people (CLT introduced only at the end of the 1950s a radio programme of a few hours per day in Luxembourgish, which even today has not yet become a 24-hour programme; as far as TV in Luxembourgish is concerned, the offer has been even more minimalistic; at the end of the 1970s CLT launched a TV programme called *RTL Hei Elei* on Sundays only and only for approximately 3 hours; in 1991 this programme became a daily, one-hour service).

CLT's monopoly came under fire in 1984 when the government initiated a project aimed at delivering TV programmes via satellite all over Europe (known today as the Astra system). Not only was CLT not involved in this project, but it opposed it openly, together with the French government, arguing that the Luxembourg government was breaking unilaterally the franchise agreement and its exclusivity clause by granting a franchise to use fixed satellite service frequencies to Coronet, the company that promoted this satellite system. CLT even started a court action against the government and Coronet in August 1984.

The government chose to go ahead with the project. But in early 1985 it gave in to pressures from the other EC countries, who complained that Coronet was too much under American influence, and it set up a new operating company, Société Européenne des Satellites (SES), comprising only European shareholders and a governmental stake of 20%. SES launched successfully its first satellite late 1988 and by 1996 it operated six satellites, with three more to be launched within the next two years. The company is clearly the market leader in its field and eager to become the main platform for digital television.

CLT suffered some serious setbacks in the 1980s as far as its expansion in France was concerned. In November 1985 and in January 1986 the French government chose to disregard CLT's application for the new commercial fifth and sixth French TV channels. This followed the non-implementation of an earlier governmental agreement (October 1984) between France and Luxembourg to give to CLT two out of the four transponders on the French DBS satellite TDF1 accompanied by a commercial exclusivity on that satellite. This declaration of intent appears in retrospect as an attempt to get rid of the Coronet threat or at least to delay it sufficiently so as to make sure that TDF1 would be in orbit first.

Following the 1986 change of government in France, CLT was able to make up some of the lost ground by getting a stake in the sixth TV channel M6. This was, however, only a small compensation for its frustrated plans to become the leading commercial TV operator in France. The company was more successful in Germany with the launch of RTL Plus together with Bertelsmann in early 1984. This German language channel used in the beginning Luxembourgish terrestrial frequencies, allowing only for a limited penetration into Germany. Following its distribution via satellite in 1989, it considerably extended its reach, enabling it to achieve break-even point in 1990. Today, the channel, renamed RTL Television, is the most popular German programme. CLT launched a second German programme, RTL2, in 1993. Due to German anti-concentration rules, it had to limit its stake to 24%. In French-speaking Belgium, the company was able to retain its strong position on cable networks by obtaining the exclusive commercial licence in 1987 for RTL-TVi. CLT managed to involve the Walloon newspaper publishers (Audiopresse) in RTL-TVi and to set up together with public broadcaster RTBF a common agency to collect advertisements. Despite these consolidation moves, RTL-TVi suffered badly from the entry on Belgian cable of the new French commercial channels. Following its German strategy to preempt competition, CLT set up a second Walloon channel, Club RTL, in 1994. In early 1990 CLT launched a new and very successful Dutch TV channel aimed at the Netherlands, RTL Véronique (now called RTL4), that was able to circumvent the restrictive Dutch media legislation by the fact that it was labelled a Luxembourgish channel, broadcast out of Luxembourg and distributed via Astra. In the Netherlands as well CLT pursued its preemptive strategy by setting up a second Dutch channel, RTL5, in 1993. Plans to further expand and to team up with the Endemol group as well as Veronica within the Holland Media Group have, however, been opposed by the anti-trust branch of the European Commission.

This CLT strategy to diversify its activities outside of Luxembourg has led to a dislocation of its programming activities away from Luxembourg. Only the group headquarters remain in Luxembourg. Apart from a considerable loss of fiscal revenue for the state, personnel employed in the broadcasting field tend to stagnate. This has been compensated only partially by the advent of SES. The growing internationalization of CLT and the dislocation it entailed led the government to realize that something had to be done to improve the broadcasting offered to the resident population. The considerable success of pirate radios since the early 1980s clearly indicated that there was a demand for local broadcasts not fulfilled by the minimal programmes CLT proposed. The government presented an ambitious liberalization scheme in 1990 that became the new electronic media law of 1991.

The press

Press legislation is rudimentary. The constitution mentions freedom of the press with hardly any limitations. An antiquated law of 1869 deals with infractions committed by the press and regulates the right of reply in a not very satisfactory way. A 1976 law introduced direct subsidies to the press in order to safeguard diversity. There are no ownership rules nor limitations. No particular content rules are applicable except for offending comments, dealt with by the 1869 law.

The press is entirely in the hands of private interests which are closely linked to political parties or trade unions as far as ownership and editorial policy are concerned. The largest newspaper, *Luxemburger Wort* (approximate circulation 80 000), belongs to the Catholic Archbishop of Luxembourg and it has close links with the dominant Christian-social political party (CSV). The *Luxemburger Wort* is published by the Imprimerie Saint-Paul, the country's largest printing outfit, which also controls the largest weekly, *Télécran* (approximate circulation 37 000), the commercial radio station DNR and a number of other periodical publications plus extensive book publishing activities. The second-largest newspaper, *Tageblatt* (approximate circulation 26 000), belongs to the socialist trade unions OGB-L and FNCTTFEL; it has close links with the Socialist Party (LSAP). The *Républicain Lorrain* (approximate circulation 10 000) is a local edition of the Metz-based French regional newspaper with the same name. The *Lëtzebuerger Journal* (approximate circulation 6000) is owned by the Liberal Party (DP). The *Zeitung vum Lëtzebuerger Vollek* (approximate circulation 3000) is owned by the communist KPL. The weekly *Revue* (approximate circulation 25 000) is indirectly controlled by CLT. The influential weekly *d'Lëtzebuerger Land* (approximate circulation 7000) is the only truly independent publication, together with the satirical weekly *Den Neie Feierkrop* (circulation 6000). The weekly *Grënge Spoun* (approximate circulation 3000) has close affiliations with the Green Party (GAP).

The advertising market in Luxembourg has been estimated at around 50 million ECU in 1995 (source: IPL). The market share of the press is still at about 70% despite the introduction of commercial radio stations. The reason for this high share has to do with the slow start made by the new commercial radio stations and limitations on CLT's advertising revenues out of its Luxembourg broadcasting activities. Another reason can be seen, of course, in the limited TV and radio outlets CLT offers to the resident population as well as local advertisers. The new Media Law of 1991 has however led to a doubling of direct state aid to the press in order to compensate for possible loss of advertising revenues following the liberalization of the radio landscape. The law also contains a provision that calls for periodic review of the level of press subsidies (in 1995 subsidies amounted to nearly 2 million ECU).

Electronic media

The new Media Law ('loi du 27 juillet 1991 sur les médias électroniques') formally abolished the monopoly CLR/CLT had enjoyed on a contractual basis since 1930. It also introduced into national law the stipulations of the 1989 EC Directive on 'television without frontiers'. Furthermore, it introduced regulations about new services such as teletext, videotex, cable networks, transmission via satellite and the access to terrestrial frequencies. Its main provisions, however, concern the liberalization of radio. This became technically feasible in 1984 when Luxembourg obtained supplementary FM frequencies following the Geneva ITU conference. It also became politically necessary considering the need to regulate somehow the pirate radio stations that emerged in the early 1980s. In 1990 there were close to 30 pirate radios on the air, some of them very popular (RFM for instance).

The two supplementary FM frequencies that were coordinated internationally according to the needs of CLT were attributed to CLT in order to enable it to achieve at long last a comprehensive coverage of the country for its programme in Luxembourgish, RTL Radio Lëtzebuerg, which remains the most popular station with an estimated audience share close to 50%. CLT had to share one of these frequencies, however, with the newly created public radio RSC (Établissement Public de Radio Socio-Culturelle). RSC uses this frequency, 100.7 FM, between 14 and 22 hours each day. This station, which benefits from public funding (around 2 million ECU per year in 1996) and which pursues an ambitious, rather elitist programme policy, was launched in 1993. So far, its audience share has not exceeded 1%, a fact which in the eyes of its critics proves the point that it is superfluous in a liberalized environment.

The interconnection of local frequencies made possible the establishment of four so-called regional radios with a coverage that comes close to encompassing the whole territory. These frequencies were allocated in 1992 to four consortia, involving press groups for two of them. In order to prevent undue concentration, stakes are limited to 25% of the capital. Eldoradio, the most successful of the new stations, with an estimated audience share of

12%, is indirectly controlled by CLT/RTL. Other shareholders are the *Tageblatt*, the *Lëtzebuerger Journal*, *Revue* and the *d'Lëtzebuerger Land*. Eldoradio is a typical music station, targeting the younger audiences. Information or current affairs programming is limited to the strict minimum. Den Neie Radio (DNR), with an estimated audience share of 4%, has amongst its shareholders the Imprimerie Saint-Paul, Luxembourg's leading press group, some Catholic associations, the Christian trade union LCGB and some business interests. This station aims, rather unsuccessfully, at competing with RTL Radio Lëtzebuerg. DNR offers extensive news and current affairs coverage. Radio Latina, with an estimated audience share of 7%, addresses itself primarily to the foreigners residing in Luxembourg (32% of the population). Its shareholders are immigrants' associations and IP Luxembourg, CLT's advertising agency. Radio Ara (estimated audience share 3%) is owned by organizations belonging to the so-called associative movement. It is the only radio station that tries alternative programming, taking into consideration the needs and desires of all kinds of marginal groups.

None of these four regional networks operates profitably three years or more after their launch. The need to bring in fresh capital has become obvious in all four cases. A report published in May 1996 by the governmental Service des Médias et de l'Audiovisuel on three years of radio liberalization mentions the need to 'stabilize' the existing operators. In order to make investments more attractive, it proposes to drop the 25% ownership clause. Fears that the press would suffer in its advertising revenues from the new commercial radios have not materialized so far. Protectionist measures such as a limit on advertisement in the case of RTL Radio Lëtzebuerg and RTL Hei Elei are questioned the more so that the press benefits from a doubling of direct subsidies. Until 1995 RTL Hei Elei was authorized to cover only one-third of its operating costs (around 7 million ECU per year) via advertisements. The remaining two-thirds were compensated by governmental subsidies. Following the new franchise agreement signed between the government and CLT, CLT has to support the costs of its local TV programme. The advertisement ceiling has been only slightly modified to its advantage. In return, however, CLT has been freed from payment of the licence fee.

The law identified a third category, the so-called local radios. In theory, some 40 locations are possible, but in 1996 only 12 were in operation, most of them broadcasting only for a few hours a day or a week. These local radios have to respect strict technical limitations (power of 100 Watt, radius of 5 kilometres) and they are subject to restrictions as far as advertisement financing is concerned.

The law enables the government to grant TV franchises besides those held by CLT. This provision has, however, not been applied for the obvious reason that advertising revenues are too limited to support another local TV programme. One franchise has been granted to a high school on an experimental basis (Uelzechtkanal). It broadcasts on cable networks in the southern part of the country for a few hours a month. Special mention is made of franchise agreements for international radio and TV programmes, pursuing Luxembourg's tradition of offering a 'flag of convenience' to international broadcasters. For the time being CLT continues to benefit exclusively from this system. The company finds it convenient to make use of the Luxembourg nationality for some of its programmes aimed at foreign audiences. It is thus able to circumvent the stricter regulations that apply to radio and television in most of its target countries. In television, the following programmes make use of this facility, which amounts in most of the cases to them having a double nationality: RTL Television (Germany), RTL4 and 5 (The Netherlands), RTL9 (France), RTL-TVi and Club RTL (Belgium).

The law establishes also supervisory or regulatory bodies such as the Independent Broadcasting Commission (Commission Indépendante de la Radiodiffusion), in charge of granting authorizations and controlling the application of the legal prescriptions, an advisory Programme Commission (Conseil National des Programmes) and a consultative Media Commission.

The new franchise agreement signed in April 1995 between the government and CLT establishes a contractual relationship for the next 15 years. All the existing radio and TV licences are prolonged for that period. CLT continues to enjoy a certain commercial exclusivity for its international operations. The government pledges to grant licences to third parties only if they do not compete with CLT activities. CLT managed to be freed of most of its public service obligations, including the requirement to maintain a symphony orchestra (at the beginning of 1996 the government took over the existing RTL symphony orchestra), as well as of the requirement to pay franchise fees (because of the dislocation of most of CLT's programme activities, franchise fees had become symbolic in the last years, about 1 million ECU per year). In return for these favours, CLT has pledged to keep some activities in Luxembourg, among them a technical centre for digital television, and to offer TV and radio programmes for local audiences (the cost of this has been estimated at 120 million ECU for the duration of the franchise agreement).

The new contractual arrangements oblige the company to maintain a homogenous company structure with its headquarters in Luxembourg. CLT has unsuccessfully tried to obtain more flexible structures combined with a larger autonomy for its operating companies. CLT's board has been reduced and the statutory majority of Luxembourg citizens abolished. Among the 20 board members Luxembourgers are left with only three seats. The chairman of the board will have to be a Luxembourger. The Director-General has to reside in the country. The government's controlling influence on the company's ownership has also been reduced. Under the previous arrangements 75% of the shares had to be nominal ones. Their sale had to be authorized by the government. The new arrangement has reduced the number of nominal shares to two-thirds. Their change of ownership is still subject to a governmental authorization.

The company's ownership has undergone considerable changes since 1994. Since 1974 the company has been controlled by two dominant shareholders, the Belgian Groupe Bruxelles Lambert (GBL) and the French Havas group. They use a holding company, Audiofina, to control CLT. Audiofina itself is controlled by Compagnie Luxembourgeoise Multimédia, owned by GBL (60%) and Havas (40%). By the end of 1995 Audiofina owned about 97% of CLT's capital. In the beginning of 1996, this Belgian-French alliance came under severe strain when Havas, which is also a major shareholder of Canal Plus, opposed CLT's autonomous digital TV plans. Havas favoured a rapprochement between CLT and Canal Plus. CLT chose to pursue an independent strategy and tried to join forces with BSkyB. This plan was defeated, however, in March 1996 when BSkyB decided to team up with Bertelsmann, Canal Plus and Havas. In April 1996, Bertelsmann and CLT announced their intention to merge their TV activities, including their digital TV plans. Bertelsmann will get a 50% stake of CLT's capital. When completed, this reshuffling of CLT's capital will reduce considerably French influence within the company.

This move to bring in a major German partner at the expense of French interests has been overdue for quite some time. Over the past ten years, CLT has changed considerably the nature and the geographical spread of its business. Up to the mid-1980s, CLT was mainly engaged in radio and it drew a majority of its revenues from its French radio operations. Today, television accounts for more than 80% of turnover and Germany, thanks to RTL Television (jointly owned by CLT and Bertelsmann) has become the most important market, with close to 70% of turnover, followed by Benelux (22%) and France in third position with declining importance.

Statistics

(1 ECU = 40 francs)

Population (1995)

Number of inhabitants	406 600
Geographical size	2586 km²

Broadcasting (1995)

Number of national radio channels	1
(4 regional networks with a quasi-national coverage)	
Number of TV channels	(44% audience) 1
Percentage of TV households connected to cable	87.3%
Foreign TV programmes on cable	39
(depending on capacity of networks)	
Market shares of the main channels	
RTL Television	17%
ARD	8%
ZDF	7%

The press (1995)

Number of daily newspapers	5
Total circulation of daily newspapers	(estimate) 125 000
Total advertising expenditure (all media)	(estimate) 50 m ECU

Market shares of the main categories of media	
Press	74%
Radio	17%
TV	7%

References

Anon (1995) 'Le secteur audiovisuel au Luxembourg', *Bulletin du STATEC*, no. 7/1995.

CLT (1996) *Annual Report 1995*. Luxembourg: CLT.

Goerens, Pierre and Zens, Jean-Paul (1996) 'Bilan de la loi de 1991 sur les médias électroniques'. Luxembourg: Service des Médias et de l'Audovisuel, Ministry of State.

Kugener, Jeannot (1995) 'Les antennes collectives au Grand-Duché de Luxembourg'. Luxembourg: Service des Médias et de l'Audiovisuel, Ministry of State.

Maréchal, Denis (1995) *Radio Luxembourg, un média au coeur de l'Europe*. Nancy: Presses Universitaires de Nancy.

Service des Médias et de l'Audiovisuel (1996) *Rapport d'activité 1995*. Luxembourg: Ministry of State.

SES (1996) *Annual Report 1995*. Luxembourg: SES.

11

The Netherlands

Kees Brants and Denis McQuail

National profile

The Netherlands are small and densely populated – 15.4 m people inhabit 41 000 km^2, or 443 per km^2. The highest point is just over 300 metres above and the lowest a few metres below sea level. All parts are easy to reach by broadcasting or cabling and, being approximately 240 km long and 190 km wide at its broadest points, the country as a whole is very accessible (or vulnerable) to cross-border broadcasting with (or without) satellites. To the south it borders with Belgium, whose northern half is Flemish (Dutch)-speaking, and to the east and southeast with Germany. Over-the-air broadcasts from both countries can be seen in a fair part of the country, but with a cable density of more than 85% there seem to be more borders crossed than just these two. There are two official languages, Dutch and Friesian, the latter only spoken in the province of Friesland, which has just over half a million inhabitants. More than three-quarter of a million people of non-Dutch nationality live in the Netherlands (some 5% of the population), the largest groups being Turkish (203 000) and Moroccan (165 000).

The Netherlands is one of the richer countries of Europe, linked to Germany both economically and communication-wise (shipping and road transport). With a gross national product of Dfl630 bn (1995; 274 bn ECU), a positive trade balance, a per capita income of Dfl44 400 (1994; 19 320 ECU), a private consumption of Dfl311 bn (1995; 135.2 bn ECU) and a low rate of inflation (3%), the Netherlands counts as one of the more successful OECD stories. On the other hand, unemployment is relatively high (464 000 in 1995, or 7.3%) and those on a more or less permanent sick benefit number almost double that. The extensive (and expensive) social security system is under scrutiny and revision.

The political system, with four large and six small(er) parties and never a clear majority for one party, has created a situation of permanent coalition governments. The 1980s were characterized by Centre–Right governments, with both a Christian Democratic media minister and prime minister. Since 1994 the PvdA (Labour) and two liberal parties (VVD and D66) have been in power, the first providing the prime minister, the last the media minister. The Netherlands is a constitutional monarchy.

Development of the press and broadcasting since 1945

The recent history of press and broadcasting is closely intertwined with the socio-political developments of the past 90 years, summarized in that one word for the kind of social system almost unique to the Netherlands: 'pillarization'. Dutch society between the beginning of the twentieth century and the mid-1960s (and notably the first 20 years after the Second World War) was a principal example of 'segmented pluralism', with social movements, educational and communication systems, voluntary associations and political parties organized vertically (and often cross-cutting through social strata) along the lines of religious and ideological cleavages. Unlike the two religious groups – Calvinists and Catholics – the Socialists incorporated only one class on the basis of a clearly class-bound ideology. From a social-economic point of view, the liberal 'pillar' was the mirror-image of the socialist one.

The press in those years had strong links with political parties, both formally – the editor of the newspaper often being the party leader as well – and informally – political journalists getting their news from party officials of the same 'pillar'. About two-thirds of the press had interlocking directorships with one of the four pillars, creating a fairly closed political communication system in which the press functioned as the platform for the pillarized elite. Next to these was a politically more neutral press with, however, a rather conservative undertone.

The origin of Dutch broadcasting lies in the 1920s, when there was a coming together of radio amateurs and the telecommunication industry (Philips). But it was not long before representatives of the pillars quickly moved in. In 1930 the government made special rules for radio in which only broadcasting corporations with strong ties to these 'streams in society' were allowed on the air: the VARA for the socialists; the KRO for the Catholics; the NCRV and the VPRO for the Protestants. The AVRO, originally born out of commercial interests, aspired to be a national broadcasting corporation, but in reality had strong links with the bourgeois-liberal sphere.

This polarized structure changed dramatically towards the end of the 1960s, with the loosening of religious and ideological ties; both party press and broadcasting systems were 'depillarized'. While political parties had to change their campaign politics, press and broadcasting engaged in a struggle for as big a public as possible, while radio and TV pirates disturbed the tenuous balance of the system by broadcasting from the North Sea.

The press

The newspaper situation at the beginning of the 1970s was dominated by tendencies to press concentration, affecting both partisan and more neutral papers. The socialist *Het Vrije Volk* – shortly after the war, the largest daily – was reduced to a Rotterdam local paper and in 1991 merged with another Rotterdam paper (to lose its name). *Het Parool*, emerging as a socialist underground paper during the war, dropped its radical tone at the end of the 1960s and is now struggling to hold its major position in Amsterdam. The communist *De Waarheid*, originally another resistance paper and for a long time supported financially by the party, first became a weekly, but ceased to exist in 1991.

Of the two Catholic dailies, *De Volkskrant* changed its tune, to successfully become the paper of the better educated liberals, while the more conservative *De Tijd* changed first into a weekly (1974), to merge 15 years later with another weekly, *HP. Trouw*, Dutch Reformed and also set up as a resistance paper, is holding its ground, but its publisher merged with that of *De Volkskrant* and *Het Parool* to form a new Perscombinatie NV. Partly as a reaction to the gradually more liberal line of *Trouw*, orthodox Christians started in 1975 the conservative *Reformatorisch Dagblad.*

Of the neutral newspapers *De Telegraaf* is the largest, in spite of its being closed for four years after the war because of its collaboration with the German occupiers. The *Algemeen Dagblad* filled the gap originally left by *De Telegraaf.* Both papers grew in circulation in the 1970s. The liberal-conservative *Nieuwe Rotterdamse Courant* and *Algemeen Handelsblad* merged in 1970, to become the largest and fastest growing evening paper, *NRC Handelsblad.*

Broadcasting

In broadcasting, advertising had already been an issue before the war, but particularly in the late 1950s and early 1960s financial and press interests had lobbied for advertising-financed media. One Cabinet had proposed a dual system based on the English model but this was successfully resisted by supporters of the broadcasting status quo. A Cabinet fell in 1965 because of the broadcasting issue, and two years later a Catholic–socialist Cabinet produced a Broadcasting Act which bore all the marks of a compromise. In 1969 the Act came into effect, opening up the system and introducing cooperation and mixed financing. Blocks of advertisements (outside the actual programme) were allowed, commercial broadcasting companies were not. A special non-profit foundation (STER) was set up to handle advertising, the proceeds of which went proportionally to the broadcasting organizations and partly to compensate newspapers for their losses in advertising revenue due to the coming of STER.

The Act did not do away with the 'pillar' system, as the five original organizations remained on the air, but the system was opened up to new licensees as long as they aimed 'at satisfying cultural, religious or spiritual needs felt among the population' and added to (not duplicated) the existing pluriformity within the system. The allocation of broadcasting time was based on the number of members and/or subscribers to the broadcasting magazines produced by the different organizations. A Dutch Broadcasting Foundation (NOS) was founded alongside the existing organizations which was to have a much more independent position than the previous cooperative bodies. The NOS was to provide coordination and technical services, but also so-called 'meeting point programmes' and programmes which are explicitly suited to a collective approach (national occasions, sports, news). The Board of the NOS was to have government-appointed members, including the chairman, and representatives from the broadcasting organizations.

This neat setup, designed to open up and, at the same time, to protect the existing order, turned out to favour a concealed form of commercialization and also those opting more for entertainment than for culture, information and education, four elements which, according to the Act, were supposed to characterize broadcasting in a 'reasonable ratio'. The ideologically neutral TROS (originating from a TV pirate station and aiming at a more general public) and, later, the ex-radio pirate Veronica (VOO) entered the door opened by the Act and grew explosively in audience and number of members. On the other hand, a new evangelical broadcasting organization (EO) showed that not everyone had 'de-pillarized'.

Commercial pressure

In the 1980s foreign stations, sometimes with advertising explicitly aimed at a Dutch audience, were relayed via cable which had, in fact, put an end to the scarcity of channels. A Centre–Right government, and particularly the conservative coalition partner VVD, seemed to be more in favour of commercial developments, but at the same time tried to protect the old system. Some argued that the end of scarcity made publicly regulated broadcasting obsolete. Moreover, commercial interests and particularly the publishers, felt unjustly excluded and the success of TROS and VOO seemed to prove a public demand pressing for more entertainment than the system could provide.

A government White Paper in 1983 exposed the split between the Christian Democrats favouring the existing public system and the conservative VVD, which was all for commercial free enterprise in broadcasting. The new 1986 government, with the same Centre–Right coalition partners, agreed in principle that there should be room for commercial television, but surrounded its potential introduction with so many ifs that a plan made by three of the public broadcasting organizations together with four publishers was quickly aborted. As a means of protecting the national market and the existing system, the same government banned satellite advertising in Dutch and subtitling of foreign programmes transmitted via cable, but the European Court ruled this ban discriminatory and in violation of the Treaty of Rome.

In 1988, while starting a third public TV channel to strengthen the position of the existing organizations *vis-à-vis* the growing number of foreign (commercial, satellite) channels, the government introduced a new Media Act (unsuccessfully) trying to satisfy both public and private needs. The public broadcasting organizations now had to adhere to a 'full programme', of which minimum percentages were set by law: 25% information, 20% culture, 25% entertainment and 5% education. Commercial television was not mentioned but a deregulatory trend was set in motion. Besides privatizing part of NOS, the Act introduced a new Commissariat for the Media, which is responsible to the Minister for Culture. It controls the finances of broadcasting, the issuing of licences and the division of air time. It can impose sanctions on public organizations that do not uphold the law, e.g. through product placing or blatant sponsoring. The rules for the latter are, however, relaxed.

At the end of 1989 the tenuous balance was shaken again. From Luxembourg a commercial, Dutch-language, satellite station (RTL4, partly owned by CLT SA and partly by the Dutch publisher VNU, originally in combination with Elsevier) started broadcasting. Within one year it had attracted a quarter of the average audience and prompted the then social-democratic Minister of Culture to react. A proper dual system was inevitable this time but with the Luxembourg company in full command, the question was whether the duality would include a commercial Dutch channel too.

A first change of the Media Act allowed for more advertising on the public channels: the ban on advertising on Sunday was lifted, more advertising blocks were introduced and advertisers, who previously might find their spots on the channel of the evangelical broadcasting organization, now could place their advertisements next to more popular programmes. In a second change the system was opened up for national commercial broadcasting via cable, provided the station had at least a 60% reach and would possess no more than 25% of the newspaper market. It took until 1995 – and two years after RTL5 was launched to reach the young and better educated male audience RTL4 did not attract – before five stations took the step. The most prominent one was VOO, which left the public system and returned as Veronica to the commercial nest.

In line with a McKinsey research rapport, the Media Act was changed again in 1994 to strengthen the public broadcasters who seemed to lose in the competition with the commercial stations. Cooperation of the public broadcasters sharing channels was to be the formula and a concession for five years would allow for more long-term planning than day-to-day reacting to the competition and worrying about losing members and subscribers. The NOS would be split up again: the old part would provide the usual news, sports and 'meeting point programmes' on all three channels, a new NPS would cater for culture, information and minority programmes on the third channel. The strict percentages of the 'full programme' obligation were somewhat watered down, and as long as the channel provided a balanced range, the individual broadcasters could deviate in the specifics.

The press

The post-war years have seen an overall decline in the number of independent national and regional newspapers; of the present titles about half can be considered independent. Between 1946 and 1997 the number of independent publishers declined from 81 to 10 and the number of dailies with their own editor in chief from 60 to 38. The partisan tradition, with interlocking directorships between parties, unions and media, has come to an end too, albeit papers still have an editorial political stand.

The total circulation of daily newspapers is 4.7 million, covering a declining number of households: from 87% in 1983 to 74% in 1996. There are eight national dailies combining 44% of the total circulation of Dutch newspapers (see Statistics section) and 48 (65 in 1990) regional papers, 12 of which have a circulation of over 100 000. The one-paper city is a common feature in the Netherlands, with 55% of the more than 700 communities being served by only one paper. Some of the national papers are very small, like the two orthodox Christian ones, while *Het Parool*, although claiming to be national, draws 90% of its readership from Amsterdam and relies partly on local news. The *Telegraaf* and *Algemeen Dagblad* cover the whole socio-economic range of the population, while *De Volkskrant* and particularly *NRC Handelsblad* are strong in status class A.

Although there are 56 titles and 38 editorially independent papers, the market is controlled by only a few publishers (see Statistics section). The four largest control 88%, with concentration continuing. At the end of 1995 Reed Elsevier sold the *Nederlandse Dagbladunie* – with the two national dailies *Algemeen Dagblad* and *NRC Handelsblad* and three regional papers – to the Perscombinatie, publisher of *Volkskrant, Trouw* and *Het Parool*. Perscombinatie now owns 31% of the newspaper market. With the growing possibilities for TV advertising, there is a marked decline of income for the press; however, family magazines have suffered most from commercial TV. The introduction of local TV advertising in 1991 is affecting the regional press, which has already seen a diminishing readership since 1980, to an even larger degree.

In comparison to German or British newspapers, all Dutch dailies should be characterized as 'quality press', since tabloids and their sensationalism do not exist in the Netherlands. The emphasis – also with the regional press – is on national and international news. Less than half of the news is local or regional. Especially the Friday and Saturday papers have several supplements; for *De Telegraaf* and *De Volkskrant* 100 pages is not abnormal. The growth in size has meant strong competition for the weekly opinion press, which has shown a steady decline. Because of the weeklies and the extensive supplements, but also because traditionally the majority of readers (some 90%) subscribe, Sunday papers are considered not to be viable. All newspapers (and most broadcasting organizations) subscribe to the one national news agency ANP (Algemeen Nederlands Persbureau), which was founded in 1935. It also represents (and translates) foreign press agencies like Reuters, UPI, AP, AFP, DPA etc. Associated Press has its own news agency in the Netherlands.

Diversity and media pluralism have for several decades been part of the logic of state policy. Government interference with the press is limited to supportive measures for economically weaker papers, especially since the introduction of TV advertising in 1967. Papers with a financial loss can receive compensation or apply for subsidy from an independent Press Fund, which derives its income from a levy on television advertising. Until 1980 newspapers did not pay VAT; at present they pay 6% on subscriptions. In spite of trade union pressure, there is only self-regulation and no press merger law in the Netherlands. In 1993 the combined publishers agreed that none of them would own more than one-third of the newspaper market. Ownership by publishers of commercial TV stations is limited to one-quarter.

Electronic media

Broadcasting

Since Veronica went commercial in 1995, seven main broadcasting organizations, the NOS, NPS and a considerable number of small organizations share the three national public TV channels. There are five radio channels with specific profiles: information, easy listening, pop music, classical music and services for particular groups. The allocation of TV airtime operates via a three-tier system based on membership levels. To become a member, a person either takes a subscription to a programme guide of the respective organization or pays an annual membership fee of Dfl10 (4.30 ECU). The success of these magazines depends on their (still) having the monopoly on detailed programme information. Airtime is apportioned on a 5:3:1 ratio, respectively for so-called class A broadcasters with over 450 000 members, class B broadcasters with between 300 000 and 450 000 members, and class C broadcasters with between 150 000 and 300 000 members.

At present all seven are class A broadcasters and under that condition will receive a five-year concession. AVRO, KRO and NCRV share Nederland 1, TROS, NOS and EO (and until 1995 VOO) share Nederland 2, and Vara, VPRO and NPS, Nederland 3. Each channel has between 11 and 15% of the viewing time. Next to these public, member-based broadcasters, non-member NOS (mainly news and sports) and NPS (mainly culture), there are some 20 small non-member (religious, humanist etc.) organizations and there is airtime for school, party political and government information.

To be able to compete with the commercial stations, the 'full programme' provision is somewhat relaxed. By law, all member corporations are obliged to present in their programming 30% information and education and 20% culture, 10% of which should be devoted to the arts. The Escort system of the European Broadcasting Union is used for the operationalization of this balanced programme obligation, to which all stations – after initial hesitance – adhere. Home-produced, Dutch-language programmes are the most successful. Until the end of the 1980s the language barrier was sufficient protection against loss of audience to foreign commercial stations, but with the introduction of national commercial television (and before that with RTL) that no longer is a discriminating feature. Mainly due to NOS programming, domestically produced output for TV in 1994 was 71.5%, 6% more than in 1990, for which a total programme budget is available of just over Dfl1.5 bn (609 m ECU) annually for all corporations; an amount that excludes costly (drama) productions by the individual organizations. Dutch language output of the commercial stations is much lower: RTL in 1994 broadcast 41% domestically produced programmes, while 49% originated from the US.

For national public broadcasting there are three revenue sources: licence fee (64%), advertising (36%) and membership dues and magazine subscription. Advertising comes in short blocks before and after news bulletins and with 'floating' blocks adding up to 10%, with a maximum of 20% per hour at prime time. This generated an annual revenue of around Dfl450 m (194 m ECU) before the coming of RTL4, in 1988. The first few years after the introduction of RTL, STER revenue dropped considerably. Because there has been for a long time an unmet demand for advertising access, the coming of the different commercial stations did not affect the public broadcasters that much. Between 1989 and 1996 advertising time rose from 66 to 118 minutes per day and turnover went up as well. In 1995, however, the STER revenue dropped to Dfl445 m (185 m ECU), Dfl170 m less than the year before. With the fragmentation and consequent decline of viewers, competition for advertising and growing irritation with viewers over the number of spots on TV, a further financial drain is expected.

Commercial broadcasting was legalized in 1990, but it took several years before any new venture dared to compete, certainly after RTL4 started a new station in 1993 (RTL5). In October 1994 Euro 7 started with day-time TV, soon to be followed by TV 10 Gold and The Music Factory, all special interest stations, with light information, old soaps and series, and pop music respectively, and a penetration of no more than half a million each. The Dutch daughter of the Scandinavian Broadcasting System (of which Capital Cities is a major shareholder) started a light informative and entertainment channel (SBS6) in August 1995, but the 'going commercial' of Veronica in September 1995 was seen as the final step to a dual system. Veronica cooperates with RTL4 and 5 in the Holland Media Group, together aiming at a market share of 40%. As this is seen as a concentration of both the production and the advertising market, EC DG Directive IV opposed this construction. TV producer Endemol, the largest in Europe, has left the Holland Media Group (HMG) and RTL5 is now a news and weather channel (and not doing well).

Local and regional television has been stimulated by a government ruling in 1991 permitting advertising finance, although this income can only be used for programme costs and not for profit. Limitations on advertising are the same for regional and local as for national broadcasting. On a regional level, there are five public channels, two commercial channels and three public/private ventures. There are 13 radio stations, since the Media Act of 1988, set up as independent foundations. Some of these stations broadcast up to 12 hours per day.

Local cable television started experimenting in 1970 with six stations and has since grown to 120 and another 400 radio stations. This means that local radio has a potential reach of over 80% of the population and television about 50%. Broadcasting time ranges from a few hours per week on some of the TV stations to 24 hours a day on some radio stations. Until 1991 they were paid through local means, contributions, donations and extra cable subscription. Sometimes (as, for example, with Super Channel in Utrecht), a satellite station is asked to pay for entry on the cable and part of that money is spent on local programming. The introduction of advertising finance has largely put an end to commercial pirate stations, which, in their thousands, filled the air in the 1980s. By May 1995, 226 local stations had been licensed to carry advertisements. In 1993, the average income derived from this source was about Dfl40 000 (17 200 ECU). Of local stations licensed for advertising, about 47% of revenue comes from advertising, 18% from municipal funding and the rest from sponsoring and subsidiary activities. The government plans to put up for auction all radio frequencies not allocated to public channels.

New electronic media

Since the early 1970s cable has been a hot issue in media policy. National discussions mainly concentrated on distribution of TV programmes via cable, since the laying of cable networks was initially encouraged in order to improve reception quality, especially of foreign television channels; and to rid the environment of the numerous antennas. The development was facilitated by a change in the Telegraph and Telephone Law of 1904. This provision, established in 1969, allowed bodies other than the PTT to install and operate cable systems. This meant a considerable growth in larger cable systems, usually covering a whole town or city. At the present time, around 88% of all Dutch households are connected to a small (MATV) or larger cable network (CATV). The most densely cabled areas are the cities of Amsterdam, Rotterdam and The Hague; the areas least likely to be further cabled are the eastern corner of the Netherlands and the thinly populated northern areas. A penetration of 90% is expected to be the maximum.

Most cable viewers have a choice of 24–30 channels, including three Dutch, three German, two Belgian and two British public channels, usually one local, and up to 19 satellite stations. Some of the latter have a very low reach; CNN is, since the Gulf War, included in most cable networks. There is a 'must carry' rule for Dutch public TV channels. The bulk of the viewing time is shared by the three Nederlands and RTL4 and 5. Veronica is aiming for a share of some 13%, but so far is not reaching that target. The extension of channels (the numbers of hours of public television rose between 1988 and 1994 from 140 to 235 hours) has also resulted in more time spent on viewing television: from just over 2 hours per day in 1988 to 157 minutes in 1996, still somewhat low by international standards.

The local press and TV stations are allowed to provide cable text, of which there are now 62. Information is presented in a fixed, teletype way and advertising, in text form with still images, is allowed. Advertising revenue in 1995 for cable text was almost Dfl61 m. Cable text providers pay the cable companies an entry fee of around one guilder for every household.

Operating cable is always a local matter and the operating area can be no greater than that of a local authority area, of which there are just over 700 in the country. Would-be operators must acquire an authorization from the Ministry for a specific area. Most of these authorizations are assigned to local governments; the rest are in the hands of building firms, cooperative associations, pension funds etc. The initial investment costs are met by the operators and costs are covered by charging an entry fee and subscription. The charges vary a good deal, but the national average for the combined monthly fee is about Dfl15 (7.25 ECU), but will rise in the coming years, due to copyright costs and extension of cable net and new technologies.

The diversity and localization of cable management is reflected in the technical diversity of its systems. There are at least 14 different kinds of networks in operation, the majority being of the 'mini star net' kind. Many of the original systems were 'tree' networks, with later developments of 'branch-off' nets. Most of these networks now have combinations of two or three of these systems. Advanced optical fibre networks are being laid in Amsterdam and Rotterdam, mainly however for professional subscribers (large industries). In 1988 the Dutch government decided that in 15–20 years' time PTT and cable TV networks should merge at the local level.

New electronic services are beginning to take off. A subscription TV channel, Filmnet, which provides mostly movies, has existed for several years now, other subscription or pay-per-view channels are beginning to take form, including a Chinese channel and several music channels. A sports channel failed in early 1997. Since 1992 NOS, PTT and Philips are experimenting with a subscription channel, TV-Plus, which provides D2 MAC broadcasts that will be upgraded to HDTV before the end of the century. Until 1996 TeleSelect, a joint venture of Philips, KPN and the American Graff-pay-per-view, had 'TV à la carte' in Amsterdam, Utrecht and The Hague, providing two subscription and five pay-per-view channels. As the first in Europe, a group of enthusiasts in Amsterdam opened up a site on the Internet, The Digital City, comparable to the free nets in the US. Digital City is interactive and provides access to a whole range of services, from libraries, the local administrative and public information systems to discussion groups and, of course, Internet. Digital Cities have sprung up elsewhere in Holland too.

Video and telematics

Video recorders are today found in a majority of Dutch households. Although the main reason for acquisition is for 'time-shift' viewing, renting films is also very popular and not expensive. However, the total turnover of rented tapes has decreased with the extension of satellite stations (notably RTL); research indicates that it is only a relatively small number of consumers that accounts for the majority of rented tapes. The sale of prerecorded cassettes – a hitherto unexploited market in the Netherlands – is growing rapidly: in 1993 6.8 million copies were sold and in 1994, 7.4 million. The success of *The Lion King* and other Disney films is expected to bring the total sale well into the double (million) figures.

The penetration of teletext and videotex is slow but steady. Especially Teletekst, a non-commercial service provided by the NOS and transmitted together with broadcasting signals, is growing. Since 1980, when it was introduced, almost three-quarters of Dutch households have a TV set with a receiver, with around 50% of the Dutch consulting the service on average for 240 minutes per month. Teletekst provides information on news, weather and sports and a subtitling service for the deaf and hard of hearing. Access to Teletekst is free and there is no advertising. RTL and local stations have their own teletext services, which are, however, not as succesful as the NOS one.

Videotex has less general public interest; the majority seems to be for commercial and professional use. The government provides only a limited subsidy for technological developments; development of the consumer service is considered to be a task for private initiative. Videotext NL, a private company partly owned by the PTT, started in 1989 and has now an estimated 250 000 users, mainly industrial groups. It recently 'migrated' to the Internet and is now more widely available. Apart from this national system there are several, more local services, based on hybrid systems, using a combination of telephone and cable networks. They are limited in their possibilities, but relatively cheap and on offer in most big cities.

Policies for press, broadcasting and telecommunications

In the area of communication there seems to be a growing convergence on three levels. On the technological level there is a convergence of modes: cable and digitalization have blurred the traditional distinction between the different sectors press, broadcasting and telecommunications. On the economic level, the ownership structure in the different sectors is converging as well: publishers are entering broadcasting, cable infrastructure providers are beginning broadcasting and telecommunication services and KPN (PTT) is experimenting with broadcasting. These developments have had their effect on a policy convergence. The traditional press, broadcasting and common carrier policy models are slowly but steadily integrating with the realization that borderlines are being torn down like the barriers of the European Union. On the whole, however, each still has its policy domain.

Commercialization has pitted the adherents of a market-led media system against political parties (however, several have become market adherents) and the majority of the public broadcasting organizations. The regulation issue follows the commercial demarcation lines and also covers matters of press concentration, cross-ownership and diversity. In broadcasting, however, most issues centre round the focal point: the prolongation and protection of the existing public broadcasting system. How far should the Government go in order to maintain or reassert the principles of public service and diversity which the system was intended to serve?

Part of the discussion about the issues and problems surrounding cable and satellite centred around the possible threat which these potentially commercial and lucrative media might pose to the existing broadcasting system. When, as proposed, the programme guides published by the public broadcasters lose their copyright on programme information and subscription to the guides ceases to count as membership, this will mean a blow to membership, on which allocation of broadcasting time is based. The five-year concession, meant to stabilize a system in flux, will mean the end of the openness of the system, both with members and possible new entrants. The financial blood-letting from the STER, originally only to RTL4 but now to a growing number of commercial competitors, might endanger part of the financial basis of the system, especially since raising the licence fee is a politically sensitive issue and a substantial rise is not likely.

Publishers are eager to profit from cable and commercialism, but are equally afraid of losing the STER-compensation if they join a national commercial station. Furthermore, no one really knows what this will mean to press and magazine advertisements. In 1995 the gross advertising expenditure for the media amounted to over Dfl7.5 bn (3.3 bn ECU), which was 7% more than in the previous year (see Statistics section).

Conclusion

Government policy has been characterized by constant hesitations and decisional hiccups. With the press there is a growing fear that a diminishing number of publishers will monopolize the market. The adage 'government keeping its distance' and hesitation to interfere in press matters, however, has prevented consecutive Cabinets from taking action; the present Centre–Left government adheres to self-regulation too. With broadcasting the government was, on the one hand, aware of financial possibilities and the chance that advertising money would otherwise cross the border, on the other there was a traditional hesitation about advertising in general and commercialization in particular and, also through traditional ties, it tried to stay put in preserving both the existing system and the principles it was supposed to embody. The coming of RTL4 shook the shaky pillars of

Hilversum, so to speak. The government reacted with several plans and actions:

- The introduction of a third public channel.
- Privatization of the NOS technical facilities (NOB).
- Cooperation per channel between the traditionally competing public broadcasters.
- Giving concessions of five years to the existing public broadcasters which would enable them to put themselves in order.
- Aiming for fewer organizations and preferably for one public broadcaster after the five-year period.
- Aiming for a restructuring of the broadcasting organizations, so that above the boards, who have a direct link with the members, a management team should run the organization.
- Relaxation of the 'full programme' provision which, in the near future, can also be achieved per channel and not per broadcasting organization, or even between channels.
- Giving up its resistance to advertising on Sundays, commercial broadcasting and to local advertising.
- Giving more flexibility to the STER to compete with the commercial broadcasters.
- The introduction of a special fund to stimulate Dutch cultural productions by the public broadcasters. It is paid for by STER means – 6% of its revenues per year.

The Netherlands stands in a similar position to other smaller West European states, whose media systems are vulnerable to cross-border flows and whose economies have less to gain from liberalization than those of some larger countries. In adapting to change, Dutch media policy can be described as the typical product of a 'Hans Brinker' attitude: putting a finger in the dike to prevent the flood from coming in. The future will tell whether the boy's finger did the trick once more. The present trend of development for the public sector is a strong movement towards cooperation, which most likely will result in the end of the pillarized system and in its place a single general public service.

Statistics

(1 ECU = 2.30 Dutch florins, Dfl)

Population (1997)

Number of inhabitants	15.4 million
Geographical size	41 000 km^2
Population density	443 per km^2
Number of households	6.5 million

Broadcasting (1997)

Number of national public TV channels	3
Number of TV hr daily for the national public (combined av.)	16
Number of national private channels	8
Average viewing time per day (min)	157
TV penetration	98% (colour 97%)
TV licence cost	Dfl186
Local TV channels	120
Number of hr on local TV	a few per wk to a few per day

Number of households with video cassette recorders (m) (1995)	4.1	36%
Number of households with teletext decoders (m) (1996)	4.6	75%
Number of videotex subscribers	250 000	
Number of cabled households (m)	5.7	88%

Source: NRC Handelsblad, February 1997

TV offer and viewership (Ned.1, 2 and 3, and RTL4 and 5)

Programme type	Broadcasting share (%)		Viewing time (%)	
	Public	Private	Public	Private
Information	38	26	33	23
Art	4	0	1	0
Drama (fiction)	23	45	21	41
Entertainment	12	10	17	18
Sports	8	5	17	3
Children's	7	3	4	2
Advertising	9	12	7	13

Source: NOS/KLO, 1996

Reach and audience of the most important TV stations (1996)

	Reach (%)	Audience share (%)
Nederland 1	98	13
Nederland 2	98	15
Nederland 3	98	11
RTL4	88	22
RTL5	88	6
Veronica	88	8
SBS6	88	6
Other	88	18

Source: NOS/STER/Intomart, 1997

Number of national public radio channels	5
Number of commercial (cable) radio channels	9
Number of hr on public radio	17 (Radio 5) to 24 (Radio 1)
Local and regional radio channels	467
Number of hr on local radio	a few to 24 per day

The press

Number of independent national dailies	8
Number of independent regional dailies (titles)	48

National daily press in the Netherlands (1996)

Title	Circulation	Orientation
De Telegraaf	760 000	Conservative
Algemeen Dagblad	401 000	Conservative
De Volkskrant	368 000	Progressive
NRC Handelsblad	272 000	Liberal/conservative
Trouw	121 000	Progressive/Christian
Het Parool	95 000	Progressive
Reformatorisch Dagblad	57 000	Christian/conservative
Nederlands Dagblad	30 000	Christian/conservative

Source: Cebuco

Market share (%) of publishers (mid 1996)	
Perscombinatie	30.9
Holding De Telegraaf	24.5
Elsevier/NDU	19.8
VNU	17.9
Wegener	14.9

Source: Cebuco

Gross advertising expenditure (1995, Dfl m)	
TV	1070
Radio	264
Newspapers and free sheets	2730
Periodicals	1402
Cinema	25
Outdoor	235
Cable text	61
Other	1759
TOTAL	7546

Source: Adfojaarboek, 1997

Bibliographical note

A lot of data can be drawn from (Dutch language) specialized magazines such as *Adformatie*, *Informatie & Informatiebeleid*, *Mediaforum*, *Media Markt* and special publications by NOS and others.

References

Bakker, Piet, Van den Oetelaar, Sabine, Rood, Nick, and Scholten, Otto (1997) *Communicatie-kaart van Nederland*. Amsterdam: Vakgroep Communicatiewetenschap.

12

Norway

Helge Østbye

National profile

In some respects, Norway is a monolithic country. With the exception of a small Lapp population, the inhabitants come from one ethnic group. The state school system is dominant, and the Lutheran State Church includes more than 90% of the population. On the other hand, fjords and mountains have divided the country into a variety of separate communities with different dialects and local culture. Total area is larger than, for example, Great Britain or Germany, but large parts of the country are uninhabitable, and the population is only 4.4 million.

During the union with Denmark from 1400 to 1814, Oslo became the cultural, political and commercial centre. Nationalist opposition against the union with Sweden (1814–1905) got much of its strength from the periphery. One lasting outcome of this peripheral protest is two official languages: *bokmål* (literary Norwegian), based on the dialect of the upper class in Oslo and strongly influenced by Danish, and *nynorsk* (new Norwegian), which is based on countryside dialects from the western parts of Norway (Haugen 1966, 1968). *Bokmål* is now used by 80–90% of the population as their written language.

The industrial revolution reached Norway later than most Western European countries, but the industrialization process went very fast. Now, less than 6% of employment is in the primary sector and 20% in the secondary sector (*Statistisk Årbok*, 1993: 136–7). Norway has a mixed economy, where private capitalism is combined with a few nationalized industries and a lot of public regulations in the economic sphere. Norway is among the richest countries in the world (GNP per capita), but a process of transformation is taking place in several sectors, and the unemployment rate is higher than before, though lower than in most European countries.

The largest political party, the Labour Party (Arbeiderpartiet), is a social democratic party of the Northern European type. Labour was in government almost continually from 1936 until 1965, most of the time with a majority in the parliament. Since 1965, Labour has been in and out several times. There are three parties to the left of Labour, but only one of them, the Left Socialists (Sosialistisk Venstreparti), is represented in the parliament.

There are four major non-socialist parties: the conservative Høyre is the largest. Important changes in Norwegian media structure took place after the formation of a Conservative minority government after the election in 1981. The basis for the government was broadened in 1983, when the Christian People's Party (Kristelig Folkeparti) and the Centre Party (Senterpartiet) joined. The Christian People's Party represents the interests of the fundamentalistic, Lutheran type of Christianity. The Centre Party is an agrarian party. The Progressive Party (Fremskrittspartiet) is a right-wing party which represents an anti-tax, anti-bureaucracy and anti-immigration protest, with substantial support in the population.

In 1986 the coalition government was replaced by a Labour minority government. A new bourgeois government was formed after the 1989 general election, but it lasted only one year, and in November 1990 Labour took over again.

The Norwegian people has twice (1972 and 1994) rejected proposals to join the European Union. On both occasions, the two major parties, the leadership of the trade unions and the employers' associations were in favour of joining. A coalition between the periphery and urban radicals resulted in a defeat for the power elite.

Development of the press and broadcasting since 1945

The press

The Second World War represents an important point of change in the development of the press system in Norway. Before the war, all the major political parties had their own, small newspapers in most cities and towns. During the war more than 60% of the newspapers were stopped by the authorities (Hjeltnes, 1990: 15). Some of these papers never restarted. Most of the Labour press never regained their pre-war strength, especially on the advertising market.

The post-war years are characterized by monopolization. The largest newspaper in each town has survived, and increased its share of local advertising and circulation. Smaller papers often have a downward trend, and some of them have been closed down. New newspapers have appeared, but only papers started in smaller places with no previous paper have had any success. The total number of newspapers has been reduced in the post-war period, but the number of towns with their own paper has been slowly increasing. The combined effect of these trends has been a dramatic reduction in local competition. On the other hand, national tabloid newspapers have shown a considerable increase in their circulation outside the capital (Høst, 1991, 1995).

The close links between the newspapers and political parties continued during the first post-war period. As a result of competition and monopolization, most non-socialist newspapers have declared their party-political independence, partly in order to attract readers from all parties. The Labour press, which is owned by trade unions and the Labour party, now has an informal affiliation with the party, and it is acting much more independently than in the 1950s and 1960s (Høyer, 1974; Høst, 1991; Østbye, 1991).

The electronic media

The 1933 Broadcasting Act established Norsk Rikskringkasting (NRK) as a national, public service broadcaster in the BBC tradition.

After the liberation in 1945, NRK immediately continued the well-established programming from the 1930s. Many of the voices from the London war-time transmissions continued in NRK, giving the broadcasting company a strong legitimacy and popularity. The first aim was to build new transmitters in order to reach all parts of the country. In the 1950s, 1960s and beginning of the 1970s there was a widespread acceptance of NRK's role, although some specific programmes created some minor moral uproars.

The first experiments with television took place on the initiative of NRK in 1954. There was a lot of discussion concerning if and when Norway should establish a television channel, but no one objected to the idea of NRK running the service. Norway was the third last European country to establish a national television service (only Iceland and Albania were later). The service was officially opened in 1960.

From 1933 on, NRK invested its limited resources to create a national network. Small regional offices produced programmes for the national network. In 1957, these offices were given permission to transmit regional broadcasts, but for ten years few resources were allocated to this task. Since 1970, NRK has increased the number of regional offices, and each office has got more time (in particular for regional broadcasting) and more staff (5% of the staff worked in regional offices in 1970, more than 25% in 1990).

Until the early 1980s the NRK had a monopoly position, in television as well as radio. In both media only one channel was available to the audience. In 1981–2 the new Conservative government introduced three new elements in the broadcasting system: local, independent radio, local, independent television and cable distribution of satellite channels. Formally, local radio and television were introduced on a preliminary basis, but everyone knew that the process could not be reversed.

The most successful part of the liberalization of broadcasting was the introduction of local radio (*nærrradio*) in eight communities. In 1984 the number of permissions exploded, and local radio was established as a permanent part of the Norwegian media system. From 1988 the stations were allowed to carry commercials, but they had to have a local basis.

In 1981, the Conservative government also permitted a few community antenna companies to produce local television for cable distribution (some cable networks were already in operation, most of them in order to extend the area where reception of Swedish television was possible). The number of licences for local television increased dramatically in 1984, and some stations were licensed for terrestrial transmission. Commercials were not permitted on the local channels, and local television has had severe economic problems. Most of the stations closed down. Audience ratings show that local programmes are popular, in particular when they cover smaller areas (Werner et al., 1984: 38).

Retransmission on cable of television programmes via satellite was also introduced in 1981–2. The use of direct broadcasting satellites had been on the political agenda since the early 1970s. The Nordic Council (which consists of parliamentarians from Denmark, Finland, Iceland, Norway and Sweden) regarded transmission of the national channels to all five countries as the most efficient way to improve cultural exchange between the countries. An investigation and discussion on the possibility of using direct broadcast satellites for this purpose started in 1972, but it was never possible to reach a decision (NU A, 1979: 4E). After the Danish decision to withdraw from these Nordsat discussions in 1981, the original plan was more or less dead. A Swedish company developed a DBS satellite called Tele-X, and for some time this vitalized discussions of a mini-Nordsat, but the satellite is now used for transmission of the private Swedish channel TV4 and NRK's radio and television programmes to oil rigs in the North Sea and Norwegian settlements in Svalbard. Telenor (the Norwegian PTT) transmits the two national Swedish television channels for redistribution on cable in Norway. Passing several stages of liberalization, cable distribution of satellite channels is now virtually unregulated, with the exception that the content must comply with Norwegian legislation (e.g. ban on advertisements for alcohol or tobacco). Sky Channel, which was the first channel to be transmitted, has disappeared from Norwegian cable networks, but a lot of other channels are now available. In addition to British, French and German programmes, there is also one Norwegian satellite channel, TVN, which has some own production, but most programmes are imported and subtitled in Norwegian. TVN is aimed directly at Norway. One Swedish channel, Scansat TV3, also tries to attract a Norwegian audience and advertisers. The closest any has come to a fulfilment of the culturally based Nordsat idea is the pan-Scandinavian, commercial satellite channel Scansat TV3. Most of its content is imported, and the only possible, positive cultural effect is a marginal improvement in the mutual understanding of Scandinavian languages. It is interesting to note that a commercial company may have achieved more for Nordic mutual understanding than the politically and culturally more ambitious Nordsat idea, which was opposed by intellectuals and artists.

Video represented the first challenge to the Norwegian broadcasting monopoly, but it had a slow start before a breakthrough in 1980 and 1981. In October 1988, more than 40% of the population had access to video (Haraldsen and Vaage, 1988). When video was introduced, it was less regulated than the more established branches of the media industry, and the first batch of pre-recorded video cassettes on the market was dominated by pornography and violence. From 1985, video is regulated by the Film and Video Act. Local authorization of cassette dealers and a central registration of all cassettes for hire in order to ease content control and to reduce the distribution of illegally copied cassettes were introduced. According to a survey in 1983, the average viewing time for video was 6 minutes per day (37 minutes for households with video, 2 minutes for those without) (Høst, 1983). The number of video cassette players is now several times higher than in 1983, but the average time spent on video viewing is almost at the same level. Also the pattern (with youth as the heavy consumers) has remained unchanged (Haraldsen and Vaage, 1988).

The press

Structure

There are approximately 180 newspapers in Norway. Most of them are small, and have a local orientation. The larger papers have a broad coverage of national and international news, but with the exception of two tabloids and a few party political organs, distribution is mainly regional or local.

Norwegians read a lot of newspapers. Each household buys 1.8 papers per day on the average (excluding Sundays – Sunday newspapers were prohibited in 1919, but reintroduced in 1990). Subscription is the most common form of buying newspapers.

Legal framework, ethical rules and policy framework

Broadcasting, film and video are regulated by specific legislation, but there is no press law in Norway. The Constitution grants a basic right to print. The Norwegian press legislation specifies that the principal editor has the legal responsibility, that there is a limited right to reply and a limited protection of sources. There are some restrictions on communication in general: prohibition of dissemination of state secrets, libel, racial discrimination etc., but no legislation gives the journalists any special protection. On the other hand, every citizen has the right to look into letters and documents in the civil service, and this is an important tool for the journalists.

The press is divided on several policy issues, such as press subsidies, restriction of foreign ownership and the development of newspaper chains. The introduction of new technology has, in most newspapers, united the owners, the editors and the journalists against the typographers.

Ownership and finance

Most of the press and other print media are organized in private stock companies. Some newspapers and publishing houses have a very limited number of stockholders. Ownership of the press has traditionally been local, and very few owners control more than one paper.

Labour newspapers were founded and owned by local trade unions and party branches, but very early they started a strong technical, economical and editorial cooperation. In 1992, 32 newspapers merged into one holding company. The labour press is stronger in Norway than in other Western countries. One out of six sold newspaper copies comes from this chain. The party political content of these papers has been reduced since the 1950s.

One newspaper group is larger than the labour press: the mainly family-owned Schibsted group. In 1860 *Aftenposten* was founded by Amandus Schibsted. During most of this century, *Aftenposten* has been the largest newspaper in Norway, with two separate editions each day (morning and afternoon). In 1966, the Schibsted group bought *VG*, a small evening paper, with serious economic difficulties and a circulation of less than 30 000. The new owners developed *VG* into a modern tabloid, and had great success in the market place. *VG* became the largest newspaper in Norway in 1981. The daily circulation in 1994 was almost 390 000, which means that more than one in three Norwegians read this newspaper on an average day. The Schibsted group also owns a minority of the shares in four of the largest regional newspapers (*Fædrelandsvennen*, *Bergens Tidende*, *Stavanger Aftenblad* and *Adresseavisen*). The group is also engaged in book publishing. Plans to expand by acquiring some local newspapers have been called off, and companies for video production, local radio and television, and a new newspaper in Oslo have all failed. But, if we include the regional newspapers, the group accounts for more than half of the total Norwegian newspaper circulation and *Aftenposten* and *VG* alone account for almost 40% of the newsprint.

A more recent development in the Norwegian newspaper structure is a chain of non-socialist newspapers, mostly with local monopolies. The Orkla group (based on consumer goods and finance) has bought 20 newspapers. The Orkla group also publishes several weekly magazines, and was for some time the owner of a satellite television channel (TVN).

Until recently, the newspaper industry was the territory for idealists with a message (political or ideological). During the post-war period, a lot of the papers have made a loss most years. Some newspapers, however, made a substantial profit, but most of the surplus was reinvested in the paper. Recent changes in ownership have led to an increased focus on profit in some parts of the industry; newspapers have become business.

Several newspapers had to close down in the 1960s, and the industry's organizations turned to the government for subsidies. The Labour and the Centre Parties' press would gain most from the press subsidies, and these parties backed the proposition, while the conservative Høyre opposed it. Newspapers were already exempted from VAT, and from 1969 some newspapers have received money directly from the state. Several kinds of subsidies were introduced, but the most important is production subsidy, where the papers receive a certain amount per sold copy. Rules were made in order to channel the subsidies to papers with the weakest structural position on the market (the smallest papers and papers with a minority position on the local market – second-ranking papers), but with preset rules so that there should be no fear of state interference with editorial policies.

In total, the subsidies account for less than 2% of the industry's total income (NOU, 1992: 48). But it means survival or death to a lot of newspapers, especially the second string ones. The system is important in the protection of local competition. Since 1981 the Conservatives have proposed a reduction in the subsidies, but have met opposition from their coalition partner, the Centre Party. In real terms, there was a small reduction in subsidies from 1983 to 1986, and an increase in 1987–8 during the Labour government. In 1989 and 1990 the press subsidies again became an issue in media politics because the Conservative government announced that it wanted to scrap the whole system of press subsidies along with reduction of subsidies to other industries. With Labour back in government from late 1990, this debate is less topical.

Advertising revenue is the major source of income for the Norwegian press. It accounts for 51% of the total income, compared to 39% from circulation (NOU, 1992: 48).

Electronic media

Structure

After eight years with regional, independent, private broadcasting, the Broadcasting Act of 1933 established a national broadcasting company in the form of NRK (Norsk Rikskringkasting), in the public service broadcasting tradition. The Norwegian Broadcasting Corporation was owned by the state, and was given exclusive rights to broadcast oral messages, music, pictures etc. The monopoly lasted for almost 50 years. Now, NRK transmits one television channel and three radio channels. Regional broadcasts are transmitted for several hours per day on one of the radio channels.

Transmission of satellite television channels via cable, and local, independent radio and television was allowed in December 1981. Local radio has become a success. More than 400 stations have been on the air. Local television, however, has found it difficult to survive, and only a handful of stations are transmitting on a regular basis. Some of these are owned by foreign companies.

In 1988 two satellite channels started, aiming at Norway: a group of Norwegians started TVNorge (TVN) and the Swedish company Kinnevik started a channel in the Norwegian language in its TV3 network, transmitted from London (thereby covered by British legislation, which is more liberal than the Norwegian) and with some Norwegian programmes. In 1995, Kinnevik extended its supply of 'Norwegian' channels, but these channels were closed down in less than one year.

The most important changes appeared in the early 1990s, when a mixed system or duopoly was established. In 1992 the first national, terrestrial, private and commercial television channel, TV2, was started. Parliament insisted that its headquarters should be located in Bergen. In 1995 the Schibsted group started a satellite channel, TV+, which, after problems finding an audience, was taken over by TV2 and finally shut down in 1996. In 1993 a national, commercial radio channel started its operations from Lillehammer.

Norwegians listen to radio for between two and three hours per day (different methods for data collections give different estimates) and watch television for two hours. The introduction of local television and satellite channels had little influence on the viewing of NRK's TV channel. But since the introduction of the second terrestrial channel, the total amount of television consumption has increased by 10 or 15 minutes per day, and in Spring 1995, NRK's share of the total viewing for the first time fell below the important 50% mark.

Local radio was an immediate success, especially among young people. The commercial channel P4 and NRK's third channel started in the autumn of 1993. NRK's third channel was aimed at young people, and NRK took over much of the youth audience from local radio. P4 is attracting listeners from young and middle-aged adults, and local radio has been squeezed considerably, and is in deep trouble.

Legal framework

The Constitution secures everyone a right to print, but according to a Supreme Court decision, the same right does not apply to broadcasting. The general criminal laws put the usual limits to the journalistic freedom: libel, blasphemy, some kinds of pornography and portrayal of violence etc. are prohibited.

Legislation grants NRK independence from the government in matters concerning programming, but the administrative ties between the broadcaster and the Ministry of Cultural Affairs were tight until 1988. Then, NRK was granted a more independent position. Only the Director-General was to be appointed by the government, and NRK was freed from the strict rules of appointment procedures and wages which apply to civil servants.

The Broadcasting Act made it possible for the Conservative government which came to power in 1981 to allow private, local radio and television stations on a temporary basis. In 1987 the Broadcasting Act was changed in order to make local radio permanent. Local radio was regulated by the Local Broadcasting Act (Lov om nærkringkasting) of 1987 (Ot. prp. no. 47 1986–87; Innst. O. no. 3 1987–88). This act made local radio permanent and accepted advertising in local radio, but introduced a tax on revenues from broadcasting advertising. The income from this tax was used to subsidize local radio stations in areas where the economic foundation is too weak to support a station, but this procedure was undermined or boycotted by most rich local radio stations. The introduction of advertising seems to favour stations with music and local news at the expense of stations with a more idealistic basis. The Act states that local radio should, as a general rule, not cover an area larger than one commune (Norway has 450 communes, the smallest have a population of less than 1000), and the municipal councils are authorized to issue licences for transmission. The Act also established the Local Broadcasting Council, which is appointed by the Ministry of Cultural Affairs and has an independent secretariat. This council can withdraw licences to transmit for both local radio and local television.

The Local Broadcasting Act treated local television in the same way as local radio, with one major exception: local television was not allowed to transmit commercials. This was changed by the Advertising in Broadcasting Act (Lov om reklame i kringkasting m.v.) of 1990 (Ot. prp. no. 55 1989–90).

In 1992 a new Broadcasting Act was passed (Ot. prp. no. 78 1991–92), replacing four previous laws, and giving a more tidy legislation in this area. The new act took into account Norway's membership in the European Economic Area and established a separate administrative body for the media: Statens medieforvaltning, which is responsible for the routine administration. The culture ministry is responsible for the policy-making.

NRK's organization

NRK is a hierarchical organization with 3000 employees. In economic, administrative and technical matters, the Director-General shares the overall responsibility with NRK's board of governors, but nobody (except in the case of a court decision) can overrule him in matters concerning programmes and programming policy. The Director-General is appointed for an eight-year period, and cannot be renominated for the position.

The Ministry of Cultural Affairs is the most important policy-making body outside NRK. Especially in periods with non-socialist government since 1981, the Ministry has been active in media policy issues. Before 1981, NRK had a lot of influence on the broadcasting policy. The Ministry also handles major changes in the structure of NRK's organization and new services. The appointment of the Director-General is regarded as an important question which involves the political leadership in the Ministry as well as the rest of the Cabinet.

The board of governors is also appointed by the Cabinet. The board has the final word in matters concerning economy, administration, personnel etc., and it can influence the selection of the Director-General. In periods when there is a conflict between the Ministry and the NRK, the board is more politically important.

The Broadcasting Council is appointed by the parliament (eight members) and the Ministry of Cultural Affairs (six members). The council has changed from an expert group to a reflection of party politics. The council discusses programmes and programming policy. Its decisions have the form of advice to NRK, and there are several examples where the broadcasting company has disregarded its advice (Østbye, 1977). The council also takes part in the nomination of the Director-General.

NRK operate three radio channels and two television channels. The second television channel started in 1996. The channels are run independently of each other, but they share some resources. Regional programmes are produced by 18 regional branches, each with a head office and substations located in other parts of the region. One branch produces programmes in Lapp for distribution in the northern region and for the national networks. The other 17 branches also divide their attention between regional radio programmes and productions for national radio and television. For some years there has been regional television, but neither personnel nor equipment allows for more than 15 minutes per day.

TV2 and P4

TV2 and P4 are private joint-stock companies. Their boards have a more direct influence over programming than is the case for NRK. TV2 has a small organization – approximately 320 employees, of which 100 are journalists or editors: 200 work in the main office in Bergen, 110 in Oslo. With the exception of news and a few other programmes, the programmes are made by independent production companies.

Ownership and financing

NRK is owned by the state, but was in 1987 given a more independent position *vis-à-vis* the Ministry of Cultural Affairs. The three main owners of TV2 are important actors in other media businesses: Schibsted (33%) and A-pressen (22%) mainly in newspapers, and the Danish company Egmont (33%) is the biggest actor in the Norwegian magazine business. The Swedish company Kinnevik (satellite television: TV3) is the most important owner of P4.

Advertising is banned in NRK's radio and television broadcasting. NRK is financed from two sources: a TV licence and a special tax on radio and television equipment, which is now being phased out (NRK, 1995). Before 1987 NRK's total budget was decided by parliamentary vote; since 1988 only the licence fee is set by the parliament, and it is up to NRK (the board and the Director-General) to decide how the money thus raised is spent.

TV2, the satellite television channels, P4, and local radio and television are financed mainly by advertising. Commercials were allowed on local radio from 1988 and on television from 1991.

Programming policies

Like other public service broadcasting institutions, NRK is trapped in a triangle of influences: the political authorities, the audience and the journalists all represent challenges to ideas like balance, relevance, quality and independence. To rely heavily on only one of these bases will easily transform the broadcasting company into a political commissariat, a purely commercial company, or a paternalistic institution. For NRK, autonomy is an important goal. The Broadcasting Act abandons any external censorship, but a lot of institutions try to influence NRK's programming policy. Parliament is one of these, having the authority to change the Broadcasting Act and, for example, introduce clauses imposing specific goals on NRK, introduce censorship, reduce NRK's budgets etc. Until now, the parliament has done little of this kind, but some parliamentary discussions may be understood as warnings. In order to avoid intervention, NRK is possibly practising self-censorship with more narrow limits in the programming than an external controller would be able to exert in an open, democratic society.

NRK broadcasts 3000 hours of television. One-third is news and information. In the early 1980s, between 55 and 60% was Norwegian productions, but this has been reduced to 50%. Almost all the Norwegian productions are produced by NRK itself. Most of the imports come from the USA and the UK. Imported programmes are subtitled. Dubbing is used only in children's programmes.

TV2 and P4 have their rights and obligations *vis-à-vis* the state laid down in the Broadcasting Act and in specific franchise agreements with the culture ministry. The broadcasters have to fulfil some public service obligations, and there are restrictions on advertisements (max. 15% of total airtime, max. 20% per hour, all commercials have to be placed between programmes, political commercials and commercials aimed at children are banned etc.).

Telematic media

The development of new telematic media increased the interest in mass media issues in Norway towards the end of the 1970s. The first issue to raise the interest in media politics was satellite television: plans for a Nordic exchange of television programmes by means of direct broadcasting satellites. The second issue was home video.

The Norwegian PTT (Televerket, now Telenor) has been operating a videotex system (Teledata) since 1978. Private use was mainly tested in a pilot project in one area, Bergen, where the largest newspaper played a leading part by delivering general news. The pilot project was closed down in 1981, and indicated that private households were not likely to become heavy users of videotex. The permanent system is mainly for commercial information. Internet services have taken over much of the same functions.

For some time, there have been plans for an integrated telecommunication network for telephone, data and video transmission. A Royal Commission has proposed that Telenor should have the responsibility for the development of the national network, but that private companies should compete with an independent branch of the PTT for the local networks (NOU, 1983c; NOU, 1984). Later trends indicate that there will be increased competition in telecommunications. In order to retain its strong position, Telenor is using its last years as a monopoly to expand into surrounding areas, like cable television and satellite operations. Almost all the present cable networks are only transmitting television pictures. But the telephone system is gradually being upgraded to ISDN standards.

Policies for the press and broadcasting

The traditional struggle between the national centre and the periphery in Norway could be extended to include conflicts along a local–national–international dimension. A second range of issues concerns the conflict between monopolies and demonopolization. This conflict was solved in 1990, when a broad coalition in the parliament agreed on the establishment of radio and television duopolies (allowing for one private television channel, one private and one new, third, public service radio channel).

A third, underlying, dimension in most media politics is a conflict between a focus on economy or technology vs. a focus on cultural factors or media content. A fourth dimension is latent rather than manifest: a conflict between media as commodities or as public goods. If media are regarded as commodities, private ownership, deregulation and free market competition is a sensible policy. If, on the other hand, the media are regarded as means to reduce gaps between different segments of the population (information gaps and differences in the supply of culture and entertainment), then state ownership and regulation can be justified in order to avoid the consequences of free competition.

Main actors

Within the context of the four dimensions elaborated above, the political parties are one group of important actors. The parties are often working in cooperation with other associations like Christian organizations, trade unions etc. The parties and some of the organizations are interested in a broad spectrum of issues in media politics. Along the centre–periphery dimension, the Progressive Party and the Conservative Party represent one pole, with the Centre Party and probably the Christian People's Party at the opposite pole. The Progressive–Conservative alliance represents one pole on the remaining three dimensions, but in this case with the Labour Party and the Left Socialists at the opposite pole. The conflicting location of the parties along different dimensions has made it difficult to construct a broad coalition in media politics.

A second important group of actors are the media themselves. The formation of conglomerates makes the picture difficult to read. In general the existing media, with the exception of NRK, have favoured the introduction of new media and new channels. The press was important as owners in the early stages of local radio and television and cable networks, and big newspaper groups have all been involved in television (Schibsted and A-pressen are main shareholders in TV2, Orkla dominated TVN for some time). The press also, in general, supported the new media. Conflict of interest was hardly discussed as an ethical theme in these matters.

The Norwegian electronic industry used to play an important role as a pressure group in media politics, often acting in cooperation with trade unions and employers' associations. But now almost all radio receivers, TV sets, video recorders etc. are imported, and the industry plays a minor role.

The company responsible for the telephone monopoly (which is to be abandoned), has become an important actor in satellite and cable television. Film producers and associations for advertising agencies and advertisers have tried to influence decisions on advertising in local media and national television.

Main issues – integration or disintegration?

The broad coalition behind the broadcasting policy in the 1950s, 1960s and beginning of the 1970s disappeared in the 1980s. The Conservatives proclaimed in the election campaign in 1981 that they promoted a second television channel financed by commercials and organized outside NRK (*Høyres arbeidsprogram* 1981–5: 89). Since the formation of the Conservative government in 1981, most decisions on broadcasting politics by non-socialist governments can be interpreted as steps towards this goal. The decision to allow local radio, cable transmission of satellite programmes and local television broke the monopoly and put the question of financing on the agenda. At the same time, the government weakened NRK by allowing only insignificant increases in the licence fee leading to cuts in NRK's budgets, rather than allowing a strengthening of the institution in order to meet the new competition. The Labour Party has tried to strengthen the NRK (Østbye, 1995).

A broad coalition has emerged in support of the local media. But for a long time this coalition could not agree on two of the major questions concerning the organization of a second television channel: organization inside or outside NRK, and financing – commercials or increased licence fee (Vaagland and Østbye, 1986). Since the agreement in 1990, the TV2 question has been solved. A broad coalition, including Labour but excluding the Progressives, accepted the establishment of a private, second channel, financed by advertising. In order to secure some of the PSB goals, there are a lot of regulations on form and content of both programmes and commercials. It is far from certain that a station with these restrictions on advertising will make it financially possible for the company to produce and distribute a national channel.

Local radio and television is still on the agenda. Since the start in 1981–2, the area covered by each station has usually been limited to one commune. The size of each commune varies, from less than 1000 inhabitants up to 20 000–25 000, with some exceptions. The first local radio stations were run by organizations, very often with much unpaid work. Several radio stations shared one transmitter, dividing the day between them. Small, local radio stations were well suited for this system. When advertising was permitted in 1988, a distinction has emerged between idealistic and commercial local radio stations. The present areas are too small for local television and for commercial, local radio. Lack of available frequencies makes it impossible to allow for much competition. The government has proposed a system where the area covered by each station is extended, and one commercial channel will be allowed in each area. In addition, idealistic stations are allowed on separate frequencies, or allotted time slots on the commercial frequency (St. meld. no. 24 1994–95). This system has met opposition in the parliament. Questions concerning ownership will become important when franchises for the new system of local radio and television are being discussed.

TV2's satellite channel, TV+, and the two 'Norwegian' satellite channels, TVNorge and TV3, are competing for agreements with the local television stations. The local stations will retransmit programmes from the satellite channel on their terrestrial transmitters.

The press subsidies represent another topical theme. The Conservatives would like to abandon most of the subsidies. The Labour Party is the strong defender of the subsidies, usually with some support from the Centre Party when it is not in government with the Conservatives. Labour and Centre Party newspapers would be likely to suffer most if the subsidies are abandoned. Estimates show that local competition would remain only in a few cities. Also most of the smallest newspapers (circulation less than 2000–3000) would be likely to disappear (NAL, 1990).

The press is adapting to the changing media environment in different ways. Some newspapers are available on the Internet, while others are involved in local radio and television stations.

The creation of the independent radio and television channels has, however, focused on another issue: concentration of ownership control. Legislation against concentration in radio, television and newspapers separately is likely, but regulation of cross-ownership is regarded as more difficult to impose (NOU, 1995).

The government has started a campaign to promote ethical standards in the media. Primarily, it expects the internal rules in the media to be strengthened and more rigorously enforced, but there is also a threat to include new legislation to give better protection of privacy (St. meld. no. 32 1992–93).

Technical innovations, results of competition and import of new media and new ideas create the challenges to the Norwegian mass media system. The solutions are affected by Norwegian traditions and political culture.

Statistics

(1 ECU = 8.14 Norwegian kroner, Nkr)

Population

Number of inhabitants	4.4 million
Geographical size	387 000 km^2
Population density	14 per km^2
Number of households	1.9 million

Broadcasting (1997)

Number of national, terrestrial television channels	
Public service (NRK)	1
Commercial (TV2)	1
Number of local television channels (permissions)	101
Number of satellite channels	
In Norwegian language	7
Other channels cleared for redistribution via cable	40
Television penetration	98%

Number of national, terrestrial radio channels	
Public service (NRK: P1, P2, Petre)	3
Commercial (P4)	1
Number of local radio stations	379 franchises in 212 areas

Television licence fees	
Black-and-white	Nkr600
Colour	Nkr1480

Market share and number of hours on national television		
NRK (terrestrial)	43%	3609 hr
NRK2	1%	
TV2 (terrestrial)	32%	4160 hr
TVNorge (satellite/cable)	7%	
TV3 (satellite/cable)	6%	

TV+, TV6 and ZTV (satellite/cable channels, established in 1995, very small market share and were closed down in 1996)

Market share and number of hours on national radio		
NRK/P1 (excl. regional)	30%	7272 hr
NRK/P2	8%	8722 hr
NRK/Petre	13%	6628 hr
P4	21%	8736 hr
Local radio	15%	

New electronic media

VCR penetration	61%
Satellite channels	50%
Cable	40%
Own dishes	10%
Personal computer	33%

Advertising revenue	Nkr (m)
Newspapers	3600
Weekly magazines	550
Journals	220
Cinema	65
Commercial radio (P4 + local)	215
Commercial TV (TV2, TV3, TVN)	1700

The press

Number of independent newspapers	
6–7 days per week	63
4–5 days per week	21
2–3 days per week	81
1 day per week	47
Combined circulation for 212 newspapers	3 170 000

Circulation of the 10 largest newspapers	
VG (Verdens Gang) (indep., Oslo, national tabloid)	386 137
Aftenposten (indep. cons., Oslo, national/regional)	279 965
Dagbladet (indep., Oslo, national tabloid)	228 834
Aftenposten aftenutgave (indep. cons., Oslo, regional)	188 544
Bergens Tidende (indep., Bergen, regional)	95 415
Adresseavisen (cons., Trondheim, regional)	89 516
Stavanger Aftenblad (indep., Stavanger, regional)	72 097
Dagens Næringsliv (indep. business, Oslo, national)	53 533
Fædrelandsvennen (indep., Christian, regional)	47 170
Drammens Tidende & Buskeruds Blad (cons., regional)	43 813

* Data relate to 1994 unless stated otherwise. Most of the data about radio, television and advertising is provided by MediaNorge (NORDICOM/Norge). Data about newspapers come from Høst (1995).

References

Haraldsen, Gustav and Vaage, Odd F. (1988) *Radiolyttingog fjernsynsseing*. Oslo: Statistisk sentralbyrå (Rapport 88/27).

Haugen, Einar (1966) *Language Conflict and Language Planning*. Cambridge, MA: Harvard University Press.

Haugen, Einar (1968) *Rikssprâk og folkemål* (translation of Haugen, 1966). Oslo: Universitetsforlaget.

Hjeltnes, Guri (1990) *Avisoppgiøretener 1945*. Oslo: Aschehoug.

Høst, Sigurd (1983) Videobruk i Norge vinteren 1983. Oslo: Institutt for Presseforskning.

Høst, Sigurd (1991) 'The Norwegian newspaper system', in Helge Rønning and Knut Lundby (eds), *Media and Communication*. Oslo: Universitetsforlaget.

Høst, Sigurd (1995) *Avisåret 1994, Flere aviser, stabilt opplag*. Fredrikstad: Institutt for Journalistikk.

Høyer, Svennik (1974) *Norsk pressemellom 1865 og 1965 (del I og II)*. Oslo: Institutt for Presseforskning.

Høyer, Svennik (1982) 'Pressen – økonomisk uTViklingog politisk kontroll', in NOU, *Maktutredningen. Massemedier*, 1982: 30.

Høyres arbeidsprogram 1981–85. Oslo: Høyre.

Hultén, Olof (1984) *Videoi Svenge*. Stockholm: Sveriges Radio.

Lund, Sissel (1985) *Billedmedier i Norge*. Oslo: NRK/Forskningen.

McQuail, Denis (1990) 'Caging the beast', *European Journal of Communication*, no. 2–3: 313–31.

Mathisen, Kjell Olav (1982) *Teledata brukererfaringer*. Kjeller: Televerkets forskningsinstitut.

NAL (1990) *10 teser om pressestøtte* (Ten theses on press support). Oslo: Norske Avisers Landsforbund.

NOU (1983a) Report no. 3: *Massemedier ogmediepolitikk*. Oslo: NOU.

NOU (1983b) Report no. 9: *Lov om film ogvideo*. Oslo: NOU.

NOU (1983c) Report no. 32: *Telematikk*. Oslo: NOU.

NOU (1984) Report no. 29: *Organisering av televirksomheten i Norge*. Oslo: NOU.

NOU (1992) Report no. 14: *Mål og midler i pressepolitikken*. Oslo: NOU.

NOU (1995) Report no. 3: *Mangfold i media*. Oslo: NOU.

NRK (1990) *Programregler*. Oslo: NRK.

NRK (1984) *Årbok 1983*. Oslo: NRK.

NRK (1995) *Tall og Fakta 1984*. Oslo: NRK.

NU A (1979) Report 4E: *Nordic Radio and Television via Satellite*. Copenhagen: The Secretariat for Nordic Cultural Cooperation.

Nymo, Birger (1984) *Publikum og fjernsyn over kabel*. Kjeller: Televerkets forsknmgs-institutt.

Østbye, Helge (1977) *Norsk rikskringkasting*. Bergen: Senter for medieforskning.

Østbye, Helge (1982) 'Norsk rikskringkasting – et monopol, to medier', in NOU, Report no. 30: *Maktutredningen. Massemedier*. Oslo: NOU.

Østbye, Helge (1991) 'Dimensions in Norwegian mass media politics', in Helge Rønning and Knut Lundby (eds), *Media and Communication*. Oslo: Universitetsforlaget.

Østbye, Helge (1995) *Mediepolitikk*. Oslo: Universitetsforlaget.

Ot. prp. no. 47 1986–87 'Lov om nærkringkasting'.

Ot. prp. no. 55 1989–90 'TV2 – Lov om reklamei kringkasting m.v.'

Ot. prp. no. 78 1991–92 'Lov om kringkasting'.

Rokkan, Stein (1975) 'Sentrum og periferi, økonomi og kultur' in *Sentrum og periferi i historien* (Studier i historisk metode X). Oslo: Universitetsforlaget.

Ryland, Stig (1990) *Reklame i nærradio*. Volda: Møre og Romsdal DH.

Seip, Jens Arup (1959) 'Det norske system i den økonomiske liberalismes klassiske tid', *Historisk tidsskrift*, 39.

Seip, Jens Arup (1975) 'Modellenes tyranni' in *Sentrum og periferi i historien* (Studier i historisk metode X). Oslo: Universitetsforlaget.

Smeland, Sverre (formann) (1973) *Tilråding fra nærkringkastingsu TV alget*. Oslo: NRK.

Statistisk årbok 1993 (Statistical Yearbook 1993). Oslo: Statistisk sentralbyrå.

St. meld. no. 84 1984–85 *Omny mediepolitikk*.

St. meld. no. 32 1992–93 *Media i tida*.

St. meld. no. 24 1994–95 *Nærkrinkgasting*.

Syvensen, Trine (1985) *Forsøk med lokal radio og fjemsyn i Norge (utkast)*. Bergen: Senter for mediefag.

Tofte, Tor Jørgen (1985) *Program 2i NRK/radio. Kulturpolitikk eller lokaliseringspolitikk?* Bergen: Senter for mediaforskning.

Vaage, Odd Frank (1995) *Kultur og mediebruk 1994*. Report 95/15. Oslo: Statistisk sentralbyrå.

Vaagland, Olav and Østbye, Helge (1986) 'Slutten på NRK-monopolet – og hva så?', in *Pressens årbog 1985:2*. Copenhagen: Reitzel.

Werner, Anita ([illegible]) *Ungdom og video våren 1987*. Oslo: Institutt for presseforskning.

Werner, Anita, Høst, Sigurd and Ulvær, Bjørn Petter (1984) *Publikums reaksjoner på satellitt og lokalfjernsyn*. Oslo: Institutt for presseforskning.

13
Portugal

J.-M. Nobre-Correia

National profile

The state of Portugal covers 92 028 km^2 – the Azores and Madeira included – and has a total of 9.9 million inhabitants. The country's population density is moderate at 107.4 inhabitants per km^2. According to the 1991 census, 20% of the population is younger than 15 and 13.5% is older than 65. Forty-four per cent of the people live in municipalities with less than 1000 inhabitants and a mere 11% live in conurbations having more than 100 000 inhabitants. Ten per cent of the population work in the primary sector, 36% in the secondary and 48% in the tertiary sector. The unemployment rate is 6.1%. The gross domestic product per head of the population amounts to 887.5 m escudos.

With regard to the media, Portugal's linguistic homogeneity is unique in Europe. The 114 000 foreigners who legally reside in Portugal do not challenge this homogeneity. However, Portugal's illiteracy rate is the highest in Europe, with 11% of those over 10 years old not fully literate. This situation partly accounts for the fact that the country's press readership is very small.

In 1140 Portugal became an independent nation, and between 1580 and 1640 Spanish sovereigns succeeded to the throne. Very shortly afterwards, in 1641, the *Gazeta*, the first Portuguese monthly, was published. The first daily newspaper, the *Diário Lisbonense*, only came into being in 1809. The freedom of the press was decreed in 1821, but underwent a number of changes until the Republic, established in 1910, reaffirmed the principle of the freedom to inform. When the Republic gave way to a dictatorship in 1926, censorship was reimposed. This censorship lasted until the 1974 revolution.

After that time Portugal's regime became a semi-presidential, parliamentary democracy. The president is elected for a five-year term, and the single-chamber parliament for four years. After ten years of Centre–Right government – with the social-democratic party in power – the socialists assumed power after the legislative elections of October 1995. After giving two mandates to a socialist head of state, the Portuguese people elected another socialist in the presidential elections of 1996.

Portugal has been a NATO member since 1949 and member of the European Union since 1986. During 1996 a process of centralization of the administration was started, with the government intending to add nine new regions on the mainland to the autonomous regions of the Azores and Madeira – which were created in 1976.

The press and broadcasting since 1945

The press

Until the dictatorship was established in 1926, the history of the Portuguese press was not unlike that of the press in the other European countries, except that the major 'turning-points' happened a few years later. Under the Salazar dictatorship the press was forced to keep a very low profile. Several newspapers disappeared. New general newspapers were rare, and when they came into being they did not last long.

Of all the newspapers that existed before Salazar assumed power, only three succeeded in not becoming the government's official mouthpieces. These three newspapers were, in particular, *República*, but also *Diário de Lisboa* and *O Primeiro de Janeiro*. A number of regional weeklies originally adhering to the ideas of Salazarism afterwards changed over to the opposition, especially after 1958. This was true for the *Jornal do Fundão* and the *Notícias da Amadora*, but also for *Comércio do Funchal*, the *Jornal do Centro*, *Opinião*, *Independência de Agueda* and *Voz Portucalense*.

Salazar created a quasi-perfect duopoly by dividing the media into the regime's media on the one hand and the media of the Catholic Church on the other. When Marcelo Caetano became Prime Minister in 1968, the situation changed slightly. When it came to the assimilation of foreign news a certain degree of freedom was tolerated, but the changes introduced in that period were often cut short later on. The greatest novelty was the weekly newspaper *Expresso*, launched by Francisco Pinto Balsemão on 6 January 1973. Modelled on the British Sunday newspapers, *Expresso* adopted a new tone formerly unknown to the Portuguese press. It provided quality information, seriously elaborated dossiers and communicated a wide range of opinions. Its success triggered a new type of press and a new concept of journalism. It also affirmed the existence of a new social ruling class that was cosmopolitan, more interested in Europe than in Africa, and no longer satisfied with the current government's policies.

In the meantime, the end of the 1960s and the beginning of the 1970s saw a considerable press concentration. The major newspapers ceased to be family businesses and became jointly controlled business companies that were tightly controlled by the financial power. At the time of the coup d'etat on 25 April 1974, Lisbon had nine dailies. Five of these were morning newspapers: *Epoca* (which belonged to the single political party), *Diário de Notícias* (Caixa Geral de Depósitos), *Jornal do Comércio* (Banco Borges & Irmão), *Novidades* (Catholic Church) and *O Século* (Banco Intercontinental

Português). The remaining four newspapers were evening newspapers: *A Capital* (Banco Borges & Irmão, Banco Espirito Santo & Comercial de Lisboa and the biggest economic group in Portugal, CUF), *Diário de Lisboa* (two-thirds owned by the Ruella Ramos family and one-third by the Banco Nacional Ultramarino), *Diário Popular* (Banco Borges & Irmão) and *República* (representing the socialist opposition to the regime).

Compared to Lisbon, the daily press in the city of Oporto comprised merely three titles – all morning papers: *O Comércio do Porto* (Banco Borges & Irmão), *Jornal de Notícias* (Caixa Geral de Depósitos) and *O Primeiro de Janeiro* (Pinto de Azevedo family). In addition to these titles, the daily press consisted of nine other newspapers in continental Portugal (three in Evora, two in Beja and two in Braga) and ten on the islands (seven in the Azores). These 'provincial' dailies communicated only the opinions of the local elites (modest size, simple content and low degree of professionalism).

The state of the periodical press resembles that of the daily press. In Lisbon three tri-weekly sports newspapers were published, only one escaping the move towards concentration: *A Bola* (private, with participation of the editors), *Mundo Desportivo* (Caixa Geral de Depósitos) and *Record* (Banco Borges & Irmão). The only two illustrated weeklies, *Flama* and *O Século Ilustrado*, also belonged to the Banco Intercontinental Português, which also controlled the weeklies *Vida Mundial* (supplying general information), *Modas & Bordados* (a women's magazine that later became *Mulher*), *Jacto* (attracted younger readers) and *Cinéfilo* (its main topic being the cinema). The weekly magazine *Vida Rural* (a magazine on agriculture) was owned by the Caixa Geral de Depósitos, whereas *Radio-Televisão* belonged to the Banco Borges & Irmão.

Following the revolution of 1974 the freedom of the press and the right of information was restored. However, in the period of turbulence in the aftermath of the revolution the press was not always properly run, and the 1974–5 events immediately had two important consequences. First, the number of newspapers, especially those that did not appear daily, grew considerably. Secondly, the state became the owner of several newspapers after the nationalization of all the banks, decreed in March 1975.

The first papers to be published for the general public were those edited by political organizations. It was not until 1975 that a new type of general informative press came into being, when the dailies *Jornal Novo* and *A Luta* were launched. At that same time, weeklies were launched, some of which became highly successful, such as *O Jornal* and *Tempo.*

Immediately after the counter-coup d'etat of 25 November 1975, most of the dailies remained unpublished due to the state of siege. In the aftermath of the 'counter-coup' a new press appeared: the dailies *O Dia* (in December 1975) and *O Diário* (in January 1976) and the weekly magazines *O País* (in January) and *O Diabo* (in February). All of these titles were ideologically marked and were situated at the extremes of the political range. The period of agitation was followed by a period of relative calm. In 1976 the outcome of the legislative elections in April and the presidential elections allowed Portugal to adopt a regime of moderate democracy. There was a period of intermission in the media which permitted it to reflect on its future.

In 1979 things began to change. Finally there were attempts to launch intervention dailies such as *A Tarde* (which was the successor of *Jornal Novo*, both of which were controlled by the confederation of employers) and *Portugal Hoje* (unofficial newspaper of the Socialist Party after *A Luta* disappeared). More importantly, on 19 March *Correio da Manhá* was launched, deliberately positioned in terms of industrial and commercial content rather than in terms of politics.

There was clearly a need to do away with the influences of the old regime and its censorship. As a result the diversity of the press was accentuated and the new press itself clearly addressed an elitist readership. The modernist financier Belmiro de Azevedo initiated the launching of *Público* on 5 March 1990, the first quality newspaper in Portugal. This new newspaper triggered off the restructuring of the old *Diário de Notícias* (1864). It took on a new formula in 1992 to become as sociologically diverse as its young competitor. These two newspapers can be considered the structural vectors of the new leading circles.

Broadcasting

The first radio stations in Portugal appeared in 1914. Compared to the radio stations in Europe they have had their own idiosyncratic history. In Portugal, the public Emissora Nacional, instituted in 1935, has always cooperated with the influential private stations such as Rádio Clube Português, officially recognized in 1933 and Rádio Renascença, instituted in 1938, and other more regional ones (Emissores Associados de Lisboa, Emissores do Norte Reunidos), even local ones (Emissora das Beiras, Rádio Altitude, Rádio Alto Douro and Rádio Ribatejo). This situation generated concepts of radio and language use that was highly original.

When the first television programmes were broadcast in 1957, the Salazar regime was still in power, and as a consequence they merely voiced the opinions of the established regime. In contrast to the rest of Europe, where television arose from the public sector, the Radiotelevisão Portuguesa was set up as a private company. Its shareholders were not only the state, but also nine private radio stations, 12 banks and one 'natural person'. The RTP has always had recourse from the very beginning to advertising, unlike most of the public broadcasting corporations in Europe.

When Portugal became a democracy again in 1974, the history of the radio evolved in a counter-current to 'proper' history. Radio broadcasting in Portugal was nationalized while in a large number of European countries it lost its monopoly. Its proper process of demonopolization only started in 1979 – illegally. It was not until 1989 that the first local radio stations were recognized. The creation of TSF on 29 February 1988 – on the eve of the legalization – was the first step towards redefining the media landscape.

TSF, an information radio station, tried to address the new need for information; investigative journalism and live, on-site reports.

The first private television broadcasting was not launched until 1992–3 – significantly later than in the rest of Europe. Sic started its broadcasts on 6 October 1992, TV1 on 20 February 1993. The first cable networks were installed on the Azores and in Madeira in 1992, and in 1994 on the mainland.

The press and broadcasting today

The press

Twenty-two years after Portugal became a democracy again, real changes in the daily press are limited to Lisbon. The three general titles in Porto have not changed (*O Comércio do Porto*, *Jornal de Notícias* and *O Primeiro de Janeiro*). In Lisbon there are five general dailies left (*Correio da Manhã*, *O Dia*, *Diário de Notícias* and *Público* – all morning newspapers, and *A Capital*, the only evening newspaper). To these titles one might also add *Diário Económico*. The innovations and changes carried out in the provinces are not significant. In total there are now fewer general daily newspapers (20) than in the Salazar epoch (30).

The evening newspapers were once quite important, but have now vanished except for *A Capital*. The quality newspapers give priority to news on politics and the economy rather than culture. In the popular newspapers culture is simply non-existent. However, one can detect two important changes. First, the titles that are predominant in the popular daily press as well as in the quality daily press appeared after democracy had been reinstalled (*Correio da Manhã* and *Público*). Secondly, Portugal has no less than three sports newspapers: *O Jogo* (launched in 1985), *A Bola* and *Record* (both of which became dailies in 1995).

The proliferation of the weekly press has caused a great diversity, both in ideology and in journalistic approach. The most important general newspaper, both in the daily and weekly press, is still *Expresso*. Its most important competitor is *O Independente*, which started in 1988 and appeals to a younger readership. Both *Tal & Qual* and *Visão* are fighting for the third place. Both belong to the Edipresse group. *Tal & Qual* is a popular magazine, which started in 1980, and *Visão* is a news magazine, which was launched in 1993 and which took the place of *O Jornal*. Both are trailing far behind the first two.

Although new titles are thriving – magazines on women, television, cars and business are abundant – the state of the Portuguese press is on the whole mediocre. It is only fair to say that the press again reflects a multiplicity of ideologies and a freedom of style that are invaluable for a country that for 48 years lived with heavy censorship. Nevertheless, the situation is still bad. The rate of illiteracy remains high, editorial content is Lisbon-centric, and to a lesser degree addresses the issues of the larger coastal cities. Thirdly, newspaper distribution is limited and slow. The papers are delivered late in the inland cities of the country and often do not arrive at all in rural locations. Prices are excessively high and still increasing. In 1974 the price of a daily was 2.5 escudos; now they cost between 100 and 150 escudos (0.5–0.8 ECU). *Expresso* was sold at 5 escudos; now its cover price is 400 escudos (2 ECU). Penetration of the press is extremely low; 39.3% of adults read the newspaper of the previous day, 46.6% read the weeklies of the previous week and 31.4% the monthly magazines of the previous month.

Broadcasting

After the radio sector became state-controlled, with the exception of Radio Renscença, which belongs to the Catholic Church, free radios came into existence from 1979 onwards. The state itself decided to privatize part of the radio channels grouped under the name Radiodifusão Portuguesa in 1993.

At present, Portugal has 287 radio stations, most of which are local. The public RDP has three national programmes (Antena 1, general, Antena 2, cultural, and Antena 3, which focuses mainly on a younger audience). Besides RDP, there are also RDP Internacional and RDP Africa. The catholic Rádio Renascença offers two national programmes (RR Canal 1, general, and RFM, which addresses a younger audience), several regional programmes (among which Rádio Lisboa) and an international programme. Rádio Comercial is responsible for two general programmes (RC OM and RC FM). Finally, there is TSF, which is information-oriented, as well as NRJ Energia and Rádio Cidade.

In Portugal there are only three television broadcasting stations. First, there is the public RTP, which has two national channels – RTP1, mainly focusing on general news, and RTP2, culturally oriented; two regional programmes – RTP Açores and RTP Madeira – and one international programme – RTPI. Apart from RTP, there are two private stations: Sic and TVI, both of which are general in nature. Since May 1995, Sic, created by Francisco Pinto Balsemão the founder of *Expresso*, has become the top station of these four national programmes, both in terms of viewing figures and advertising revenue. Unable to compete, TVI occupies a modest third place, far behind Sic and RTP1. This led TVI to introduce pay television by the end of 1996.

The new television stations forced the old RTP to abandon its deadening routine. It reacted to the challenge by making its offer of information more dynamic, but at the same time it accentuated the weaknesses of Portuguese television by adopting a populist tone. To enliven the information programmes, the television stations attribute an excessive importance to small news items. As for their programming policy, the stations have copied all the mediocre items from foreign stations: the live shows and the game shows and quizzes and above all the Latin American – more specifically Brazilian – 'telenovelas' series, as they are referred to. These shallow drama series have invaded the television screen, mainly in prime time.

The major groups

Seven groups form the backbone of the daily press. Lusomundo is the most important one – one of its minority shareholders being the Irish group, Independent Newspapers. It controls *Jornal de Notícias* and Lisbon's *Diário de Notícias* and holds important positions in Funchal's *Diário de Notícias* and *Açoreano Oriental* (Ponta Delgada). Other powerful groups are Presselivre, with *Correio da Manhã*, Controjornal, with *A Capital*, Soci with *Diário Económico*, and Investec with *Record*. Added to these are the financial groups Sonae and Banco Português de Investimento, which control *Público* – in which group the Spanish Prisa and the Italian L'Editoriale Espresso hold minority positions – and the Catholic Church, with *Diário do Minho* (in Braga), *Correio da Horta* (în Horta, Azores), *A União* (in Angra do Heroismo, Azores) and *Jornal da Madeira* (in Funchal).

Clearly, the state of the periodical press is rather more complicated. Six groups are important. Of these, Controjornal, with *Expresso* and a number of specialized magazines such as *Autosport*, *Caras*, *Exame* and *Turbo*, holds the top market position. There are also Soci, with *O Independente* and several economic periodicals – *Fortuna*, *Semanário Económico*, *Valor*. Furthermore, there is Impala, with several specialized magazines (*Maria*, *Nova Gente*, *TV 7 Dias*), and the Swiss Edipress (*TV Mais*, *Visão*, *Tal & Qual*). The Catholic Church is still very influential in the regional and local press, with no less than 635 titles, and the state itself, via TV Guia Editora (a subsidiary of the RTP), with a large number of telemagazines (*Telejogos*, *TV Guia*, *Telguia*).

In the radio sector only three groups are important, not taking the state into account (RDP). First of all there is the Catholic Church, with Rádio Renacença and a large number of local radios. Next there is Presselivre, with Radio Comercial and Radio Nostalgia (which plays music from the 1960–1980s). Finally there is Lusomundo, with TSF-Radio Press, NRJ Energia (playing music for a younger taste) and XFM (playing music for minority groups). The financial group Sonae took an interest in the sector and created Rede Nova de Rádio in 1995.

The state also has a finger in the television pie with RTP. Controjornal controls Sic, of which the Brazilians behind Globo are shareholders as well as several financial institutions. The Catholic Church is in theory TVI's major shareholder, but has in reality lost its control to anonymous foreign investors.

Policies for the press and broadcasting

Legal framework

From a legal point of view, the media situation is regulated by the decrees and laws of 26 February 1975, 9 March 1976 and 24 October 1988, as well as by the law of 25 May 1995. These laws constitute a legislative whole, with principles ensuring the right to practise journalism without any form of administrative repression. This journalistic activity is solely dependent on the power of judgment of a court of justice. Another principle concerns the existence of 'editorial councils' elected by the journalists themselves and which have to decide on any appointment of an editor-in-chief. Furthermore, there is a principle concerning the right of natural and moral persons to reply to any published piece of writing. Another principle establishes the journalists' rights to have access to sources of information, the right to their professional secrecy and the right to a 'conscience clause'. Finally, one principle allows the establishment of a 'Press Council' (after the example of the British Press Council), which later became The High Authority of Social Communication. The totality of these principles are guaranteed by the Constitution itself and give evidence of a particularly modern and progressive concept of the right of information.

As far as the ownership of the media is concerned, no legal principle impedes the initiatives of the players. There is no limit whatsoever in the press, and in the radio sector real life has made the legal framework obsolete. Moreover, no one is capable of monitoring the legal maximum of 25% for shareholders of private television stations.

Indirect state subsidies to the media and especially the written press are considerable. The state pays the postal costs almost entirely. It partly refunds the transport costs of journalists and funds their professional training. It supports the technological modernization of the media (graphics equipment, telecommunication and information technology). The sum of 310 m escudos was allocated to 73 regional newspapers in 1995 alone.

Nevertheless, 22 years after the return of democracy to Portugal, the overall progress report is not entirely positive. The daily press remains an extremely fragile sector, its circulation rates are far too low for a population of the size of Portugal's. The regional daily press is especially sleepy and insignificant in supplying information. The audiovisual landscape does not offer the variety it should. Television stations offer above all entertainment, seeing the viewing public as consumers rather than as citizens. On top of that, the television licence fee was abandoned on 1 January 1991. The stations' own audiovisual production is almost non-existent; they depend to a great extent on American and Brazilian productions.

There are two positive things to mention, however. With the exception of Rádio Renascença, the media are independent and are not mouthpieces of either political parties or labour unions. After 48 years of an authoritative regime and 19 months of revolution the need to become independent has become a primordial demand of the Portuguese journalists.

Main issues

In the rest of Europe, a technological revolution has swept the media. Portugal, however, experienced a political revolution which generated considerable socio-cultural repercussions. Protected by the language barrier and its geographical setting on the edge of Europe, it was only quite late that Portugal discovered what was at stake in the international media scene.

Confronted with this new situation, the public company Portugal Telecom – which began privatization in May 1996 – plays an essential role in the field of mobile telephone (TMN), data communication (Telepac) and cable networks (TV Cabo Portugal). In this latter sector it almost has a position of monopoly, operating via nine regional enterprises such as TV Cabo Douro, Porto, Mondego, Tejo, Lisboa, Sado, Guadiana, Madeirense and Açoreana. These enterprises had about 100 000 subscribers in May 1996 and hoped to attain 170 000 by the end of the year in a total of 52 towns. In the Braga region, in the north of the country, Bragatel is a fellow-operator. Multicanal, an initiative of Lusomundo (50%) and of United International Holdings (50%), remains in the planning stage.

Despite the delay in terms of cable networks in Portugal, only 270 000 households – 9% of those who have a television – have satellite dishes.

Statistics

(1 ECU = 195 escudos)

Population

Number of inhabitants	9.9 million
Geographical size	92 028 km^2
Population density	107.4 per km^2
Number of households	3.5 million

Broadcasting

Number of national radio channels	8
Number of national television channels (RTP, Sic and TVI)	3
Pay-TV (TVI)	1
Number of local television channels	4
Number of cabled households	100 000
Number of local radio stations	ca. 280
Number of households with TV	3 million
Households with satellite TV	270 000

The press

Number of national daily newspapers	20
Press penetration	
Adults reading the newspaper of the previous day	39.3%
Adults reading the weeklies of the previous week	46.6%
Adults reading magazines of the previous month	31.4%

Data relate to 1995.

References

Kleinsteuber, Hans, McQuail, Dennis and Siune, Karen (eds) (1986) *Electronic Media and Politics in Western Europe: A Euromedia Research Group Handbook of National Systems*. Frankfurt: Campus Verlag.

Østergaard, Bernt S. (ed.) (1992) *The Media in Western Europe – The Euromedia Handbook*. London: Sage.

14

Spain

Rosario de Mateo

National profile

Spain covers 504 782 km^2 and has a population of 39 433 942 inhabitants. Population density is 78 inhabitants per km^2. However, the population distribution is very unequal: in the coastal regions the density is 100 inhabitants per km^2, whereas in the interior of the peninsula it is only 25. The metropolitan areas Madrid and Barcelona, with about 4.5 and 3 million inhabitants respectively, are the main nuclei of population, though there are four more cities with more than half a million inhabitants.

After the economic recession of 1993, the Spanish economy has undergone a slow but continued recovery, with a constant increase of the gross domestic product (−1% in 1993; 2% in 1994; 3% in 1995; 2% in 1996) and steady inflation rate control (4.9% in 1993; 4.3% in 1994; 4% in 1995; 3.2% in 1996) but with high unemployment rates (above 20% throughout this period).

The economic activity is focused in Madrid and Catalonia (service and industry), followed by the Basque Country (industry) and Valencia (industry and agriculture). However, the region with the highest income per person is the Balearic Isles. This is due to tourist income. Madrid and Catalonia rank just behind the islands. The distribution of wealth is very unequal, and the south and the inner regions are among the poorest regions in Western Europe.

With the Constitution of 1978, Spain became a parliamentary monarchy. A regime was established which recognizes the existence of different regions and cultural particularities in Spain. Seventeen autonomous regions (Comunidades Autónomas, CCAA) were set up, each having its own parliamentary and governmental system. The state administration is distributed between the central and the regional governments. The regional governments handle issues concerning culture, health, urbanism, security etc., with some variations. Defence and foreign policy are the prerogative of the central government.

The Constitution acknowledges the linguistic plurality of Spain. Spanish (or Castilian) is the official language for the whole country. Catalan, Basque and Galician are official languages in their respective regions.

In the majority of the CCAA the government is in the hands of the conservative party or nationalistic parties (Catalonia and Basque Country). A general election was held on 3 March 1996, and at the beginning of May 1996 the conservative party (Partido Popular), with the votes of Basque, Catalan and Canary nationalist parties, set up the present government.

It was the Spanish Socialist Party (PSOE) which came to power in 1982, that brought Spain into the EU and active participation in the NATO alliance. This has brought Spanish international politics in line with the rest of Western Europe. At the same time, Spain has been obliged to restructure its legislation in economic affairs, adapting it to the EU. The new situation in Europe has made it easier for foreign capital to enter most branches of production. This situation has also allowed Japanese companies to invest in Spain.

Development of the press and broadcasting since 1945

The mass media in Spain in 1945 worked on the premises imposed by Franco's regime after his victory in the Civil War (1939). Until 1966, the conditions for the development of the media were tightly controlled. From then until the dictator's death in 1975, they were, apparently, more liberal. In 1975 the transitional period to democracy started, and old and new values coexisted for a time. This gave way to the formation of the present structures in the mass media.

The main concern of Franco's government was the ideological function of information. Therefore, the state tried to control the mass media through laws and regulatory measures and in many cases through the ownership and management of the media.

The press, according to the law of 1938, was considered a national institution and its organization was under state control. Radio information services were also under strict control following the rules of 1939. The organization of this medium was set down in the law of 1934. These rules implied the reduction of the freedom of speech, because of imposed censorship of news. Private companies were required to apply for administrative licences in order to set up radio and press activities.

This control was strengthened when the state took over a great number of newspapers, magazines and radio stations. On 28 October 1956, the first official television broadcasting began. Television was constituted as a public state monopoly dependent on the government. Its regulation was essentially based on the existing legislation for radio broadcasting. In 1965 the second official television channel was launched.

At the end of the 1950s, the financial oligarchy and technocratic economists from the Opus Dei (a Catholic lay order) became leading and influential figures on the political and economic scene. The Stabilization Plan of 1959 marked the beginning of a phase of economic development which presupposed the existence of a European market. However, this international expansion was not possible as long as Spain continued with its dictatorship system. Thus a programme of institutional reorganization was carried through, a reorganization that had the appearance of a political liberalization of the Franco regime.

The Press and Printing Law in 1966 can be viewed in this context. The aim of this law was to liberalize the written press, though censorship and regulation of journalistic enterprises continued. Broadcasting own information was forbidden for radio stations, which were obliged to broadcast the official news bulletins of the public radio station, Radio Nacional de España. However, the bill of 1964 was important because of its rationalization of the Spanish radio sector. This bill fixed and defined the public and private broadcasting of national, regional (referring to the area formed by some townships) and local media. Afterwards the setting up of FM radio stations was relatively liberalized, and a pattern for the financing of radio companies was established.

Television continued to be a national public monopoly, lacking a legal entity of its own, since its management was under a general office of a ministry. Televisión Española (TVE) had its own technical network, while in the rest of Europe the broadcasting function was in the hands of the PTT. The financial sources of TVE were the General State Budget and advertising.

After Franco's death (1975), the state was removed from the management of the printed press. The existing restrictions in this field were eased with the law of 1984, which also provided the press and the news agencies with economic state help.

In the radio sector public and private ownership and management coexisted, and freedom of information was introduced in 1977. However, all legal structures and the organization of radio were maintained until 1987, when the Telecommunications Act (Ley de Ordenación de las Telecommunicaciones, LOT) was passed.

Television reached adulthood in 1980, when the Radio and Television Statute was promulgated. This statute invalidated the previous television regulation, which was chaotic and partial. From this year onwards, management was progressively decentralized. First of all, the monopoly of the state administration ended, with the approval of a law in 1983 which allowed the CCAA to have their own channels. Secondly, in 1988, the private television law was passed, and the public monopoly of television ended.

The press

Legal framework

The press in Spain is not controlled by any specific legislation since the promulgation of the 1978 Constitution. Formerly, the law of 1966 was an impediment to the normal development of press activities. The activity of the press is now free, subject only to legislation protecting honour and individual privacy, the new penal code, approved by parliament in

November 1995, and the Constitution. Therefore, there are no limitations to the ownership or the financing of publications. However, the participation of press companies in radio and television is regulated in order to guarantee the plurality of these two media and to avoid monopolization.

In 1986, the entry of foreign capital into the Spanish press was liberalized, so as to adapt Spanish legislation to the regulation of the European Union. Since then many press groups have started activities in Spain, for example Bertelsmann, Hachette, Bauer, Springer, VNU and Hersant (most of them in the field of non-daily papers). Other groups were established in Spain earlier, by taking advantage of some openings in law, like Gruner & Jahr.

Although the Spanish press is financed through advertising and sales, it became necessary in 1984 to establish a legal framework for state subsidies. This regulation had its origins in the crisis of the press sector during the early 1980s and it was based on the circulation of the newspapers, the consumption of Spanish paper and technological renovation. At first these measures were intended to make it easier for newspapers to survive during the crisis and only wholly-owned Spanish enterprises could receive support. This led to accusations of unfair competition by the EU, and subsidization was gradually reduced from 1988 onwards, in such a way that today there is no help from the state, directly or indirectly, to the press (only a reduction in post and telecommunication rates).

The governments of some CCAA with their own language (Catalonia, the Basque Country) give economic help to the press (magazines and newspapers) to make up for the difficulties in sustaining a press with a language different from Spanish.

Press ownership and financing

Until 1984 some newspapers were owned by the state and they competed in the market with the private press, which was mostly run by family-owned companies. Sales and liquidation of the newspapers created by Franco's regime (in all the main cities) have left the sector completely in private hands. At the same time, the Constitution sheltered the freedom of speech and free enterprise, so that the market was rearranged at the end of the 1970s and the beginning of the 1980s.

During this period, the Spanish press went through a very severe crisis, along with a general economic crisis in Spain. This forced a number of well-established newspapers to close, because they were not able to switch to new technology. At the same time, new newspapers, not run by family-owned companies, were created and they have become market leaders within a few years. These newspapers are for example *El País* (created in 1976 by PRISA, which is now one of the leading communication groups in Spain) and *El Periódico* (created in 1979 within Grupo Zeta, one of the leaders in the magazine market). Along with these new companies, only the main newspapers of great tradition survived, for example *ABC*, *La Vanguardia*, *La Voz de Galicia* or *Heraldo de Aragón*. These are all family-owned companies. At the end of the 1980s a new national newspaper, *El Mundo*, was created with great success: after only five years it had become the third most popular newspaper by its circulation.

In 1986 the admission of foreign investment in the press sector was allowed, opening the way for the most important European press groups to become active in Spain, either by buying existing publications or by creating Spanish versions of the most popular magazines in their country of origin. The most important ones, among others, are Bertelsmann, Gruner & Jahr, Axel Springer, Bauer, VNU and Hachette. These groups now have the largest non-daily press sales, together with some Spanish-owned companies such as Grupo 16, Hymsa or Grupo Zeta, which have also received foreign investment in recent years.

Foreign capital has found it much more difficult to enter the Spanish daily press. Several foreign groups, such as Hersant, Rusconi, Murdoch, Expansion, Dow Jones, Rizzoli and the Guardian, have formalized their presence in newspapers by buying part of the capital in newspaper publishing companies. None has created its own newspapers. Only the deal between Prensa Española (publisher of *ABC*, with the second largest circulation) and Springer to launch a new popular newspaper, *CLARO*, in 1991, changed the transnational way of penetrating the Spanish press for a while, but it was not successful.

At the same time, PRISA (owner of *El País*, the highest circulation newspaper, radio network SER, part of Canal Plus, etc.) began expansion in 1989 into foreign press markets. Among the Spanish media groups, PRISA has the most important strategy of direct investment. It owns part of the capital in the companies publishing the *Independent* (UK), *Público* (Portugal) and *La Prensa* (Mexico). PRISA also has an agreement to exchange information products with the newspaper publishing companies of *Le Monde* (France), *La Repubblica* (Italy) and the *Independent* (UK).

There is a tendency towards the concentration of ownership and production in the Spanish newspaper industry: only 20 among more than 100 daily newspapers control nearly 72% of the circulation of the newspapers and two-thirds of these newspapers are owned by daily press groups like Prensa Ibérica and Unidad Editorial, among others, or by media groups like PRISA, Zeta and Bilbao Editorial.

Regarding the financing of the press (newspapers and magazines), revenue comes from selling copies and from advertising. Advertising contributes 50–70% of the income in the main Spanish newspapers and magazines, implying a great advertising dependence among publishing companies, although advertising revenue has been lower for Spanish newspapers in recent years. In 1987 advertising contributed 63% of the income in Spanish newspapers, but by 1994 this contribution was down to 52% because of stagnating advertising revenues combined with rising sales prices (10%), and increased sales of newspapers (3.5%). In 1995 and 1996 advertising contributed about 50% of the income of Spanish newspapers. On the other hand, the state press subsidies, created in 1984 to help newspapers survive the crisis, were deemed to be unnecessary in 1990, and were therefore stopped.

The circulation rate of daily newspapers in Spain is among the lowest in Europe but has been growing slowly in recent years. In 1987 this rate was 79 copies per 1000 inhabitants, while in 1996 it had grown to 106 copies per 1000 inhabitants. This rate is lower, however, if we only consider general information daily newspapers and disregard sport and economic dailies. In this case the circulation rate went from 69 copies per 1000 inhabitants in 1987, to 90 copies per 1000 inhabitants in 1996. In the northern regions the rate is higher – in Catalonia it is about 115 copies. Low levels of newspaper reading are in part due to the fact that Spain has a poor reading tradition and that there are no populist newspapers (yellow press), as in other countries.

From the mid-1980s there has been a trend among leading newspapers to seek new readers, those not used to reading, by printing specialized supplements and using a lot of graphics and illustrations. Newspaper reading has indeed slowly increased every year since 1986. By including magazines in full colour and other supplements in this way, the leading papers have increased the circulation of their Sunday editions by 70–100%.

In 1996, *Marca*, a daily sport newspaper, had the highest national circulation – 475 002 copies. The next three daily newspapers (general information) with the highest circulation, *El País*, *ABC* and *El Mundo*, have a national distribution but in most CCAA they are exceeded in sales by the main regional newspapers. Among these newspapers we find *La Vanguardia* (Catalonia), *El Periódico* (Catalonia), *El Correo* (Basque Country), *La Voz de Galicia* (Galicia) and *El Diario Vasco* (Basque Country). Other newspapers with a national distribution are *Diario 16*, with decreasing sales in recent years, and *As*, a sport newspaper. All the newspapers with a national distribution are published in Madrid. Of the 102 newspapers in Spain in 1994, only a handful of national newspapers – or regional for Catalonia and the Basque Country – had a daily circulation of more than 100 000.

In order to overcome the economic consequences of low circulation and increasing costs, especially of paper, newspapers created a number of parallel strategies in the 1980s, continuing in the 1990s. Some of the national newspapers publish special editions in some CCAA (*El País*), in order to increase their sales regionally. Some publishing groups have collaboration agreements with local newspapers to exchange national and local news (Grupo 16). A third strategy is to establish new press groups, publishing regional newspapers in some CCAA and sharing news with other CCAA papers (Grupo Z, which publishes *El Periódico de Cataluña*, *La Voz de Asturias*, *El Periódico de Extremadura* and *El Periódico de Aragón*; Prensa Ibérica, with newspapers bought from the state in 1984; COMECOSA, set up by *El Correo* and regional newspapers).

Most of the 100 or so daily newspapers are published in Spanish. Only six are in Catalan and one in Basque, and a few more are bilingual, Catalan/Spanish, Galician/Spanish and Basque/Spanish. Newspapers printed in

Catalan receive economic help from the government of Catalonia, in order to mitigate their economic difficulties. The circulation rate of these newspapers is 17 copies per 1000 inhabitants.

A large number of daily press and magazine titles are available on the Internet.

Structure and organization of non-daily press

In the wide field of non-daily press, Spain has an enormous quantity of journals. There are about 350 journals; most of them have a small circulation, with only a few exceeding 500 000 copies. Contrary to newspapers, most magazines have a national reach. This fact makes it easier for them to survive. In Catalonia there is a local press written in Catalan.

General information weeklies normally belong to groups. These groups often have publications in many fields. Grupo Zeta (the Murdoch Corporation owns 25% of the capital) has magazines of general information – *Interviu*, *Tiempo* and *Panorama* – and travel, sports, economic and sex magazines besides. Grupo 16, also with foreign capital (Hersant, Rusconi), publishes a weekly of general information, *Cambio 16*, which competes with those belonging to Zeta and others with a smaller circulation. Grupo 16 also publishes magazines on travel, history and cars, among other specialities. The yellow weeklies press (*Prensa del Corazón*) has the highest circulation of non-daily press. The majority of publisher companies of non-daily press have an important amount of foreign investment.

Electronic media

Legal framework

In the 1980s there was an important change in the legal regulation of television, radio and the other electronic media. Its effects continue in the 1990s.

In television, the 1980 statute established the RTVE monopoly in Spain. Under the control of parliament, RTVE developed the state jurisdiction in television, and also managed the public radio channels (Radio Nacional de España, RNE). In 1983, the passing of the 'third channel law' allowed the CCAA to create a channel for their geographic area in addition to the two RTVE channels and under the same charter as RTVE. The regional parliaments were in control and could use the Third Channel broadcasting network of RTVE. Retevision has the monopoly to broadcast all terrestrial television signals until 1999; it is a public institution but its privatization is planned.

A law passed in 1988 allowed private companies to run three national channels. Foreign participation was limited to 25%. The same limit applied to Spanish newspaper publishing companies. The transmission network is provided by the public company Retevision (controlled by Telefónica and RTVE among others). Retevision was created by splitting up the RTVE network into the management functions of television channels and the broadcast of signals. At the end of 1992 a law was passed in order to regulate television through the Spanish satellite Hispasat.

In spite of initial rejection by the private television companies, in July of 1994 'the television without frontiers law' was passed, bringing the Spanish legislation in line with EU Directive 89/552.

After more than two years of debate a law regulating cable telecommunications was passed in December 1995 and the technical directions for the execution of this law were approved in February 1996. The law defines cable communications as a public service. Operating licences are awarded by a Commission with representatives from the state, the CCAA and the municipalities. Cable service franchises area will have between 50 000 and 2 million inhabitants, and consist of one operator in addition to Telefónica (a semi-public telecommunications company under the control of the government). Cable operators, with previous licences, can offer basic telephony services from 1 January 1998 in accordance with the EU telecom deregulation timetable. But paradoxically the cable operators will only operate at the end of 1998. There are about 17 companies, with foreign and national capital, preparing to enter a cable market with 12 million potential consumers.

The next area of broadcasting regulation will be local television, with many viewers in specific regions.

In 1987 the 'telecommunication regulation law' (LOT) was passed. Radio broadcasting is considered a public service, with state control of operating licences. The CCAA can provide licences to operate on the FM band. This law liberalized non-basic services (value-added services and some others) while protecting the fundamental position of Telefónica. The same law governs radio broadcasting and specifies that public stations (state AM radio and state and CCAA stations in the FM band) must coexist with private ones (in both AM and FM). Rules were incorporated to avoid ownership concentration among privately owned radio stations, and foreign capital was accepted, but in a very limited way.

After 12 years without any regulation, in April 1991 a law was passed allowing municipalities to broadcast local radio financed by their own budgets and local advertising.

The future promises a partial reform of the LOT of 1987 and the Telecommunications by Cable Law of 1995, and also new laws, including legislation for digital television.

Television organization and structure

Until 1989, when private channels started broadcasts in Spain, there were two RTVE television channels with national coverage. These channels were managed by TVE SA, a public company owned completely by RTVE. The regional third channels are also managed by public companies and dependent on the CCAA parliaments. In 1983, Basque (ETB) and Catalan (TV3) channels started broadcasting, and the Galician channel (Television de Galicia, TVG) started in 1985. By the end of the 1980s some other third channels had started operations: Andalucía (Canal Sur), Valencia (Canal 9), Madrid (Telemadrid TM3). Also, at this time, the Basque Country and Catalonia created their second channels (called fourth channels), although the legal status is unclear.

In 1989, private television (Antena 3, Tele 5 and Canal Plus) gradually began competing with public channels, starting in the bigger urban areas. Canal Plus is a pay-TV channel.

So, in the whole of Spain, there are today two public channels and three private ones, one of which must be paid for whereas the others are financed by advertising. In the Basque Country and in Catalonia viewers can also watch regional channels in their own language (one in the Basque Country, and two in Catalonia). Five CCAAs each have a regional channel. These channels are financed by advertising and the CCAA Budgets. The other CCAA do not have regional channels at present, so they only receive the five national channels. However, regional channels often cover adjacent CCAA partially.

There are about 500 illegal, local television stations in Spain, but only about 30 of them transmit regularly. They are mainly located in Andalucía (131), Cataluña (81), País Valenciano (45), Baleares (22), Madrid (17) and Galicia (15).

The 1980 legislation specified that cable and satellite television were to be used by RTVE. For this reason, TVE broadcast part of their programming to Western Europe and to Latin America, since 1990, on a single channel, TVE Internacional. The three private channels broadcast over satellite too. The Catalan television channel (TV3) has broadcast via satellite since 1995. This channel and three other public regional channels – Canal Sur, ETB and TVG – plan satellite broadcasts in 1996. RTVE has not taken any action in the cable television field, and the existing experiments were initiated some time ago by small municipalities; over the past two years the larger municipalities have also become involved. Telefónica and different companies, including media groups such as PRISA, are waiting for the end of 1998. Some important towns like Barcelona also have projects for cable television, all of which will have to adapt to the cable telecommunications law of 1995.

Radio organization and structure

The structure of radio in Spain has to be studied from two different points of view: ownership and coverage. Radio channels with local coverage can be publicly owned (*radio municipal*) or private stations; some regional radio stations are owned by public companies, which belong to regional radio and television corporations; others are private radio stations which have established regional or national networks. There is also the public national network of Radio Nacional de España (RNE), in the RTVE corporation.

In 1983 and 1990 the central government and the regional governments (where they have jurisdiction) increased the number of licences for radio stations. This has led to a strong growth in radio programming in Spain. The following are the main enterprises and corporations in this sector.

RNE (RTVE ownership) has 459 radio stations: 105 are on AM working in a network and 354 are on FM, working in four networks, one of which broadcasts different programming in each region (in Catalonia in the Catalan language). RNE also owns Radio Exterior de España, the premier short wave Spanish language station, and the third short wave station in the world, after the BBC and Radio Vaticano.

SER is the most important private radio broadcaster. It has: SER Conventional, nucleus of the commercial activity of the SER; 40 Principales, transmitting pop–rock music and an absolute audience leader in 'formula radio' in Spain; CadenaDial focusing on music in Spanish; M-80, 'formula radio' playing well-known music; Radio Olé, broadcasting Spanish music; and Sinfo Radio, started in May of 1994, which combines specialized music (classic, jazz etc.) with news. SER is almost always the leading network in audience ratings, with its standard programming and its 'formula radio' channel (classical, folk, rock and other music genres, news, health, information etc.) SER broadcasts on AM and FM. Since 1992 the media group PRISA (publisher of *El País*) has attempted to acquire Antena 3 Radio, owned by Grupo Godó (publisher of *La Vanguardia*). In 1993 SER and Antena 3 Radio became Unión Radio, owned by PRISA (80%) and Grupo Godó (20%). Now SER has about 430 radio stations and the other radio groups criticize this business operation because this concentration of ownership is against the law.

COPE (created by the Catholic Church radio stations in most towns) has over 80 stations on AM and FM, either associated or fully owned. COPE broadcasts 'formula radio' and 'conventional radio'. In 1992 it sold its participation of about 50% of the capital in Cadena Nova (formerly Cadena 13) in Catalonia. After 1993, when it expanded its capital, COPE's shareholders were: Catholic Church, 72.7%; Cartera de Medios (owned by three people, Galdón, Abelló and Loizaga), 9.7%; Caja Cantabria, 6.8%; Caja de Córdoba, 3.4%; the Spanish state, 2.4%; Información por Ondas, owned by the publisher company of the newspaper *Diariode Navarra*, 1.9%; Inversiones Estega, 1.5%; workers of COPE, 1.2%; and Autocartera, 0.4%.

Onda Cero Radio (created in 1990 by merging the RATO network and acquiring new concessions) has 178 stations on AM and FM. It is owned by ONCE, the Spanish organization for the blind.

Besides these networks with national coverage, there are regional radio FM networks, connected to the CCAA radio and television corporations, and some private networks in Catalonia and elsewhere. There are also some private stations (AM and FM) with local coverage that are not syndicated to networks, and some 400 local *radio municipal*, run by municipal councils.

Ownership and economic aspects

Public and private radio and television companies base their income on advertising. There are no radio or TV licence fees. However, public broadcasting corporations can receive funds from the state and CCAA if they do not receive enough income from advertising to finance themselves. From 1982 to 1992 TVE did not receive any state funding because of its high advertising revenue. Since 1993 RTVE has received public funds, and RNE, including Radio 5, originally financed by advertising, has also moved to state funding. Canal+ is a pay-TV channel with 1 400 000 subscribers.

Canal Satellite Digital, owned by Sogecable (Canal+) 85%, and 15% by Antena 3, has started to broadcast cinema and football by pay-per-view digital television since the beginning of 1997.

Public radio stations are financed via transfer of funds from the radio and television corporations, as they do not generate sufficient revenue from advertising.

Public media are organized in radio and television corporations, which combine the activities of both media, either nationally or regionally, in accordance with the laws of 1980 and 1983.

The private media are integral parts of multi-media groups due to market dynamics and the opportunities made available through legislation. So, the three private television channels have among their main shareholders communication groups that represent the 25% of capital that the law allows.

Antena 3 has changed its ownership several times. The ownership now is: 15% by Renvir, a member company of one of the media groups, Zeta; 25% by the press group Prensa Regional; 13% by International Investors through New York Bank; Bank of Santander, 10%; Constructora San Bernardo, 12%; the audiovisual producer José Frade, 5%; Banco Central Hispano (BCH), 6%; Obetago (owned by BCH ENDESA), 8%; Aseguradora Musine, 1%; others 3%; and 2% of capital from the bank Baresto is to be sold.

Tele 5 has the following shareholders: media magnates Berlusconi and Leo Kirch each hold 25%; [illegible] (owns the Spanish media group Correo), 25%; [illegible] (Bank of Luxembourg), 13%; Prensa Española (owns the majority of the capital of the daily newspaper *ABC*), 10%; and others, 2%.

Canal Plus has as main shareholders the French Canal Plus and the PRISA group (publisher of *El País* and one economic newspaper, books and also owner of the radio network SER; it also invests in foreign press, among other business). Each has 25% of the capital. Other shareholders are Grupo March, 15.79%; the bank BBV, 15.79%; Bankinter, 5.26%; Caja Madrid, 5.26%; Eventos, 7.89%.

Programming policies

Television programming is highly dependent on advertising income, forcing public and private enterprises to choose programmes likely to attract a large audience: light entertainment (talk shows, variety etc.), films, series and sports. Rarely do cultural programmes get shown and never in prime time, except on the two public television channels, La 2, national, and Canal 33, regional. Among the other television channels there is not a big difference between the public and the private programming policies. The only exception is the pay-television channel Canal Plus, which does not rely on advertising and broadcasts basically films and sport.

The open private television channels have created a new form of programming: contra-programming. Often no one knows which programme is going to be aired. This competition has different consequences, among them that television magazines have lost audience and money, and television channels are buying foreign programmes at the high price they have in the international market. In 1994 Spanish people spent 204 minutes a day watching TV.

Of the films shown on television channels, public and private, 58% were from the United States and only 18% were Spanish. The remaining 24% is self-production, mainly fictional (drama) output. This trend is expected to continue, due to the high audience interest in this type of programme, together with football and 'true-story' reality shows.

In the radio field, programming has two different trends: public and private radio stations on AM and some radio stations on FM base themselves on informative programmes, informal talk-shows, light entertainment shows and competitions and programmes with telephone participation from part of the audience. The other trend is the FM radio stations which specialize in 'formula radio' (classical, folk, rock and other music genres, news, health information etc.). In 1994 Spanish people spent 90 minutes a day listening to radio.

Several television and radio channels have led the way in utilizing the Internet.

Reception of foreign programmes

The use of satellite antennae has increased in recent years. There are now near 400 000 satellite antennae.

Nevertheless, the increase in Spanish television channels (to five or seven channels depending on the regions) will make it more difficult for foreign broadcasting to enter Spain. In some municipal areas, however, small cable systems are usually able to distribute satellite channels. Future development of cable and satellite will undoubtedly affect today's television industry.

Local radio and television

The law regulating television broadcasting in Spain does not permit local television, but since 1980 this kind of television has increased in many areas of Spain. Today there are about 500 local television channels, some using terrestrial broadcasting, some via cable (the majority of these stations are called *video communitario*). The majority of terrestrial stations are, in general, non-profit institutions and in some cases they receive economic support from local administrations. The cable stations operate as pay-TV with an audience of about 450 000 or 500 000 people per day. It is expected that in the near future their existence will be legalized. It had seemed that the legalization of local television was coming, but the process has been stopped by the conservative party, which wants to reform the Cable Law of 1995.

In the radio field, the law recognizes the existence of local radio stations with low power transmitters. Since 1934 there have been local radio stations, though most of the time they are used as re-broadcasters of national or regional radio programmes, either public or private. As a reaction to the lack of attention given to local radio, *radio municipal* (owned by town councils) began to proliferate after 1981, mainly in Catalonia but also in other areas of Spain. The law of 1991 allowed this kind of radio. The hottest issue was that of including advertising because it threatens the private radio stations.

Telematic media

The development of telematic media is very much in its early stages in Spain, although there have been many experiments in the fields of videotex and teletext from 1982 and onwards.

The videotex system (named Ibertex) is managed by Telefónica. It has not been very successful among either the professional or the domestic public. Nevertheless some economic sectors, such as banking and general stores, have shown interest in the system for use in developing relations with the public, and the Telefónica advertising campaign will foster future development. In 1990 there were nearly 150 000 customer equipment installations.

The teletext system depends on the television organizations, which are in charge of implementation and production of news and information given through this medium. In 1989 TVE started to offer its public service, while some regional channels (like TV3 in Catalonia) did not start until 1990. Now each public or private, national or regional, television channel offers this service. Until now, however, the lack of advertising campaigns has contributed to the poor use of teletext in Spain.

Policies for the press and broadcasting

The dynamics of the mass media in Spain are based on the interests of the publishing companies and the socialist administration. Press companies want to have a powerful position in radio and in television through the creation of multi-media conglomerates. Socialist policy is based on balancing public and private participation.

Therefore, press groups trying to gain a dominant position in television faced legal opposition from the socialist government, limiting participation to 25% ownership in the concessionaires and prohibiting a company from taking a share in more than one channel. Although the companies protested at first, most have finally decided to participate in the competition for private television.

The government has not objected to the entry of press companies into radio (even with a dominant position, as in the case of SER), but the telecommunications law of 1987 (LOT) limits the number of radio stations that a company may own in the same geographic area, in order to promote diversity.

At the same time, the regulation of mass media has in recent years tended to allow the participation of foreign companies in the ownership of media. This has been the case with the press since 1986 and television since 1988.

The government has also encouraged the involvement of the public sector in media activities, with the exception of the press. In this way, not only does TVE keep its two channels, but there are also public companies with regional channels. So, instead of giving the third channel to private enterprise, the public sector has been introduced into regional television. At the same time, central government and some CCAA governments have granted an important number of radio station licences to public networks in order to increase their presence, and municipal radio is being allowed to broadcast.

Owing to the different regulation of the television industry, it is difficult to get a picture of the whole. Following the Conservative victory in the 1996 general elections changes in the media industry have been put in train. Two Spanish general economic trends are applicable to the media: privatization and liberalization, although the conservative party and government sometimes drops its political, economic and social contradictions. There are other interrelated media trends: cabling, digitalization (and hence from both, channel proliferation), concentration of ownership and media activities, convergence between telecommunications, cable and television.

The debate surrounding the cable telecommunications law lasted more than two years because foreign and national lobbies have sought to get into the cable industry, their interest stemming from the possibilities of convergence between telecommunications, cable and television.

Statistics

(1 ECU = 164.5 pesetas)

Population (1995)

Number of inhabitants	39 433 942
Geographical size	504 782 km^2
Number of inhabitants	78 per km^2

Broadcasting (1996)

Households receiving terrestrial TV	99%
Number of national TV channels	5
Public (TVE1, TVE2)	2
Private (Antena 3, Tele 5, Canal+)	3

Number of regional channels (all public)	9
ETB1, ETB2, TV3, Canal 33, Canal 9, Canal Sur, Telemadrid, TVG, Telemurcia	

Audience share

Total				26.362 million	
Percentage	1992	1993	1994	1995	1996
TVE1	32.6%	29.8%	27.6%	27.6%	27.7%
TVE2	12.9%	9.6%	9.8%	9.2%	9.2%
Regional channels	16.5%	15.6%	15.2%	15.5%	15.4%
Private channels	37.2%	44.4%	46.6%	—	—
Antena 3	14.7%	21.1%	25.7%	26.0%	25.0%
Tele 5	20.8%	21.4%	19.0%	18.5%	19.5%
Canal Plus	1.7%	1.9%	1.9%	1.9%	2.0%
Others	0.8%	0.6%	0.8%	—	1.2%

Radio

Number of national channels	15
Public (RNE)	5
Private (6 SER, 2 COPE, 2 Onda Cero)	10

Audience share

	1992	1993	1994	1996
SER Conventional	2677	2691	3193	4007
SER Fórmula	2989	2907	3102	3790
CadenaDial	930	1164	1385	1672
RNE	3211	3218	3086	3274
COPE	1928	2891	3548	4056
Onda Cero	1510	2282	2543	2726

The press

Circulation of the 10 principal newspapers

	1992	1993	1994	1995
El País	407 269	401 258	408 267	420 934
ABC	304 089	334 317	321 571	321 573
El Mundo	173 766	209 992	268 748	307 618
La Vanguardia	206 829	208 029	207 112	203 026
El Periódico de Catalunya	180 992	185 517	193 576	215 581
El Correo Español	136 616	133 954	137 647	135 840
La Voz de Galicia	106 678	107 446	113 086	108 753
Sports newspapers				
Marca	287 646	333 396	421 294	475 002
As	151 512	140 213	121 793	113 559
Sport	78 201	88 972	100 405	101 193

Advertising share (%)

	1992	1993	1994	1995
Television	36.2	39.0	39.2	39.5
Newspapers*	27.3	26.3	27.07	36.2
Magazines	23.0	16.2	14.2	13.9
Radio	6.5	9.7	9.8	10.3

*Including Sunday and other supplements.

References

Anuncios (weekly). Madrid.
Boletín de la Oficina de Justificación de la Difusión (monthly). Madrid: OJD.
Estudio General de Medios. Annual Report. Madrid: EGM.
Fundesco (annual). *Communicación Social/Tendencias*. Madrid.
Mateo, Rosario de, et al. (1993) *Els Mitjans de Communicació Social als Quatre Motors per a Europa*. Barcelona: Centre d'Investigació de la Communicació, Generalitat de Catalunya.
Noticias de la Communicación (monthly). Madrid.

15

Sweden

Karl Erik Gustafsson and Olof Hultén

National profile

Sweden is sparsely populated: only in the metropolitan areas does the population density exceed 100 per km^2. About 0.5 million inhabitants, 6% of the population, are citizens of other countries. About 20% of them come from Finland. Other large groups with foreign citizenship come from former Yugoslavia and Iran.

Swedish mass media can be, and are, used in the neighbouring countries of Denmark, Norway and Finland, and vice versa. Finnish is, however, completely different from Swedish, while in Finland there is a large Swedish language minority, about 6% of the population.

For more than 40 years, until 1976, Sweden was governed by the Labour Party with coalition governments on two occasions, both headed by a Labour prime minister. In the 1976 general election the non-socialist parties in parliament gained the majority. Since then the majority in parliament has switched several times, often with narrow margins. In the elections of 1988 the Greens gained seats in the parliament for the first time. In 1991, the Christian Democrats reached the same goal. Since September 1994 the Labour Party has again been governing, but without a majority of its own.

The Swedish political structure in practice consists of two blocks: Labour and the Left Party (formerly the Communist Party) face the Centre Party (formerly the Farmers Party), the Liberals, Christian Democrats and Conservatives. The Greens were for some time not recognized by the other parties as a partner in any agreements, until 1994, when the Labour minority government negotiated for its support. Historically, however, Labour and the Centre Party have often made common cause.

Since the 1950s economic life has been characterized by free enterprise and free competition. An Antitrust Ombudsman can intervene against forms of restrictive business practices which are judged to be harmful, and remove these by negotiation. These rules hold for the mass media industry as well, but the transition period from fair to free competition took longer in this sector of the economy than in other sectors. Until the mid-1980s there were two media-related monopolies left unchanged: national terrestrial broadcasting and telecommunications.

Following Sweden's entry into the European Union on 1 January 1995, the entire legislation had to be harmonized with EU rules and directives. This has caused some controversy in the mass media sector, but has in practice not yet led to any significant structural changes.

Development of the press and broadcasting since 1945

Birth of radio and television

As far back as the 1920s, the newspaper industry had already achieved a superior position in the nation, not only according to press doctrines but by actual readership. When radio was established as a public service national monopoly in 1925, it was partly on conditions set by the newspaper industry. The publishers organizations also became major shareholders in the new radio corporation.

Television came relatively late to Sweden (1956), but it quickly reached a high penetration. After five years the number of licence holders was 1.5 million, equivalent to two-thirds of Swedish households at the time, many times higher than expected. Radio had, after five years (1930), reached a penetration of about 30%. As in its efforts to influence radio, the newspaper industry succeeded in preventing the new medium from becoming advertising-supported. The two broadcast media were made the responsibility of a restructured national monopoly, Sveriges Radio. Besides the previous shareholders, the press and the business community, a new group of shareholders made its entrance into the public service corporation, namely various mass organizations such as blue- and white-collar unions, Churches, consumer groups etc., all representing a cross-section of Swedish society. Between them, they now controlled 60% of the shares; the other two shareholder groups were able to keep 20% each. Parliament thought this was the best way to ensure accountability to the audience as well as to balance different influential social forces in what was to become the most prominent cultural and opinion-forming institution in the country.

Sveriges Radio was, as public radio and television in Sweden still are, totally financed by licence fees. The rapid penetration of television made it possible to introduce two new national radio services and one additional national television channel during the 1960s. This did not have any negative effects on the newspaper industry. On the contrary, newspapers benefited from the general interest in what was going on in and around television. The only medium to experience immediate negative effects was the cinema.

Attacks on the broadcasting monopoly

From 1925 until 1991, the public service monopoly held exclusive rights to national terrestrial broadcasting. Attempts had been made at various times to break the monopoly. The set manufacturers, the film industry and advertisers all had their reasons to introduce competition and commercial services. As mentioned already, the influential press lobby did not, however, like the idea of competition for their advertising revenues.

As in other countries in Western Europe, ships off the coast started pirate radio stations aimed at Sweden in 1961. There was an immediate interest from the listeners, and the new stations helped to change the content of public service radio, although not the system. In 1964, the parliament asked Sveriges Radio to start a new channel for light music. In addition to the talk and information network and one for serious music and education, this increased the number of national channels to three. Still very little local or regional information was still offered.

In the early 1960s, the demand for a second television channel was pushed by industry and advertising interests. With the British system as a model – the BBC and ITV duopoly – the industry lobby wanted a second independent channel financed by commercials. It would create competition and benefit the viewers, it was argued. The ruling Labour Party did not accept the idea of commercial funding, but liked the idea of competition. A second channel opened its regular service in 1969, owned and operated by Sveriges Radio. The two channels were managed independently – with separate news services, production units, editorial staffs and with only lightly coordinated schedules. They were joined under one Director-General and one board of governors.

Public local access radio

The change of government in 1976 – with a bourgeois coalition replacing the Labour Party – led to some changes in the broadcasting system. The first dent in the public service monopoly came in 1978 with the introduction of so-called neighbourhood radio. Non-commercial local organizations of all kinds were allocated licences to broadcast anything they liked, on condition it was locally produced and did not carry advertising.

Quickly, local groups all over the country launched their own local stations. Some had the ambition to compete with the national public service light music channel, others simply wanted to express freely (local) opinions not found on the national services. From the beginning, the Churches were quickest to use the opportunity, but gradually youth and student groups, educational and cultural groups as well as local political parties became very active. In 1992, the year prior to the introduction of commercial local radio, the number of access stations was 160 and the number of organizations licensed to broadcast exceeded 2000. Since then, a number of non-commercial licences have entered the commercial sector.

Home video

Plans by the electronics industry in the 1970s to market video cassette recorders as home entertainment aroused some anxiety among the political and cultural elites in Sweden. In 1974, a government commission was appointed to specify measures to ban or restrict advertising on video. The intent was twofold: to protect advertising in the daily press and to maintain the ban of commercials on television. The deliberations of the commission passed without reaction from the government.

The growth of the home video market, and particularly viewing among young people, made brutality and prurience on video tapes the subject of debate. Prepublication censorship of recorded cassettes was demanded but rejected by parliament. The debate did, however, lead to a new article in the Constitution in 1992 banning video violence. The only content for which approval prior to publication is required by the state is films for public exhibition.

Home video recorders have become very common in Swedish households and are today found in three homes out of four. A levy on rentals and direct sales brings some revenues to the state, part of which is used to promote Swedish film culture.

Cable and satellite

Although the modern mass media, from the introduction of radio onwards, have had a considerable impact on Swedish trade and industry, the discussion about new electronic media did not take this type of effect into account initially. Cable and satellites marked a turning point.

In the middle of the 1970s the idea of a Nordic direct broadcasting satellite – Nordsat – was launched and a joint Nordic governmental commission was appointed to develop the idea. The project was unique in a number of ways, even internationally. The project was seen as an integral part of the on-going cooperation and collaboration among the five countries of the Nordic cultural family. Nordsat would also be an extension of national cultural policies, since it would make all existing TV channels accessible to viewers in all Nordic countries. In spite of this, the Nordsat project was turned down.

Satellite communications were again discussed when a new project, Tele-X, was presented. The initiative was taken by the Swedish Ministry of Industry, taking over the responsibility for Nordsat from the Ministry of Education and Cultural Affairs, and making Tele-X an industrial policy issue.

Sweden sought collaboration with Finland and Norway in developing Tele-X. Denmark had withdrawn from the negotiations already during the Nordsat discussions and Iceland had little participation. After long negotiations on the distribution of costs and problems pertaining to employment policies between Norway and Sweden, an agreement was finally reached in March 1983. Later Finland joined the project. The other countries made a point of designing the beam so that it would reach Iceland. The Tele-X satellite was expected to be launched in 1986, was finally launched in 1989 and again became a wholly Swedish-run project.

Yet another example of the influence of industrial policy on media development can be found in the discussions regarding cable TV. The

Telecommunications Administration estimated that cable TV could provide employment for 3000 workers per year for seven years, which made the project attractive. Another reason to invest in cable TV was to protect the telephone monopoly, as cable TV could be used for telephone services. Almost all Swedish households have satisfactory TV signal reception conditions; there has been no pressure to install cable systems to improve reception of public service television.

In 1982 a government commission was appointed to analyse cable and satellite techniques from a number of points of view – maintaining the broadcasting monopoly and the ban on television advertising, the role of the daily press in the Swedish democracy, and the issue of violent videos.

The commission on cable and satellites concentrated its work on regulation of cable systems for mass media use. A cable law was enacted on 1 January 1986 (subsequently reviewed and changed in 1992).

Initially the Telecommunications Administration was the main actor on the cable and satellites scene. Gradually, this picture has changed. Other actors have shown interest in becoming cable network owners or operators – local authorities, public utility companies as well as private companies and housing cooperatives. The interest in satellite television increased after the introduction of the Swedish-owned commercial channel Scansat TV3 and the pay-TV channel Filmnet in 1987.

The press

Policy framework

In 1766 the Swedish parliament adopted a Freedom of the Press Act as a part of the Constitution. The present Freedom of the Press Act dates from 1949. Public censorship is explicitly forbidden (with the exception of films for public exhibition in cinemas) and there are no restrictions on publishing and distribution.

The press freedom is safeguarded in a number of ways. Any periodical appearing at least four times a year must appoint a responsible publisher, alone accountable for any violation of the law. Another measure is that the law explicitly prohibits the investigation or disclosure of sources. This protection is extended even to state and municipal employees. A third measure is the principle of free access to public documents (introduced in 1766), which gives anyone the right to turn to a state or municipal agency and ask to be shown any document. The right of access is guarded by a parliamentary ombudsman.

In 1916 Swedish press organizations set up the Swedish Press Council to guard against abuse of the liberties of the Constitution. The first Code of Ethics was adopted in 1923 and the present Code in 1978. The aim of the code is to uphold high ethical standards, particularly, to protect against damaging publicity as invasion of privacy, and defamation. In 1969 a Press Ombudsman was established to supervise the adherence to the Code of

Ethics. Serious cases are filed by the ombudsman with the Press Council. The findings of the council are published in the newspapers in question and in the trade press, and offending newspapers have to pay a fine.

There are no laws in Sweden against concentration of media ownership. A proposal was drawn up in 1980 by a parliamentary commission preventing mergers and cross-media ownership in the media industry, but the Labour government in power decided not to introduce any bill in parliament.

Circulation

In 1996, there were 95 high-periodicity newspapers (4–7 issues per week) and 72 low-periodicity newspapers (1–3 issues per week). The total circulation was 4.3 million copies, equivalent of 464 per 1000 inhabitants. This represents a 10% reduction compared to five years earlier. Circulation has been hurt by the recession and higher subscription prices, while daily readership has stayed the same. On an average day 72% of the population (9–79 years of age) read a morning newspaper. Morning newspapers reached their highest circulation in 1990, while afternoon tabloids have been on the decline since the early 1970s.

In Sweden the daily press has always been mainly regional and local. The only exceptions are two Stockholm tabloids (*Aftonbladet* and *Expressen*) sold on a single-copy basis.

As most Swedish newspaper editorials advocate party political programmes, the political structure of the press is also a debated issue. There is a discrepancy between the political line-up of the newspapers and the political preferences of the electorate which puts socialist parties at a disadvantage. However, the newspaper market is governed by economics, not by political power structures. Newspapers derive their revenue from sales to readers and to advertisers.

There are a number of general state subsidies to the daily press: exemption from value-added tax on subscription and single-copy sales and lower tax on advertising than other media. There are also a number of selective measures in the form of subsidies to individual newspapers. The government introduced 6% VAT on newspapers in 1996.

Permanent multi-million subsidies

The number of Swedish newspapers declined sharply during the postwar era, resulting in an increasing number of one-newspaper communities. Since the beginning of the 1960s the structural development of the daily press has been under close official surveillance. In order to prevent newspaper closures and counteract concentration of ownership a series of measures have been taken since the end of the 1960s.

By the end of the 1980s an elaborate system of subsidies was in place. In 1996, direct subsidies to 'low-coverage newspapers', i.e. those with not more than 40% household coverage in their place of issue, totalled approximately Skr400 m (45 m ECU). These selective subsidies amounted to some

3% of the total operating revenues of the newspaper industry. In addition, subsidies of about Skr75 m were extended to newspapers participating in joint distribution schemes.

The objective of the press subsidy programme, introduced around 1970 and reviewed and debated by seven press commissions, with the latest publishing its report in 1994, has largely been realized. There are still (Spring 1997) 20 communities with two competing newspapers (although besides the dominant paper most of the competitors have a low household penetration). Newspapers receiving subsidies are, however, economically dependent on the subsidies. The newspaper industry as a whole is profitable today, and the owners of the subsidized newspapers are working hard to increase their productivity, marketing skills and to secure the appropriate ownership structure.

Ownership and finance

Swedish morning newspapers, which are mainly subscriber-based, derive about two-thirds of their revenue from the sale of advertising space, and about one-third from sales to readers. For afternoon newspapers, single-copy sold tabloids, the revenue structure is the other way round: one-third from sales of advertising space and two-thirds from sales to readers. Subsidies for low-coverage newspapers give the recipient newspapers, only high-periodicity morning newspapers, an average revenue increment of 15–20%. The subsidies are financed by tax on all advertising.

The 15 biggest newspaper owners accounted for about 75% of all newspapers with at least three issues per week, as well as about 85% of their circulation. The largest newspaper group is the Bonnier Group, which includes the two metropolitan morning newspapers *Dagens Nyheter* and *Sydsvenska Dagbladet*, the tabloid *Expressen*, the business daily *Dagens Industri* and 50% of the tabloid *Kvällsposten*. These account for 24% of the Swedish newspaper circulation. The Labour Party newspaper group, The A-pressen, previously the second biggest in Sweden, ran into great financial problems and was totally restructured in 1993–4. In 1996, second and third places were held by the tabloid *Aftonbladet*, owned by the Norwegian Schibsted group (9% of total circulation) and the Hjörne family group of Gothenbourg (8%).

A new phenomenon in the Swedish press (also unique in Europe) occurred in early 1995. Kinnevik launched a free morning paper (5 days/week) in Stockholm, aimed primarily at those who travel by public transport. A small editorial office relying basically on wire news, contemporary layout and advertisements attract a fairly extensive readership. *Metro* claims a circulation of 240 000 copies, which gives it the second highest level of morning paper circulation in the capital.

The Bonnier Group is the largest media group in Sweden. Besides publishing newspapers it publishes books and weekly/monthly general magazines and trade journals, database information services, has interests in

Table 1 *Five major groups of the national and regional daily press by turnover in 1980, 1989 and 1995 (%)*

	1980	1989	1995
Bonnier Group	22.5	25.8	28.0[a]
Hjörne Group	8.1	8.7	10.0
Aftonbladet (Schibsted)	16.5	14.8	7.3[b]
Wallenberg (*Svenska Dagbladet*)	4.6	5.5	5.2
Ander family	3.5	3.6	3.8

[a] Including *Sydsvenska Dagbladet* and 50% of *Idag*.
[b] Previously the A-pressen group.

Source: The Information and Mass Media Research Unit, Gothenbourg School of Economics.

film and video distribution, cinemas, as well as television (TV4, programme production and distribution).

The Swedish newspaper industry is still predominantly controlled by domestic owners. In 1996, however, the first newspaper to be sold to a foreign owner was the tabloid *Aftonbladet*, previously trade union-owned. The new owner, the Norwegian newspaper group Schibsted, publisher of conservative newspapers in Norway, has pledged to retain *Aftonbladet*'s Social Democratic editorial orientation. Swedish publishers have become increasingly active in the neighbouring countries. Biggest investor in foreign countries is the Bonnier Group, with shares in newspapers of all the Nordic countries as well as in many of the Eastern European countries and France. It would still most likely be a sensitive decision to sell a newspaper to foreign owners, although nothing in the law prohibits it. The reason for expanding abroad is primarily structural: there is little room for expansion in Sweden.

Electronic media

Legal framework

For more than 30 years, broadcasting was regulated by the Telecommunications Law and an Enabling Agreement between the designated monopoly and the state. The Radio Act introduced in 1956 specified the privileges and obligations of the licensed national broadcaster. The Agreement contained, and still does, some additional contractual requirements. As new services were introduced outside the national public service organization, corresponding laws were introduced: for non-commercial community radio (1979), cable (1986), commercial local radio (1993) and satellite broadcasting (1993). All these separate laws were merged into a comprehensive Radio Act in 1996.

The general framework for national terrestrial broadcasting as laid down in the Radio Act of 1996 and in the operating licences issued to each broadcaster by the government requires catering to a broad range of interests and impartial information. A Radio Council is empowered to raise objections – or to consider complaints from the general public – to specific programmes after they have been transmitted. The Radio Council is appointed by the government.

The regulation for community radio and (commercial) local radio do not specify the content of programmes. Community stations may today be commercially financed but are still prohibited from networking. Commercial local radio may be networked, but the licence holders have to be autonomous; no one may own more than one. Newspapers may not control a station. In practice, however, all but a few of the more than 90 commercial stations are closely integrated into four more or less national networks.

According to the Radio Act, the building and operation of cable networks is unrestricted, as well as the supply of contents. There are two restrictions (1) a must-carry rule stipulates that all nationally licensed broadcast services, as well as one local public access channel, have to be carried on the networks; (2) cable-originated broadcasts have to adhere to the same rules on advertising as in the Radio Act.

Satellite broadcasting follows the same principles as cable: broadcasting from a Swedish satellite to audiences in Sweden only needs to follow the rules on advertising set out in the Radio Act. Conditions for satellite broadcasts originating in other countries within the European Community follow the TV Directive, which is somewhat less restrictive than the Swedish law on advertising.

There are today three general types of broadcasting in Sweden, apart from transnational signals entering the country: national public services, commercial services (satellite, cable or terrestrial, national or local) and public access local broadcasting (radio or cable).

Organization of national public service broadcasting

The organization of the Swedish Broadcasting Corporation, the national radio and television monopoly established in 1956, was changed in 1979. A parent company was created with four subsidiaries: television, national radio, local radio and educational broadcasting. In 1992, the present structure was implemented: three separate, autonomous companies, each wholly owned by a state foundation, operate television, radio and educational broadcasting services. A balance of political influence and independence is attempted through the representation on the four separate boards of governors of the foundation and the three broadcasting companies.

There are today four national public radio services operated by Sveriges Radio, each with its distinct profile. Channel One is talk and news, Channel Two serious music, minority and educational services, Channel Three youth-oriented with a mixture of music and information, and Channel Four with 25 regional stations plus network programmes for an older audience. There are two national TV networks, SVT1 and SVT2. The public broadcasters are required to produce at least 55% of their own programmes in the regions outside the capital. Sveriges Television, the public television company since 1987, schedules all regionally produced programmes on the SVT2 network.

The state has full control over the transmission networks through a wholly owned transmission company, Teracom, which also services the terrestrial commercial network, TV4.

Parliament decides annually on the licence fee to be paid by every household with a television set. Since 1990, there is only one fee, for television (1996 Skr1476 annually), collected by a subsidiary of the public broadcasters. Advertising is not allowed on public radio or television. However, sponsoring was allowed in 1992 of major live events which would take place regardless of the transmission.

In 1996, licence fee revenues totalled Skr5006 m, out of which 60% were allocated to television, 35% to radio and 5% to educational broadcasting. In addition to the licence fees, sales of programmes and technical services and sponsoring bring in some additional money.

It is very unlikely that the licence fee will be raised in real value in the future. In real terms, it is still roughly on the same level as in the 1980s and the number of licence-paying households is not growing. New services or increased costs have to be met by increased productivity. The discussions about future financing of public broadcasting have focused on two issues: introducing advertising or reducing the size of public broadcasting. The question whether public television can engage in pay-TV to augment its revenue base has been controversial. Although accepted by government in principle, it is strongly resented by the Conservative Party.

Commercial television

Commercial television had to circumvent the Radio Act, which until 1991 did not allow advertising. The first two channels to break the monopoly were TV3 and Filmnet in 1987. Both were carried by satellite to their Swedish viewers, and still are. TV3 was launched by Kinnevik, a forestry, steel and communications conglomerate. Filmnet was started by a Swedish office equipment, printing and publishing business, Esselte, as a joint venture with Dutch and US investors. Today, the pay-TV operator is owned by Canal Plus from France.

Additional advertising satellite channels were started in 1989 and 1990 respectively. One is today called Kanal 5 and is controlled and operated by US companies registered in Luxembourg (private investors and Disney/ Capital Cities). The second is called TV4, which two years later became the first (and only) licensed terrestrial channel. TV4 is today the prime rival to the public channels and its share of viewing equals them. Biggest owners are the Wallenberg group, the Bonnier group and Kinnevik.

From the humble beginning in 1988, commercial television in Sweden has grown considerably. There are today seven commercial channels and four pay channels for a market of 3.6 million households. In addition, Swedish

Table 2 *Television viewing in Sweden, 1996 (total population 3–99 years of age)*

	Av. daily reach (%)	Av. daily share (%)	Penetration (%)
SVT1	51	24	100
SVT2	45	25	100
TV3	20	9	54
TV4	48	28	99
Kanal 5	13	6	50
All other TV	—	8	Varying
Total TV	76	100	—

Average daily viewing time is 140 minutes.

Source: MMS TV-meter service

versions of some pan-European satellite channels, Eurosport Nordic and Children's Channel for example, are offered.

Swedes interest in commercial television has indeed increased, but the public channels have been able to keep their positions rather well considering the competition. There is a favourable opinion among Swedes towards the licence, 60% of the population consider it to be good value for the money; 40% are negative towards advertising. Both figures have become higher in recent years.

The three terrestrial channels (SVT and TV4) naturally have a lower share of viewing in cable and satellite households, but not more than 4 percentage points each in 1996.

In order to compete better, the satellite channels TV3 and Kanal 5 (Femman) have been forced to invest more in domestic programming, resulting in higher costs. TV3 has been profitable since 1991, but has seen net results dwindle since the first half of 1995. Kanal 5 did achieve a positive operating result for the first time in 1995, but has so far not been able to pay off its accumulating losses. It has been rescued only by several infusions of new capital. Competition in the pay-TV market is also fierce, between Kinnevik's TV1000 group and the Canal Plus Filmnet channels

Local radio and television

Local, or rather regional, radio and television services are provided by the national public service companies. In television, the ten production centres of SVT broadcast their own news on weekdays. In public radio, 25 regional stations organized in the fourth network, offer their own programming every day.

TV4 also supports a number of regional, affiliated regional stations, transmitting news and information during 'windows' in the TV4 schedule. Today, 15 affiliates are in operation, with varying degrees of success.

Non-commercial community radio stations, of which there are about 160 in the whole country (1996), have lost much ground to the new commercial stations. In communities with weak advertising markets they can still play a role as the local medium, however.

Commercial radio comprises around 85 stations (1996), organized in four networks. Licences were sold at auctions to the highest bidders in 1993–5 and they can be freely resold during the licence period. Four foreign owners have entered the market; biggest of them is the French NRJ network, controlling 21 licences. Few, if any stations, had become profitable in 1996. Intense marketing, cost reductions and restructuring in a number of networks have improved results for the leaders in the market.

Local TV services on cable are few and financially weak. Around 20 local access channels broadcast anything from a few hours per month to several hours daily. They may today accept sponsoring but not spot advertising. A cable-originated commercial channel (Kanal 21) is struggling to survive (1996). A home shopping service is reported to be in the black.

The financial base for expansion of radio and television in Sweden comes from the growth of advertising and to some extent pay-TV. From nothing in 1987, television advertising in 1996 accounted for 18% of all traditional media advertising, the volume of which also has expanded. The rate of growth of TV advertising revenues has tapered off since 1995. Radio advertising after one year reached a share of 1% of all media advertising in 1994. It is predicted to grow to a level of about 3–5% within a few years and then level off.

Total turnover in television in 1996 was about Skr7.6 bn, to be divided in three parts:

Licence fees, public service TV	43%
Advertising, commercial TV	33%
Subscription TV, pay and cable	24%

New distribution technologies and their implication

In Sweden, as in many other countries, there has been much talk about new media technologies, i.e. convergence between telecommunication and television, as well as multi-media developments. Less has materialized so far, however. Nevertheless, it is necessary to give a short overview of plans and actions because they carry the embryo of future developments both in terms of new services but, equally important, in terms of new kinds of actors and business logic in the media field.

The Swedish national telecommunications administration was renamed Telia in 1993 and incorporated as a commercial enterprise in 1994, although still 100% owned by the state. In the future, a part of its shares might be sold on the stock exchange to facilitate supply of investment capital.

Telia very early took an active part in the development of cable systems in Sweden, and today is the biggest cable operator via its subsidiary Svenska Kabel TV. In 1995, Telia created a multi-media division comprising cable, telemarketing and other information services. The telecom operator hopes that its new division, Tele Media, will account for 15% of total turnover in the year 2001. Value-added services are necessary, since basic network operation will yield less profit and be exposed to intense competition in the future.

Enhanced cable services, interactive video services and multi-media entertainment are all part and parcel of the strategy of Telia and others.

Other telecom operators are also owners of cable TV systems, such as Kinnevik's Tele2 and Singapore Telecom, which in 1994 acquired the biggest cable net in the capital, Stockholm. The Swedish capital has the highest per capita telephone density in the world; Sweden has one of the most liberal telecom laws in the world and Singapore Telecom certainly is counting on using the cable system as a basis for future value-added information services to private households as well as to businesses.

The next few years will probably see intensified rivalry between not only telecom and cable TV operators. Digital satellite service providers will launch a new line of services intended for DTH (Direct-to-Home) reception. In practice, they compete with cable services as well as established terrestrial channels. In addition to these technologies, Sweden might follow the UK and decide upon building a digital terrestrial distribution system for radio and television with expanded channel capacity. DTH and cable will then have to compete with over-the-air channels. It is impossible today to predict which of the technical scenarios will be the dominant one. Suffice it to say that the outcome will also determine the parameters for future electronic media policies in Sweden.

It is far from clear what channels and services Swedish viewers and Swedish households would like to have and pay for through all the new technologies. In the mid-1990s, it seems consumer confusion about digital services and digital standards of technology is widespread. Interactive technologies seem to have a long way to go before they pose any threat to established one-way conventional television.

What is clear already, however, is that the business climate will change as a consequence of these still embryonic technological changes. New actors bring new sets of values and different traditions. The ethos of publishing will more and more be replaced by for-profit information services with a retailing perspective. Publishers will compete directly with service packagers and marketers. Conditional access technology makes all content available at a specific fee for each individual user/household. It ceases to be a public good, as in conventional broadcasting.

Policies for the press and broadcasting

No coherent policy

Two main moves have been made towards a coherent mass media policy. In the middle of the 1970s, the Swedish Council of Culture suggested that public service broadcasting policy as well as press subsidy policy should be regarded as branches of a general cultural policy. The cultural policy goals were laid down by parliament in 1974, and imply: extended freedom of expression, a responsibility for society to further a full, comprehensive cultural life, to counteract the negative effects of commercialism, to contribute to artistic and cultural regeneration, to further decentralization, to increase people's opportunities for cultural pursuits of their own, to take into consideration the experiences and needs of neglected groups, to safeguard and bring culture of bygone times to life, and to further exchange across linguistic and national frontiers. Cultural aspects were integrated in the public service broadcasting policy, but cultural policy did not become the common denominator of mass media policies.

In 1982 a non-socialist government appointed a commission on mass media with broad terms of reference. Whether this initiative ultimately would have produced a policy for all media – or all new media – will never be known, for after the election the same year a new, socialist government altered the thrust of the commission's work. The new directives made the Commission concentrate mainly on the regulation of cable systems. This means that, in effect, all Swedish media commissions so far have been single medium commissions, although some have had more than one medium in their terms of reference. A coherent mass media policy seems beyond reach. The demand for such a policy might even be seen as an instrument to challenge the medium-by-medium policies, i.e. the prevalent public service broadcasting policy and the existing press subsidy policy.

The initiatives on media development directions taken by the other actors – the industry, the Telecommunications Administration, the public service broadcasting corporation, and so on – have pressed forward in the direction of increased commercialization of all media markets, which indirectly support the idea of a coherent mass media perspective. The fact that all media industries are commercially financed have introduced several common elements across the field, as well as direct corporate integration. Public support of certain mass media must be based on valid concepts of how media operate in and serve a modern democratic society. Key concepts in the media policy for the 1990s seem to be related to the prefix national: to protect national control of vital media institutions, to support national production and defend national cultural identity.

Main issues

At the end of the 1980s, the issue of advertising on television became the main issue on the political agenda for mass media. After several years of growing satellite and cable television activity, and subsequently also of advertising revenues, the Swedish parliament decided in 1991 to change the Radio Act and permit commercials. The main reason for this change of mind was to make sure that some of the commercial revenues could be used for domestic productions. Parliament also determined that public television would not be opened for advertising. In November 1991, TV4 was selected, among originally more than 30 applicants, by the government as the best candidate for the new national terrestrial licence. In return for the privilege of having exclusive rights to terrestrial advertising, TV4 pledged to meet the obligations of the Radio Act and of its own Enabling Agreement with the state.

Within a year after its launch in March 1992, TV4 had become an economic success and could be listed on the Stockholm Stock Exchange in 1994. Its two commercial rivals, TV3 and Kanal 5, suffer from a severe disadvantage: advertisers prefer to reach the whole country rather than just the satellite-connected half of the population. TV3's owner, Kinnevik, is subsidizing DTH equipment in private households to expand the universe of TV3.

If and when satellite distribution reaches a penetration level of more than 75% of the population (instead of 54% 1996), then the Kinnevik strategy could become a winner: the cost of distribution compared to terrestrial transmission is much lower and parliament can make no demands on expensive domestic drama, news or children's programmes. Digital satellite distribution also facilitates introduction of pay services, regarded as the most interesting part of TV in the future.

The Swedish government in December 1996 proposed that digital terrestrial television be introduced in Sweden in two phases. First, a trial period of a limited scope of up to four years from 1998, during which time different kinds of television and other digital services will be tested. On the basis of the outcome of this market test, a definitive decision will be taken on the number of multiplexes to be established and the conditions for digital broadcasting. Parliament supported this strategy in April of 1997. The reason for this cautious strategy is the great uncertainty concerning the speed and nature of the digital conversion. A recommendation in early 1996 to the government to establish quickly a fully developed digital national terrestrial network (with as many as 24 channels operating within 5–6 years) was heavily criticized because of this uncertainty as well as the perceived consequences for national broadcasting policy.

In the mid-1990s, three other issues are prominent on the political agenda for the media. One concerns the traditional press support policy, another the consequences for the media of Swedish entry into the European Union, the third issue is what the effects of interactive, multi media technologies (IT) might be on the mass communication system and society.

Since its introduction in 1971, press subsidies have been debated both as a principle and as to their practical effects on the structure of the press. The main trend in the role of the press in the past 25 years is a shift from looking at newspapers predominantly as instruments of democracy, i.e. carriers of news, information and political opinions. Gradually and increasingly, as newspapers are recognized as businesses and parts of commercial conglomerates, the question arises whether the present policy is appropriate. The newspapers cannot be viewed in isolation from other media any longer. Press support, the 1994 Press Commission wrote in one of its reports, is probably still for some time necessary to maintain a degree of competition on the few markets where there still are competing newspapers. In the long run, however, such support needs to be based on what role different mass media actually play in a democratic society today. Rather than protecting a particular structure of the newspaper industry, public support for any mass medium should be based on a general model of democracy.

Harmonization of Swedish laws on the media with the rules established within the EU touched upon many aspects, from VAT on newspapers to the constitutional protection in Sweden of access to public documents. Harmonization not only affects the media legislation outlined in the foregoing; it also has repercussions on the media through changes in the laws regulating competition, the right to privacy and, debated most intensively, public access to official documents. This access has been a part of the Swedish constitution since 1766, and it is one of the most hallowed principles set out in the Freedom of the Press Act. The principle is a mainstay of accountability in public government and important to journalists as well as citizens. The principle deviates radically from tradition within the EU.

The debate concerned the strategy for protecting the principle after joining the EU and the consequences of EU policy prevailing in cases of conflict between the two. The Swedish policy does not guarantee openness on the part of Swedish authorities. But its status and long standing has made it a vital feature of the public sphere in the country. Critics of what was seen as too lenient an attitude towards the EU's more closed tradition, hope that Sweden might be instrumental in opening it up, giving support to demands already heard from within the EU.

As in the EU, the issue of media concentration is high on the agenda. The European competition law does not seem to give much support to those who would like to stop the accelerating integration in media industries. In March 1995, the government appointed a Media Council, with a single mandate to monitor developments in the media sector. The council has been invited to suggest policy measures to hinder excessive concentration of ownership and control, should it find such measures warranted.

Interactive multi-media and the evolution of cyberspace is sending its psychological chock waves into the Swedish media industry and society as elsewhere. In economic and structural terms not much has happened. A minute minority of Swedes are equipped with powerful modems to be able to enjoy the new technologies and the services they offer. A number of consequences are tangible enough to demand public reaction. Copyright issues trouble the business through pirating of software and programs as well as controversies with producers and creators regarding future exploitation. Apart from property rights, the new technology blurs the distinction between private communication and mass communication as codified in the constitution and especially the question of who is responsible for the content. The protection of individual integrity as codified in the Swedish data protection law from 1973 is rendered obsolete by the new information technologies.

The government has started a review of several of the most important concepts in the Swedish legislation on the media and freedom of information in light of the experiences of the IT evolution so far. The problem is, of course, that such a review has to take aim at a fast-moving target. Most likely, economic self-interest will guide the developments until a new balance has been found which in its turn can be codified into new laws. To be sure, the present wave of new digital technologies will have long-range effects on traditional mass media systems that are much more dramatic than anything since the birth of the daily press 250 years ago.

Statistics

(1 ECU = 9.30 Swedish kroner, Skr)

All figures from 1996, except where noted.

Population	
Number of inhabitants	8 837 000
Geographical size	449 946 km^2
Population density	20 per km^2

Broadcasting	
Number of licence fees	3 366 000
Licence fee/year (Skr)	1476
Number of public TV channels	2
Hours per week, national	158
Hours per week, regional	29
Number of public radio networks	4
Hours per week, national	530
Hours per week, regional	1621
Community access radio stations	
Number of transmitters	160
Number of participating organizations	1600
Hours per week, total	8400
Commercial local radio	
Number of stations	85
Major networks (number of stations)	
NRJ, affiliated/owned stations	21
Radio Rix	25
Bonnier Megapol	13
Fria Media	10
Commercial TV	
Advertising channels	5
Kinnevik (TV3, TV6, ZTV)	
Wallenberg, Kinnevik, Bonnier (TV4)	
SBS (Kanal 5)	
Pay-TV	4
Canal Plus (Filmnet, 2 channels)	
Kinnevik (TV1000, 2 channels)	

Cable and satellite	
Households connected	2.2 million
Households subscribing	1.6 million
Households with private dishes	0.5 million

The press

Weekday circulation of largest metropolitan dailies (March 1996)	
Morning papers	
Dagens Nyheter (independent)	362 000
Göteborgs-Posten (liberal)	266 000
Svenska Dagbladet (conservative)	188 000
Sydsvenska Dagbladet (liberal)	119 000
Arbetet (labour)	79 000
Afternoon tabloids	
Expressen (liberal)	374 000
Aftonbladet (labour)	381 000
GT/Kvällsposten (liberal)	130 000

Advertising revenues (Skr m)

Provincial newspapers	3736
Metropolitan morning papers	3680
Metropolitan afternoon tabloids	672
Trade and business magazines	934
Popular weeklies	442
TV	2263
Radio	319
Cinema	96
Outdoor advertising	502
TOTAL	12 644

Media use
(reach per average day, % inhabitants 9–79 years)

Television	84
Radio	80
Subscribed morning papers	72
Evening tabloids (single-copy sales)	27
Periodicals	29
Weekly magazines	31
Records	30
Sound cassettes	25
VCR	16

References

Bagerstam, K. (1975) 'Kabelfernsehen in Kiruna', *Media Perspektiven*, 1.

Boethius, M. (1980) 'Lokalradio in Schweden nachdrei Jahren auf sicherer Basis', *Media Perspektiven*, 8.

Gustafsson, K.E. (1981) 'Pressepolitik in Schweden', *Publizistik*, 3.

Gustafsson, K.E. (1982) 'Die Diskussion ueber die Einfuehrung von Werbung im Schwedischen Fernsehen', *Media Perspektiven*, 12.

Gustafsson, K.E. (1984) 'Outlines of a Swedish mass media policy of the 1980s', *Mass-communicatie*, 4.

Gustafsson, K.E. (1992) 'Staatliche Förederungfür publizistische Vielfalt in Schweden', in G. Rager and B. Weber (eds), *Publizistische Vielfaltzwischen Markt und Politik*. Düsseldorf: Econ Verlag.

Gustafsson, K.E. (1995) 'La presse et le système d'aide à la presse en Suède', *Legipresse*, no. 4.

Gustafsson, K.E. and Hadenius, S. (1976) *Swedish Press Policy*. Stockholm: The Swedish Institute.

Gustafsson, K.E. and Weibull, L. (1995) 'Responsibility of television. National report: Sweden', in *Television Requires Responsibility*. Güthersloh: Bertelsmann Foundation.

Hultén, O. (1980) 'Future of broadcasting – public service broadcasting in the 80s', *Masscommunicatie*, 3–4: 109–22.

Hultén, O. (1981) 'Why Nordsat – why not?', *Media, Culture and Society*, 3: 315–25.

Hultén, O. (1984) 'The video trend in Scandinavia and Finland', *Nordicom Review*, 1.

Hultén, O. (1984) *Mass Media and State Support in Sweden*. Stockholm: The Swedish Institute.

Hultén, O. (1994) 'Festhalten an starkem öffentlich-rechtlichen Rundfunk. Schwedische Medienpolitikim Zeichen internationaler Konkurrenz', *Media Perspektiven*, 5: 224–34.

Hultén, O. (1995) 'Diversity of conformity? Television programming in competitive situations', *Nordicom Review*, 1: 7–22.

Hultén, O. (1996) 'Das Schwedische Rundfunksystem in Zeichen der Konkurrenz', in *Internationales Handbuch für Hörfunk und Fernsehen 1996/97*. Hamburg, pp. 197–207.

Nowak, K. (1991) 'Television in Sweden 1986: position and prospects', in J. Blumler and J. Nossiter (eds), *Handbook of Comparative Broadcasting*. London: Sage.

Ortmark, Å. (1979) 'Sweden: freedom's boundaries', in A. Smith (ed.), *Television and Political Life. Studies in Six European Countries*. London: Macmillan Press.

Pash, G. (1982) 'Nah-Radio in Schweden', *Media Perspektiven*, 12.

Roe, K. (1985) 'The Swedish moral panic over video, 1980–1984', *Nordicom Information*, 2–3 (Nordicom, University of Göteborg).

Weibull, L. and Anshelm, M. (1992) 'Signs of change. Swedish media in transition', *Nordicom Information*, 1: 37–56 (Nordicom, University of Göteborg).

Weibull, L. and Börjesson, B. (1991) *The Swedish Media Accountability System*. Department of Journalism and Mass Communication, University of Göteborg.

16

Switzerland

Werner A. Meier

National profile

With an area of 41 284 km^2, compared to its large national neighbours Switzerland is a small state. In 1994 the population was 7 037 800, more than 1 in 6 of them foreigners (1 318 265). This population is, however, unevenly distributed, duc to the topography of the country. Half of the population live in urban centres, which contrast considerably with thinly populated regions and peripheries. Swiss society is multilingual (German 64%, French 19%, Italian 8%, Romansch 1%, other 8%). The topography results in many more cultural segmentations. Therefore, the socio-cultural differences between urban and rural areas are quite evident; furthermore, Swiss society has moved in the past decade even more in the direction of a multicultural society.

The Swiss political system is highly differentiated and therefore especially complex. It functions as a direct democracy on three different levels: the confederation, the regional provinces (26 cantons) and the local communities (more than 3000). This system is the result of Switzerland's socio-cultural and socio-political diversity and creates not only various opportunities for political articulation but also a variety of tensions among interest groups on these three levels. In spite of linguistic, cultural and religious differences as well as considerable economic inequalities, Switzerland – governed since 1959 by a coalition of four parties – has managed to develop strategies for solving political disagreement by very elaborate political discourses and to reach a consensus on some basic political values, but by no means on such issues as nuclear energy, disarmament, joining the EU etc. Consequently, the political decision-making process is rather slow, complicated and often inefficient.

As the end of the decade nears, in general the Swiss economy is still on a relatively healthy footing. After three years of stagnation and recession, Switzerland finally embarked on a road to recovery in 1994. The real gross domestic product (GDP) rose in 1994 and 1995 by roughly 2%. Still, a recession in the early 1990s yielded a rising unemployment rate, of a record 5.1% by late 1993, and real income is actually declining for most people. Sixty-one per cent of the workforce are engaged in the service sector while 33% have a job in industry and 6% in agriculture. The EU countries, especially Germany, France and Italy, are Switzerland's most important trade partners: 57% of exports go to EU countries while 73% of imports come from the EU countries. In the light of these facts it is not surprising that the viability of the Swiss economy in the near future will be even more dependent on the quality of its relations to the EU. In its Autumn 1993 foreign policy report, the Swiss government reiterated its goal of EU accession; however, in deference to the December 1992 referendum verdict on the EEA, and to divisions within the ruling coalition parties, currently the government is concentrating on limiting the negative effects of remaining outside the EU.

In general the Swiss economy has great political influence on decision-making processes. Corporations and banking institutions sometimes influence politics more than do the political parties.

Development of the press and broadcasting since 1945

The development of the Swiss broadcasting system goes back as far as 1911, when the first licences for radio reception were issued, and to 1921 when the first public radio station began transmissions. Local corporations in the bigger cities ran the first radio stations in the 1920s, different regional interests in the thoroughly segmented confederation determining the broadcasts. Yet there was also an increasing demand for better coordination, for securing access rights for social minorities to the common good of a scarce radio spectrum, and for guaranteeing sufficient output of politically non-partisan and culturally responsible programmes for all segments of the population. Certainly one of the main structural tensions in the Swiss broadcasting system is the struggle between federalist (particularistic) and centralist forces, ever since the Swiss broadcasting corporation (SSR, Société Suisse de Radio Diffusion) was founded in 1931. Mainly it was fear of uncontrolled political influence and the resistance of the influential publishers that delayed the introduction of television until the late 1950s. The SSR did not go on the air before 1958 with its programmes on a regular basis. Radio and television were 'public service monopolies' from 1931 to 1983.

This proved to be a type of institutionalization which served the interests not only of the political system but also of the printed press. While advertising was forbidden on radio and permitted on TV in a restricted manner from 1964, the revenues of the press were not jeopardized by the electronic media. The institutionalization of a public monopoly – financed mainly by licence fees – prevented economic competition between print and electronic media and brought about a financially healthy private and a viable public system.

Pressure from pirate radio stations on the one hand and from the bourgeois parties and the advertising industry on the other, and the general trends towards de-monopolized broadcasting in Western Europe, forced the federal government in 1982 to give provisional licences to 36 private local radio stations in all parts of Switzerland. Furthermore, the acceptance of the constitutional art. 55bis of 2 December 1984 by the citizens provided the basis for the 'Federal Law on Radio and Television' (RTVG), which became effective in 1992. These decisions opened up the broadcasting system for new private enterprises, and a new era began for the Swiss media system as well as for Swiss media policy.

The press

Policy framework

In Switzerland, the press is still referred to in the Federal Constitution only in a terse sentence, 'The freedom of the press is guaranteed' (art. 55). Additionally, art. 55bis of the Federal Constitution, which regulates radio and television, explicitly calls for the protection of the written press. There is, however, no legal obligation on the Swiss press to fulfil a public service. Newspapers are private enterprises and depend on market mechanisms and on the rights of freedom of commerce and trade. Yet, they are expected to be more than just businesses. Swiss media policy thus typifies the democratic paradox of autonomy and obligations which characterizes the mass media. The conflicting goals of economy and state apparatus lead to diffuse expectations concerning the public and social obligations of private enterprises towards society.

Ownership and finance

In Switzerland all daily newspapers with a circulation over 100 000 are owned by multimedia companies. Ringier, the largest publishing company, owns the yellow paper *Blick* (335 143) and *Sonntagsblick* (tabloid), the leading Sunday newspaper (346 137). Ringier also publishes the weekly magazines *Schweizer Illustrierte* (210 585) and *L'Illustré* (84 513). The second largest publishing company – based on turnover – is TA Media AG, the owner of the leading quality newspaper, *Tages-Anzeiger*, with a circulation of 282 222 copies. TA Media AG also publishes the *SonntagsZeitung*, a Sunday paper with a circulation of 200 663, and has a minority share (49%) in the publishing company 'Berner Tagblatt'-Mediengruppe (BTM), which owns the leading newspaper in Berne, the *Berner Zeitung* (131 525). Both Ringier and TA Media AG are located in Zurich and each is financially controlled by one family. The other two important publishing companies in the German-speaking part of Switzerland are BaZ-Gruppe, publishing house of the daily newspaper *Basler Zeitung* (114 319), of *Weltwoche* (107 104), the leading weekly quality newspaper, the weekly paper *Sport* (50 081) and *der schweizerische Beobachter* (331 019), a fortnightly published magazine, devoted to consumer protection and practical advice etc., and AG für die Neue Zürcher Zeitung (publisher of *Neue Zürcher Zeitung* and *St Gallen Tagblatt*). The leading publishing house in the French-speaking part is

Groupe Edipresse, which controls two-thirds of the newspaper circulation with the four large dailies *24 heures* (91 096), *La Tribune de Genève* (78 104), *Le Matin* (68 324) and *Le Nouveau Quotidien* (39 546).

The leading daily newspapers in the Italian-speaking part are *Corriere del Ticino* (37 104), *La Regione Ticino* (30 538) and *Giornale del Popolo* (18 845).

Advertising provides 60–80% of subscription newspaper revenue. In the past years the indirect financing of newspapers by the advertising industry has grown. Therefore the profitability of newspaper production is more and more dependent on the viability of the advertising industry. In addition, the dependence is direct, because most of the newspapers – with the exception of some leading newspapers – have leased their advertisement columns to advertising companies. The biggest leaseholder company, the Publicitas-Gruppe, with a turnover of 1297 m ECU, controls more than 60% of the advertising placement business.

Structure and organization

Variety of choice cannot be measured by the number of different titles alone, but rather by the independence of the publishing house as well as by journalistic performance. The large publishing houses – all of them owned and controlled by Swiss capital and management – enjoy an increasing share of the market. The five most important newspapers, with a daily circulation over 100 000, are read by almost as many people as the 235 smallest newspapers, with a circulation of up to 25 000. More and more small and medium-size newspapers have been forced out of the market or have been taken over by large publishing companies. In 1995, the number of dailies – appearing at least five times a week – amounted to 102, but the number of fully staffed newspapers fell from 67 to 52 between 1990 and 1993 alone. Furthermore, hardly any new dailies are being launched. After the tabloid *Blick* was established in 1959, it took more than 30 years for a new daily to appear on the saturated market – the quality paper *Le Nouveau Quotidien*.

In conclusion: all common forms of press concentration – publisher concentration (a declining number of publishing houses), journalistic concentration (a declining number of fully staffed papers) and a concentration of circulation – can be observed in Switzerland. The movement towards concentration also leads to closer cooperation between publishing houses in the fields of logistics and printing. The trend seems to be heading towards a two-tier Swiss newspaper landscape. Only a few high circulation papers will serve the economic centres and the agglomerations, meanwhile many small newspapers have to fill the gaps, taking advantage of narrow local advertising and readership markets. However, the development takes its course according to the principle that the many who have little should be robbed of the little they have, while the few that have a lot should be given even more.

Electronic media

Legal framework

The organization of radio and television is based on art. 55bis of the Federal Constitution, which was passed by the citizens in the plebiscite on 2 December 1984. Legislation on broadcast media became the Confederation's task. The Act specifies information, education and entertainment – exactly in this order – as the main functions which radio and television are supposed to fulfil. The independence of the broadcasting institutions is ensured, and other media, especially the press, are also taken into consideration. Finally, it mandates an independent complaints authority (UBI). The Federal Law on Radio and Television (RTVG) sets out these demands in even greater detail. It states that electronic media should:

> contribute to the formation of unbiased opinion, to the diverse and factual information of listeners and viewers, and to their education and entertainment; and to facilitate their access to civic knowledge; take into account the diversity of Switzerland and its population, and to strenghten national unity and international understanding; promote cultural development and the participation of listeners and viewers in cultural life; facilitate contracts with Swiss living abroad and promote the presence of and understanding for Switzerland abroad; take particular account of Swiss audiovisual production, especially films; and take into account as widely as possible European production.

Within this system, the Swiss Broadcasting Corporation (SSR) has a special role to play. It has a legal right to a licence and to licence fees for the financing of radio and partial financing of television. This, in turn, commits the SSR to quality programming in all parts and language regions of Switzerland. In particular, its programmings have to promote mutual understanding and exchange between the various parts of the country, linguistic communities and cultures. For important factual programming, particularly broadcast news, whose appeal exceeds linguistic and national frontiers, the standard language – rather than the local dialect – should as a rule be used.

In addition, the SSR has to produce a radio channel as well as some hours of television programming for the Romansch-speaking population and a short-wave radio service for listeners abroad. Moreover, the SSR is allowed to participate in satellite television programming on the multilateral level (3sat, TV5 Europe/TV5 Canada, Eurosport etc.).

The Bienne-based Federal Office for Communication (BAKOM) and the Federal Transportation, Communication and Energy Department (EVED) are in charge of supervising Swiss radio and television broadcasting's performance. Since 1984 the Independent Authority for Programme Complaints (UBI), as art. 55bis of the Federal Constitution demands, has to evaluate complaints about the programmes. The eleven-member committee has developed a set of criteria, according to which it judges the individual programmes in the light of professional norms and social values. In practice, the procedure is as follows: within 20 days of its first being transmitted, anyone (in principle only individuals) can bring a complaint about a certain programme before the conciliation body of the broadcaster which put out the programme (*Ombudsstelle*). The conciliation body will then investigate the matter and try to mediate between the parties. If the person bringing the complaint is still unhappy about the conciliation body's findings, he or she can complain to the UBI. The complaint must be counter-signed with the signatures of at least 20 people. UBI decision can be challenged in the Federal Court. The UBI complaint procedure was originally designed to secure certain reporting standards. However, the number of complaints being brought via lawyers is growing and some proceedings thus take on a 'legal' dimension. The *Ombudsstelle* and the UBI have the difficult task of finding the right balance between freedom of opinion and pluralism for producers and viewers, and the responsibility of the electronic media to inform citizens reliably. In any case, the institutionalization of 'programme-controlling' authorities is an interesting as well as a problematic way to secure the quality of programmes and the interests of the viewers.

Structure and organization

Clause 29 of the RTVG makes no firm stipulation on how the SSR organizes itself. Currently, the SSR is registered as a private, non-profit organization but with a public mission. The SSR has a dual structure, comprising a 'professional organization' with a management structure (Director-General) and a 'parent organization' with a corporate structure (Central Council, Board of Central Council). The 'professional organization' comprises eight enterprises, a service undertaking and the SSR general management, and is responsible for programme services. The SSR and its regional societies are led by entrepreneurial bodies.

The 'parent organization' fulfils a two-way bridging function between the public and the SSR. It therefore represents the interests of the listening and viewing public in programme matters, and the interests of SSR as programme-producers in dealing with the public. In particular, in 1992 the SSR has set up Viewing Audience Councils (*Publikumsräte*) on a regional level which act as consultative bodies. The council comprises representatives from all walks of society but it does not represent the audience as such. These newly created *Publikumsräte* are independent bodies within SSR and no longer subordinate to the board of the respective regional companies. Armed with such new freedoms, their task is to establish closer contacts between those responsible for programmes and their audience. The *Publikumsrat* – made up of 26 members who normally meet once a month – must represent the interests of the audience *vis-à-vis* the programmes' producers. The councils can take an independent look at questions of structure and basic matters relating to the programmes themselves and can put forward observations, suggestions and ideas. It thus should fulfil a social and political function in general and a supervisory and cooperative function in particular. The establishment of a relationship built on trust between laymen controllers and the media professionals is not only a central prerequisite for effective dialogue, but also an uphill task. However, the members of the councils experience the whole spectrum of organizational/internal reaction 'from being loved to death, to ignorance on the part of those responsible for the making and doing'.

SSR's workforce comprises around 6000 personnel, of whom 60% are permanent staff and 40% freelancers. More than 90% of all SSR personnel are engaged in the programme, production and technical sector. Only 13% of all directors and vice-directors are women.

The SSR structure reflects the fact that Switzerland is multilingual as well as multicultural, and production facilities are distributed over all the language regions. The six radio studios (Zurich, Berne, Basle, Geneva, Lausanne and Lugano) as well as four regional studios (Aarau, Chur, Lucerne and St Gall) produce nine channels, altogether 83 468 hours of radio broadcasting annually (1995). The three television studios in Geneva, Lugano and Zurich produce individual, self-reliant programming for each of the three linguistic regions as well as a fourth special output in the Romansch language; their total output is 39 665 hours of broadcasting per year (1995). Swiss Radio International (SRI) produces daily schedules which are broadcast in four national languages as well as English, Spanish, Portuguese and Arabic, and which comprise approximately 38 500 broadcasting hours yearly (1995).

Ownership and financial/economic aspects

National radio and television, as offered by the SSR, is mainly financed by licence fees and television advertising. The federal government sets the radio and television licence fees. The yearly amount – for radio (96 ECU) and television (148 ECU) per household – is one of the highest in Europe. The total of licence revenues amount to 481 m ECU (1995) or around 70% of the total revenue of SSR. For its programme services the SSR receives 74% of the licence fees; the Swiss PTT keeps 23% for its services, which include construction, operation and maintenance of the transmission installations, 0.7% goes to private local radio stations and 2% is VAT.

For SSR, TV advertising is limited to 8% of the total programming time. The revenue from television advertising is 156 m ECU (1995) and constitutes about 23% of total SSR income. Advertising is operated by a private company (Publisuisse), in which the SSR holds a majority share. During prime time almost all available slots were sold to the advertising industry. On radio, advertising is forbidden – except for the private local radio stations. However, sponsorship is allowed on all radio and TV channels and brings in 13 m ECU or 2% of the SSR channels' income (1995).

There is also a financial compensation by the largest linguistic region for the benefit of the two smaller ones. To enable the French- and Italian-language regions to produce and receive as many programmes as German-language Switzerland, they receive an over-proportionate amount of financing. Although the licence fee revenues from the German-speaking population add up to 72% of the overall licence fee revenues, the programme producers in that region get only around 40% of overall licence fee revenues. Without such cross-subsidization – as a sort of contribution to national solidarity – it would be nearly impossible to set up and maintain a full line of television programmes in all linguistic parts of Switzerland.

Due to the restricted revenues, the SSR is forced to put together and produce its programmes rather cheaply. The SSR channels spend only 1964 ECU on average for an hour of radio and 20 000 ECU for an hour of television programming, eight times less than, for example, ZDF. Nevertheless, only 28% of the overall Swiss TV programmes are original productions – one of the lowest shares among the public broadcasters in Europe (1994).

The development of a competitive TV market has been very slow. In December 1992, the AG Schweizer Fernsehen International was granted a ten-year licence to air Tell-TV. The original idea was to produce 4–6 hours programming on the fourth national TV network. Studios were rented, staff hired and programme ideas developed. But in July 1993, even before its much delayed launch, Tell-TV was forced to declare bankruptcy. The project had been underfinanced from the outset. A financial success, on the other hand, was the start of a Swiss advertising window on RTL. Around 21 m ECU of advertising money are channelled from the Swiss-German market to Germany (1996). The estimation for 1997 is much higher. Three German private channels with advertising windows for the Swiss market could earn more than 60 m ECU. The second step planned by several Swiss publishers together with RTL would have been to establish a Swiss one-hour programme window on RTL. These plans were the source of contentious debate and were ultimately rejected by the Federal Council in April 1994. The applicants were told that the rejection of their licence application was consistent with the media policies pursued hitherto and reflected national political concerns. The Federal Council declared that it was taking account of the four languages and wanted to give an independent Swiss media landscape a chance in the future as well. Instead of the programme window on RTL, the Federal Council had given the publishers the opportunity to participate in the S Plus channel, but the offer was rejected both on principle and for commercial reasons. In the hope of spurring on cooperation between the SSR and private programme suppliers, as provided for by law, the Federal Council had granted a licence in November 1992 for a new SSR television channel, stipulating that programme slots were to be made available to licensed programme providers. S Plus, relaunched as S4 in March 1995 after a failure, ceased operation in the summer of 1997. It will be transformed to a second channel in every linguistic region. In the German-speaking part, SF2 will be launched – as a complement to SF1 and primarily devoted to sports and youth programmes – on 1 September 1997.

Programme policies

Undoubtedly the starting point for the development of programme policies is the SSR's charge and mission. The SSR, however, is confronted, especially in the TV sector, with some structural handicaps which have to be taken into consideration at the very beginning: the small, distinctively segmented Swiss market, steeply rising programme production costs in certain areas, mighty competitors from different neighbouring countries and lately from emerging local TV stations, limited financial and creative resources. Under such – partly new – circumstances, the SSR is developing programme policies which can be described under the headings 'helvetization, adaptation, commercialization'. Thus primarily the SSR is fostering news and information about 'Swiss' issues and problems. Secondly, the SSR is reinforcing the collaboration with major public service broadcasters in Europe; thirdly, the SSR is willing to take advantage of the new technologies; fourthly, the SSR is trying to survive in the different newly emerged transnational broadcasting markets with a more mass-audience-oriented programme profile in order to be able to compete in the new market environment. In general, the SSR – according to its newest charter – operates along entrepreneurial lines in order to optimize performance and enhance its position in a competitive environment. Its strategies, objectives and resources are focused on proficiency in the media market. Market success is an integral aim of the SSR programming mission. This success is measured in terms of audience ratings, market share and the reputation and viability of its programming.

Foreign media availability

Geographically determined factors such as poor television reception in many regions have accelerated the installation of cable systems in Switzerland since the early 1960s. As a result, 79% of all households were cabled at the end of 1994. Less than 10% of TV viewers are entirely reliant on a roof-top antenna. Thus, on average a household has access to up to 30 channels, including the four Swiss channels. As most of the cable systems are privately owned they show a strong interest in gearing the system to the consumers' preference, with an array of attractive foreign television channels. As a result, more than 80% of all households in the German-speaking part of Switzerland have access to at least nine general channels from Germany (ARD, ZDF, RTL, RTL2, Sat1, Pro7, B3, S3, 3sat), to two from Austria (ORF1 and ORF2) as well as to four from France (TF1, F2, F3 and TV5) and one from Italy (RAI1), apart from special channels in the German language like Eurosport, DSF, Arte or Viva. The high availability of more or less attractive foreign channels – especially in the mother tongue – has a distinct effect on the total viewing time and the audience share. In the German-speaking part of Switzerland 65% or 85 minutes daily of the total viewing time – 129 minutes on average per day (1996) – is dedicated to other than SSR channels, mostly to foreign channels. The situation in the two other linguistic regions is also precarious: 65% of the total viewing time in the French and 66% in the Italian-speaking part of Switzerland is spent on foreign channels. Still the SSR's TV programmes are able to keep their market leader position in every linguistic region – especially in prime time (6–11 pm). Their market shares were (in 1996) 36% (SF DRS), 35% (TSR) and 33% (TSI). These figures as well as the high availability rate of foreign channels, demonstrate the difficulties for the Swiss broadcasting system in holding its position in the new – dominant privatized and commercialized – national and European broadcasting environment.

Local TV and local radio

From the early 1970s the federal government allowed short-term experiments with local TV without any advertising. Although these limited experiments were more or less positively received by the local audience, they have been terminated as a result of lack of financial support by the communities.

In 1982, the experimental phase with local television was replaced by a government decree – namely the Ordinance on Experimental Local Broadcasting – that made commercial local radio and television possible. The test phase turned out to be an introductory phase for private local radio, fruit of a rather conservative and careful design in order to give all affected actors in the media sector (government, local broadcasters, the SSR, newspaper publishers etc.) time to adjust to the new situation.

In the first phase in 1983 around 30 licensed radio broadcasters went on the air, providing programmes and services for their relatively small local audiences in all three linguistic regions. At the end of 1995, around 40 private local stations were in operation. The market share of the local radio had reached 37% (German-speaking), 21% (French-speaking) and 9% (Italian-speaking). The stations from abroad are losing ground, with a respective share of 13%, 28% and 23%. The SSR channels are still market leaders, with respective shares of 50%, 51% and 68%.

Concerning local television channels, six private stations are on the air (end 1995) in cities like Zurich (Tele Züri, Züril, HTV), Berne (TeleBärn), Basle (Stadtkanal), Baden (M1). The transmission areas encompass between 200 000 and 600 000 households. The annual budgets come to 2–8 m ECU and the daily programme output – mainly news magazines and talk-shows amount to 2 hours. However, it is still uncertain if there is enough advertising money to keep the new stations alive in the long run.

Telematic media

In 1984 – also after a test phase – over-the-air teletext was publicly introduced in Switzerland on the basis of a licence given to the SSR and the Swiss Newspapers and Magazines Publishers Association, with each having a share of 50% in the production company Teletext AG. Currently, Teletext AG – now a subsidiary of the SSR – is providing short news and other services in German, French and Italian on all four SSR channels. Teletext staff are editing daily around 2500 pages of national and foreign news, sport, weather forecasts and tourism information. Shopping via teletext has also been possible since 1995. Furthermore, the teletext service is now engaged in subtitling of TV programmes and films.

In 1987 – after a seven-year test phase – the federal government decided to introduce videotex, which uses a connection to the telephone network as a link to a data bank, as a public service in Switzerland. The national PTT was authorized to market the system to subscribers and information providers, but the problem of converting a technical system to a useful public service has not yet been solved, despite early optimism. The diffusion of videotex has been rather slow until now. In 1990, PTT had attracted only 50 000 subscribers, roughly 35% of them private households. Although PTT started more than once an expensive marketing campaign to launch videotex, and although the charges and expenses for users have been massively reduced over the past years, the public service was always far from commercially viable. Not surprisingly, in 1995 a private company, Swiss Online AG, took over responsibility for the service, hoping to reach the break-even point within one year. In the meantime, heavy competition by other on-line systems and an massive increase of tariffs have curbed the hopes of the business community. The viability of the new on-line service is still very much uncertain.

Policies for the press and broadcasting

Main actors and interests

At least four interest groups influence the defining and enforcing of standards, norms, values and regulations in the Swiss media landscape.

- Transnational actors. Among these the Council of Europe is of particular importance for Swiss broadcasting policy, since Switzerland is not (yet) a member of the EU. The Swiss government and parliament, however, gave its approval to the European Convention on Transfrontier Television, whose traditional liberal ideal of free flow of information does not take into consideration the structural handicaps of small, multicultural states.
- National governmental actors. National authorities, mainly the federal government, the EVED, the parliament, the BAKOM and jurisdiction – among the last the UBI – contribute to the definition, protection and enforcement of norms, standards, values and regulatory activities. Typical for a government's strategy in a direct democracy is that it seeks consensus at almost all costs, to avoid plebiscites, whose outcomes are difficult to predict. The result of such a strategy is in any case very often a rather questionable and problematic compromise.
- Political parties. The political parties react – if at all – in the media sector according to their traditional platforms. The liberal and conservative parties in general favour the privatization of the whole media system, the

social-democrat party prefers newspapers to be as independent as possible from commercial pressure and a public broadcasting system.

- Media organizations. As powerful multipliers, on which the politicians depend to a certain degree, media organizations can challenge or even obstruct government strategies, regulations and values they judge unfavourable to their interests, with considerable success. Especially the privately owned media companies usually are only willing to comply with special social, cultural or political obligations as long as the market rewards such activities. The fact that these interests partly differ among the media, however, limits their influence on media policy.

Main issues

The essential concerns for the survival of most newspapers nowadays are an up-to-date marketing system with early morning deliveries and a wide range of special supplements. In order to be able to make the necessary investment in printing, marketing and editorial work, even the largest publishing houses are concentrating their forces through cooperation contracts on the level of printing, publishing, advertising and editorial work. This has, for example, resulted in several publishers editing joint weekend supplements or in joint advertising sections. The trend towards cooperation is being reinforced by the high marketing costs in competitive environments as well as by the Europeanization of the advertising market. The trend towards economic concentration is being intensified through the doubling of printing capacities in recent years by some large publishing companies, which will force some small entrepreneurs out of the market.

The demise of several projects, like European Business Channel or Tell-TV, has convinced most of the potential investors that the launching of a new TV channel or only a new programme is a risky business in such a competitive market. Indeed, the combination of different languages, a highly fragmented audience, insufficient advertising money, expensive programme production, exclusivity rights and marketing costs, the scarcity of creative resources and of technical staff, the lack of a viable audiovisual industry, legal restrictions for some advertising and sponsoring activities (bartering) and so on may prove to be real stumbling blocks for potential private broadcasters.

Small states, among them Switzerland, heavily depend on large neighbouring countries. They have to comply with many exterior exigencies because the passive balance of trade of their media sector will continue to be rather modest because of international counter-trends and because their legitimation in traditional liberal democracies is precarious.

The influence of advertising on decisions in Swiss media enterprises is bound to increase further, as competition for advertising revenues becomes harder and the audience becomes accustomed to getting media fare cheaper.

The regulation of the Swiss broadcasting system is moving in two directions: cautious opening to private broadcasters and at the same time securing the structures of a productive system of public broadcast, mainly for political and cultural reasons. Furthermore, there are distinct tendencies to maximize Switzerland's presence in international broadcasting while at the same time strengthening and multiplying the media of local and regional communication.

Statistics

1 ECU = 1.68 Swiss francs, Sw.fr (March 1997)

Population

Number of inhabitants (1995)	7 062 400
German-speaking Swiss (1990)	63.7%
French-speaking Swiss (1990)	19.2%
Italian-speaking Swiss (1990)	7.6%
Romansch-speaking Swiss (1990)	0.6%
Other languages (1990)	8.9%
Foreigners (1994)	19.3%

Broadcasting

Public broadcasting	
Radio licences	2 797 422
Television licences	2 623 082
Radio licences per 1000 inhabitants	396
TV licences per 1000 inhabitants	371
Annual fee (radio)	96 ECU
Annual fee (television)	148 ECU

Allocations of finances (1996)

	German part	French part	Italian part	Romansch part
Pop. language	64%	19%	8%	0.6%
Revenues				
Allocation to TV	43%	32%	24%	1%
Revenues				
Allocation to radio	44%	33%	22%	1%

Television

No. of public channels (SSR national network)	4
No. of private local channels	30
No. of hours per year (4 SSR channels only)	39 665

Division of TV audience (%) (1996, 24-hr market share, per person)

German part		French part		Italian part	
SF1	28	TSR	29	TSI	28
S4/Sport (SF2)	5	SF DRS	2	SF DRS	2
TSR	2	TSI	1	TSR	2
TSI	1	S4/Sport	4	S4/Sport	2
RTL	10	TF1	16	Canale 5	14
Sat.1	8	F2	12	RAI1	10

German part		French part		Italian part	
Pro 7	8	M6	8	RAI2	10
ARD	6	F3	8	Italia	8
ZDF	5	TV5	1	RAI3	5
ORF 1	5			TMC	2
ORF 2	3				
RTL 2	2				
Others	14	Others	19	Others	16

Radio (1995)

No. of channels (SSR national networks only)	10
No. of hours per year (SSR national networks only)	83 468
No. of local radio stations	38

Division of radio audience (%) (1995, SSR)

German part		French part		Italian part	
DRS1	38	La première	38	Rete 1	52
DRS2	2	Espace 2	2	Rete 2	1
DRS3	9	Couleur 3	7	Rete 3	8
Other SSR	1	Other SSR	4	Other SSR	7
Local (CH)	37	Local (CH)	21	Local (CH)	9
Foreign	13	Foreign	28	Foreign	23

New electronic media (1996)

Videotex subscribers	100 000
Teletext users	45% of adult pop.
VCR	60% of adult pop.
Pay-TV subscribers	95 000

The press (1996)

No. of newspapers publishing 5–7 days a week	99
No. of newspapers publishing 1–4 days a week	143
Circulation, 5–7 days a week (1996, SZV)	2 717 400

Leading daily newspapers (1996)

	Readership (000s)	Copies sold
Blick (Ringier AG)	804	335 143
Tages-Anzeiger (TA Media AG)	743	282 222
Neue Zürcher Zeitung (NZZ-Gruppe)	424	158 167
Berner Zeitung (BTM/TA Media AG)	323	131 525
Neue Luzerner Zeitung (Luzerner Zeitung AG)	310	129 000
Aargauer Zeitung (Aargauer Zeitung AG)		120 000
Basler Zeitung (BaZ-Gruppe)	240	114 319
24-heures (Edipresse SA)	299	91 096
Tribune de Genève (Edipresse SA)	216	78 104
St. Gallen Tagblatt (NZZ-Gruppe)	185	72 283

Leading weekly magazines (1996)

Schweizer Illustrierte (Ringier)	210 585
Schweizer Familie (TA Media AG)	205 529
Glückspost (Ringier)	193 141
L'Illustré	84 513

Facts (TA Media AG)	74 898
L'Hebdo (Ringier AG)	55 388

Advertising expenditures (1995, Stiftung Werbestatistik Schweiz)

Medium	Amount (m ECU)	% share
Newspapers	1168	56.0
Magazines	361	17.3
Outdoor	265	12.7
Television	208	10.0
Local radio	54	2.6
Cinema	20	1.0
Teletext	8	0.4
Total	2084	100

References

Beeli, Robert (1993) 'Das neue schweizerische Radio- und Fernsehrecht', *Rundfunk und Fernsehen*, 1: 43–58.

Bonfadelli, Heinz and Hättenschwiler, Walter (1989) 'Switzerland: a multilingual culture tries to keep its identity', in L. Becker and K. Schönbach (eds), *Audience Responses to Media Diversification: Coping with Plenty*. Hillsdale, NJ: Lawrence Erlbaum, pp. 133–57.

Bonfadelli, Heinz and Meier, Werner A. (1994) 'Kleinstaatliche Strukturprobleme einer europäiaschen Medienlandschaft. Das Beispiel Schweiz', in Otfried Jarren (ed.), *Medienwandel – Gesellschaftswandel? 10 Jahre dualer Rundfunk in Deutschland*. Berlin: pp. 69–90.

Dumermuth, Martin (1992) *Die Programmaufsicht bei Radio und Fernsehen in der Schweiz*. Basle: Helbing & Lichtenhahn.

Durrer Beat (1994) 'Die Strukturreform der Schweizerischen Radio- und Fernsehgesellschaft SRG', *Media Perspektiven*, 2: 57–62.

Meier, Werner A. (1994) 'Switzerland: television and the viewer interest. Explorations in the responsiveness of European broadcasters', in Jeremy Mitchell and Jay G. Blumler (eds), *Media Monograph No. 18*. London: John Libbey, pp. 147–62.

Meier, Werner A and Schanne, Michael (1995) *Media Landscape Switzerland*. Zurich: Pro Helvetia.

Meier, Werner A. et al. (1993) *Medienlandschaft Schweiz im Umbruch: Vom öffentlichen Kulturgut Rundfunk zur elektronischen Kioskware. Reihe: NFP 21 Kulturelle Vielfalt und nationale Identität*. Basle: Helbing & Lichtenhahn.

Saxer, Ulrich (1996) 'Das Rundfunksystem der Schweiz' in *Internationales Handbuch für Hörfunk und Fernsehen 1996/7* (ed. Hans Bredow Institut für Rundfunk und Fernsehen an der Universität Hamburg). Hamburg.

SSR (1995) *Charter of the Swiss Broadcasting Corporation*. Berne.

SSR (1995) *SBC in Brief*. Berne.

SSR (1995) *Geschäftsbericht 1994*. Berne.

SSR (1996) *Facts and Figures, 1996*. Berne.

VSW (1996) *Katalog der Schweizer Presse*. Zurich.

WEMF (1996) WEMF Auflagen-Bulletin/Mach Basic 96, Zurich.

Zoller, Pierre-Henri and Rickenman, René (1995) *Suisse. Les Télévisions du Monde. Un Panorama dans 160 pays*, compiled by Guy Hennebelle. Paris: Editions Corlet/Télérama, pp. 262–7.

17
The United Kingdom

Jeremy Tunstall

National profile

In the United Kingdom, geography and population distribution as well as language use all favour a highly centralized communications system. In 1996 the UK had a population of 58 million living in 23 million households. By European standards there is a negligible labour force engaged in farming. The population is 90% urbanized and concentrated between London and Manchester. Fifty-seven per cent of the population live in just four of the 14 commercial television regions – based on London, Manchester, Birmingham and Leeds. At least 97% of the population speak English as a first language. Among other first languages are Urdu and Welsh.

The UK has a centralized system of government, but Scotland has a degree of autonomy (including a distinctive legal system) more characteristic of a federal state. In media terms also, Scotland is the UK's most distinctive region.

Both the national political and economic systems still reflect the 'End of Empire', which occurred in the 1960s. The British continue to see themselves as performing some kind of entrepôt role in the world. This has more reality in the press, television, radio, music and telecommunications than in most other fields.

Development of the press and broadcasting since 1945

Characteristics of British media development

Gradualism – slow change, continuous evolution and policy consensus – has broadly characterized British media in the twentieth century. This slow-change, gradualist, tradition is in sharp contrast to what has occurred in most of the other West European countries in the same century.

In media policy Britain is a tortoise. In British media history there are very few key dates or key events. The modern era offers perhaps just two key dates, one each for newspapers and television. In 1896 the modern mass press was born in Britain. In this year Northcliffe's *Daily Mail* was launched as the first successful half-penny national morning daily. The key date for television in Britain was 1955; the launch of a new ITV channel entirely financed by advertising marked the birth of Britain's television duopoly.

BBC television had begun a pilot service in 1936, but even the BBC service which started up again in 1946 was still semi-experimental and subordinate to radio.

After gradualism, a second key characteristic of British media is a mixture of (or compromise between) 'commercialism' and 'public service'. The element of 'commercialism' is a powerful one; Northcliffe established the pattern of the publicly quoted company, complete with shareholders and multi-media properties. The arrival of ITV in 1955 expanded the pattern; nearly all British media companies of any significance – including many radio stations and advertising agencies – are public companies. But there has long been a powerful strain of non-commercialism; this is most obviously true of the BBC and the 'public service' element legally required of commercial broadcasters. A non-commercial element was also present in Northcliffe's newspaper empire. *The Times* (which Northcliffe bought) had long had a non-profit goal; so also the Manchester *Guardian*.

Thirdly, the British media have long emphasized the central and national at the expense of the regional. In general, the regional element has declined as the twentieth century has advanced. The British regional press saw a significant decline between 1918 and 1939 and this continued after 1945. Both the BBC and ITV emphasized regionalism in their early years; but in both cases the second channels (BBC2 and Channel Four) are purely national channels.

'Eyes West' is another long-running British media tradition. Britain has long looked toward North America for new ideas and innovations of all kinds. Northcliffe, himself, was fascinated by the US press. His successor rescuers of *The Times* were the American Astor family, the Canadian Roy Thomson and Australian–American Rupert Murdoch. Both BBC and ITV history involve an endless series of attempts to adopt American innovations without also accepting their full home-grown commercial logic.

Fifthly, British media policy-making has tended to be cautious and consensual. Britain has tried to follow America, but at some distance in time; policy-making has been deliberately slow. The arrival of ITV in 1955 was preceded by four full years of active debate, lobbying and legislation. Policy-making in both broadcasting and the press has relied on Royal Commissions which have taken up to three years to complete their deliberations. Both the Annan Committee on Broadcasting and the McGregor Royal Commission on the Press ran from 1974 to 1977.

In the press the British have followed the Anglo-Saxon tradition of no special body of press law. The general law of the land (such as libel) applies; no further law is believed to be either necessary or desirable. In practice this means that monopoly law is the major part of press law.

In broadcasting there is a body of law, but this traditionally has been minimalist and vague. The detailed decisions are left to the BBC governors and ITC (previously IBA) members. These are amateur regulators with only one individual in each case (the chairman) being a more or less full-time regulator. These amateur regulators are appointed by the government of the day, but for several reasons this indirect system greatly limits the government's power to intervene. Up to 1979 the appointments were not partisan; as amateurs the regulators tend to be 'captured' by their professional staffs; and in so far as they are active professional regulators, the chairmen have tended to put their independence and integrity in evidence by resisting the cruder blandishments of government.

British media policy has tended to be made by the Conservative Party. The Labour Party, when in power, tends to be too split to be able to reach any decision. In the two years 1977–9 the Labour Party failed to legislate on its two massive reports of 1974–7. The Conservatives also tend to be split between market conservatives and cultural conservatives. Typically media (mainly broadcasting) legislation moves slowly and reflects a high degree of consensus, within the Conservative Party, between Labour and Conservatives, and between the politicians and the main media industry lobbies.

Thatcher multiple-track media policies (1979–90)

Margaret Thatcher consistently pursued dual-track policies in many fields; there was one official Conservative government policy while at the same time a different, more radical, policy was being privately developed by Margaret Thatcher and her current ideological and political favourites. Indeed there were often more than merely two conflicting media policies. At various different times Margaret Thatcher turned her attention to the media and exercised her prime ministerial prerogative to dictate a variety of somewhat conflicting media policies. She favoured traditional 'public service' broadcasting; using new media to boost national technology policy; shaking up the ITV commercial TV cartel; providing a regulation-free welcome to foreign media; and favouring the British national newspapers. Finally, Margaret Thatcher had special policies for Rupert Murdoch, her political friend and favourite media mogul.

'Public Service Broadcasting' in the BBC tradition was especially encouraged during the first two years of Margaret Thatcher's period in office (1979–81). It was during this period that a fourth national television channel was approved; Channel Four began broadcasting in 1982 as a second 'minority' TV channel – in effect a second BBC2, but with advertising – aiming to achieve only about a 10% share of British TV viewing.

Another early Thatcher emphasis was upon high technology and the use of television to encourage high technology industries. This led to a public endorsement of very high technology versions of both cable and 'Direct Broadcasting by Satellite' (the title of a 1981 policy document). The Thatcher approach was to enthuse about, but not to finance, these high technology (and even higher cost and risk) endeavours. British industry declined both offers.

By 1985 Margaret Thatcher was becoming unhappy about the lack of aggressive competition in British television. She appointed a committee under Alan Peacock in 1985 which was intended to punish the BBC.

However, this particular Thatcher initiative ultimately wounded a different target, namely ITV. A Broadcasting Act was finally passed in 1990 and it aimed to reform ITV into a more commercial and competitive shape. For the first time direct competition in TV advertising sales (with Channel Four) was introduced; and the 1990 Act also proposed a fifth, advertising-financed, channel. The least welcome change of all was a blind auction of franchises in which the incumbent ITV companies had to bid in order to retain their licences to broadcast.

While even this radical shake-up took place in traditional British slow time, ITV between 1985 and 1995 underwent a revolution. Thames, the London weekday company, disappeared. A somewhat lop-sided ITV system dominated by six companies was transformed into an even more lop-sided ITV system dominated by three companies (each operating in two regions). More even than before, the ITV system was divided between rich and poor companies. Perhaps the most remarkable characteristic of ITV is that only about one-third of ITV's apparent advertising revenue goes into making programmes for the national network. The bulk of its gross revenue disappears in four other large pay-outs: to the national finances ('cash bids', 'qualifying revenue' and plain taxation); secondly, to the advertising industry (agency commissions, price discounts, sales and marketing expenses); thirdly, into local programming (most regional companies each make between 400 and 800 annual hours of local news and other programming) only viewed in their region; fourthly, ITV companies pay out generous dividends to shareholders in order to guard against the threat of hostile takeover bids. Consequently ITV's network programme budget is no longer big enough to compete against the satellite operator BSkyB for most sports or films, nor large enough to maintain its news service ITN as a major competitor to BBC TV news.

Margaret Thatcher also took to fresh extremes the traditional policy of favouring newspapers. During the 1980s newspaper sales continued to be exempt from VAT. There was also a de facto policy of allowing exemptions to the normal anti-monopoly provisions in the case of most proposed newspaper takeovers. Margaret Thatcher took further the pre-existing tendency to transform a press anti-monopoly policy into a newspaper preservation policy. The leading – but not the sole – beneficiary was Rupert Murdoch. The most notorious single case of this occurred in 1981, when Murdoch's British company News International was allowed to purchase *The Times* and the *Sunday Times* from the Thomson company. Margaret Thatcher's admiration for Murdoch increased in 1986 when he moved his two daily and two Sunday national papers to a massive new plant at Wapping in East London. The clash over the move to a high technology plant marked the defeat of Britain's previously powerful printing unions.

In addition to this help with his newspapers, Margaret Thatcher used her waive-and-wave approach at a crucial moment in the domestic history of Murdoch's Sky satellite TV activities. This was in 1990, just as the 1990 Broadcasting Act was passed and only just before Margaret Thatcher was removed as Prime Minister by the Conservative Party. In the summer of 1990 Britain had two rival direct-to-home satellite TV offerings. One was Britain's 'official' system, BSB, licensed by the official regulator and offering expensive programming with expensive technology; the other was Murdoch's Sky system, using a Luxembourg-regulated Astra satellite and offering cheap programming and cheap technology. Both BSB and Sky were losing money at alarming rates and by October 1990 their plans to merge were being completed. Margaret Thatcher was informed of these plans during a visit by Rupert Murdoch (29 October 1990). She evidently did not object, even though the merged BSkyB was radically at odds with the current 'official' policy of the Broadcasting Act 1990.

When Margaret Thatcher thus exercised her media prerogatives for the last time in late 1990 she probably did not comprehend the full implications of what was happening. But she almost certainly did recognize that she was making life very much harder for the BBC and ITV.

The year 1986 may go down in history – along with 1896 and 1955 – as a rare key date in British media history. (The year saw the move of Murdoch's newspapers to the new technology plant in Wapping and the report of the Peacock Committee.) Certainly several themes of Thatcher's seemingly self-contradictory media policies will continue to resonate.

- The BBC survived the Thatcher era more or less unscathed; 'Public Service Broadcasting' has survived comparatively well in Britain because the BBC has avoided the common public broadcaster error of becoming closely identified with one political party.
- Print (unconstrained by neutrality requirements) remains the medium which keeps politicians awake at night. The publishing industry (national newspapers, provincial newspapers, magazines, books), with a revenue in 1995 of about £10 bn, had roughly twice the revenue of the electronic media (TV, radio, satellite, cable) at £5 bn a year. (Print and electronic total = $23 bn.)
- During the Thatcher era Britain's position as a media entrepôt, and as both media importer and exporter was strengthened.

In addition, many leading American communications companies – especially the Hollywood majors, the cable majors and some big telephone companies – are commercially active in Britain. London and Britain have also become the biggest single European base of internationally oriented satellite television channels; in 1995 there were 66 satellite channels uplinked from Britain, including for example MTV Europe and CNN1.

The press

Legal framework

In Britain, as already noted, there is no Press Law. There is also no specific subsidy for newspapers, but newspapers still receive favourable treatment in terms of VAT.

Table 1 *UK-based international media players, 1995–6*

	Assets, subsidiaries, international activities
BBC	BBC World Service Radio, BBC World (TV News), BBC Prime (TV entertainment)
BRITE	Distributes programming from Granada, London Weekend TV, Yorkshire–Tyne Tees
British Telecom	Owns 20% of MCI (USA)
Cordiant	Formerly Saatchi and Saatchi, owns two world-wide advertising agency networks
EMI	Music labels such as Capitol (USA) and Virgin
News International	Owns UK newspapers and 40% of BSkyB; a subsidiary of News Corporation (Australia and USA)
Pearson	*Financial Times*, *Les Echos* (Paris), Thames TV, Grundy, Penguin, Viking (USA), Longman
Reuters	Data and news agency (print, photo, radio, TV); has 143 foreign news bureaux
Reed	Owns 50% of Reed–Elsevier, periodical and on-line publisher
WPP	Owns J Walter Thompson, Ogilvy and Mather

The only important body of law and regulation which specifically concerns the press deals with the issue of monopoly and competition. As previously described, there is a major loophole in the relevant law and in recent years a number of substantial mergers and purchases of newspapers have occurred. The Thatcher decade of the 1980s differed from previous decades only in that there were more mergers.

Structure, ownership, finance

In some respects, newspapers and the press have declined both relative to other mass media and also in absolute terms. Most British newspaper sales records were established in the 1940s and 1950s. In 1955 50 million Britons still bought 30 million newspapers each Sunday. But the national daily newspapers in 1996 were selling 14 million copies, just as 14 million were being sold in 1975.

The size of newspapers has greatly altered over the decades. The massive sales of the 1940s were of six page newspapers. Moreover, while total sales remained the same between 1975 and 1995, the average size of the paper exactly doubled. In any other industry this doubling of volume would be recognized as a doubling of sales. The British national newspapers, especially since 1985, have put on weight, especially in the form of numerous extra sections, reviews and magazines.

Of the 19 national newspapers of 1995–6 (ten dailies, nine Sundays), all but five changed ownership at least once during the previous two decades. There were more titles and also more titles per ownership. There was also a sharp polarization between downmarket tabloid newspapers financed by sales revenue and upmarket broadsheet newspapers funded mainly by advertising. It has been the mid-market newspapers (such as the *Daily Express*) which have suffered big sales losses since the 1950s. Competitive marketing expenditure reached new extremes in the early 1990s and led to aggressive price cutting during 1994–5. The price cutting was initiated by News International's *Sun* and *The Times* (down from 45 pence to 20 pence). Market segment leaders could sustain this, but it put great commercial pressure on competitors – especially since it coincided with sharply rising newsprint prices.

When the national newspaper managements defeated the printing trade unions in 1986, they made huge economies in printing and also closed their big Manchester offices. All of the national dailies now print in several centres but they have become more editorially national, with few staff journalists employed outside London.

Meanwhile the non-national press has become more and more local. There has been a meltdown of non-national (mainly evening) daily newspapers; the sales of such dailies have halved since 1955, with much of this loss being since 1975. But there has been a big expansion of local free newspapers – with 33 million distributed into the UK's 22 million households in 1995. Paid-for local weeklies have also declined. Nevertheless, 13 provincial cities had dailies which in 1995 sold over 100 000 copies; and there were 19 separate regional companies, each of which circulated over one million newspapers per week.

Despite a double polarization between national broadsheets and tabloids, and between more national nationals and more local locals, the total newspaper circulation stayed at around 170 million copies per week between 1975 and 1995. Circulations for 1995 are shown in Table 2.

In 1995–6 a typical British household of 2.5 people was each week consuming about four morning papers, one evening paper, one Sunday and two local weeklies.

Although 22 million households were consuming about 20 million daily newspapers, it would not be true to say that 91% of adults 'read a newspaper every day'. Although sales figures rarely show changes of more than 5% from year to year, the underlying picture is hugely more volatile. Some papers sell 20% more copies on Saturday; only one-third of UK daily sales are home delivered on order. Undoubtedly some people read different dailies on different days of the week – a pattern known by the industry as readership 'promiscuity'. Even the near doubling of *The Times*' sale after it

Table 2 *UK newspaper circulation (to the nearest million copies), 1995*

	Circulation per day	Circulation per week
National dailies	14	84
National Sundays	—	16
Regional dailies	6	32
Regional Sundays	—	2
Local paid weeklies	—	7
Local free weeklies	—	32
Total	20 million	173 million

halved its price in 1994 underestimates the true level of volatility, because, in addition to attracting new readers, *The Times* also lost about one-quarter of readers who claimed to read it 'almost always'.

Magazine readerships are, of course, still more volatile. The biggest press sales drop in recent years has been in weekly consumer magazines. As British companies have withdrawn from this declining and less profitable area, German publishers (like Bauer) have entered the mass sale women's weekly market; French publishers (like Hachette) have entered the magazine mid-market; and American magazine publishers have a strong presence at the glossier monthly end of the consumer field. Taking the ten leading weekly and the ten leading monthly women's magazines, only 7 out of 20 are 100% British.

In business magazines the picture is different. Britain is a substantial net exporter of business magazines, many of which are primarily aimed at specialist export markets in Africa and Asia. Between 1965 and 1995 the British business magazine total increased from 2082 titles to 5362 titles.

Electronic media

Legal framework

Official policy has continued to move forward at the traditional cautious pace. The current position largely depends on decisions in (and around) the Broadcasting Acts of 1990 and 1996. The main changes of 1990 were as follows.

- The old Independent Broadcasting Authority (IBA) was replaced by a more 'arm's length' commercial broadcasting regulator, the Independent Television Commission (ITC). The 15 incumbent regional ITV companies would have to engage in a blind auction to retain their licences. Three regional companies and the breakfast company lost their licences; the main casualty was Thames (the London weekday ITV company), which was replaced by Carlton.
- A fifth terrestrial television channel was to be set up by the ITC; after several delays Channel Five was awarded the licence, for (ultimately) a March 1997 launch. This was 14 years since the last new channel (Channel 4) launched in late 1982 and very much in line with Britain's traditional policy.
- The BBC was largely left alone by the 1990 Act apart from a requirement that 25% of its programming should be commissioned from independent producers.
- Channel Four's links with ITV were loosened, and in particular Channel Four would in future sell its advertising in competition with ITV.
- A new Radio Authority was established; but the Cable Authority was abolished. The ITC was the regulator for all commercial television, for cable and for satellite.

- A key 1990 provision was Margaret Thatcher's decision to circumvent her own Broadcasting Act and to allow Murdoch/News International to merge Sky with BSB, thus establishing BSkyB as effectively an unregulated monopoly satellite TV service.

In 1996 the Major government acted on three policy lines, already presented in previous policy documents.

- The BBC's Royal Charter and Licence were renewed. The licence fee was confirmed; the BBC would remain Britain's leading broadcast entity; it would continue as a 'public service' broadcaster. But it was required to develop still further its more 'commercial' style of the early 1990s. The BBC was also asked to pursue its export and 'world' role with added vigour.
- New 'cross-media ownership' rules would allow all but the two biggest press groups (News/Murdoch and Mirror Group) to buy into commercial broadcasting on a substantial scale; television and radio companies could also buy major newspapers.
- Terrestrial digital broadcasting was to commence in 1997 with one digital 'multiplex' (about six channels) going to the BBC, another to ITV, plus others to new broadcasters.

The other important legal framework change was a decision to set up a Department of National Heritage – effectively a Ministry of Culture, Media and Tourism. This department was run by a Cabinet minister, although there were four different holders of the post in the first four years. Other government departments (such as Trade) and government agencies (such as the monopoly and telecommunications regulators) retained some media policy significance, but the Heritage Department (established in 1992) was one of several signs of an attempt to consider media policy in a more comprehensive manner. The House of Commons also established a Select Committee on National Heritage.

Structure and competition

Britain did not follow the pattern common in 1980s Europe of suddenly doubling its number of television channels. However, since the launch of Channel 4 in 1982, TV competition year-by-year became relentlessly more competitive.

The three major players in national TV competition in the late 1990s are ITV, the BBC and BSkyB. Following the 1990 Act, ITV became a much more belligerently commercial network, with, for the first time, a single network scheduler. ITV fought hard to reduce its already diminished public service obligations; in seeking to hold on to a 38–40% audience share ITV in 1994–5 was trying to move its main evening *News at Ten* into a lower audience time slot. New ownership rules also led in 1994–5 to the emergence within ITV of three dominant ownerships – Granada–LWT, Carlton–Central and Meridian–Anglia. These three ownerships account for nearly three-quarters of ITV advertising revenue.

BBC television has also become more aggressive in pursuit of ratings and, with coordinated scheduling of its two channels, it is a formidable competitor. Increasingly the BBC also uses its five national radio channels to promote its two TV channels.

The third big player is BSkyB, whose channels in 1995 reached 20% of UK households and whose 1996 revenue reached £1 bn. BSkyB in 1995 had nine Sky channels, but also provided within its 'multi-channel' package twelve other popular (mainly American) channels, making a total of 21 channels on its Astra transponders. These same Sky and Astra channels were also the main popular provision available on cable. They, of course, have no (BBC- or ITV-style) public service obligations for local British news and British content. Sky's revenue and (even more so) its profits look certain to grow massively, and it is especially well positioned for the digital era.

The late 1990s will also see an increasingly fierce struggle between Channel Four and BBC2 to hold on to a 10% TV audience share and to prevent Channel Five from doing so. Other significant audiovisual players are the two American companies Nynex and Telewest, which accounted for 46% of all UK cabled homes in early 1996.

As the fastest-growing player on the British TV scene, BSkyB has been extremely active at making alliances. For example, BSkyB has rounded up much of British and international sport in exclusive contracts but has also made agreements which, for example, allow the BBC to continue its recorded 'highlights' coverage of football. Also in 1995 Telewest and Nynex agreed not to compete with BSkyB in the premium movie and sports channel business. However BSkyB's most enduring alliance appears to be with Granada–LWT. Granada owns some 11% of BSkyB; Granada–LWT is the main producer of British programming for BSkyB; Granada also promotes Murdoch newspapers through its hotels. Sky and Granada set up in 1996 a new company, Granada Sky Broadcasting (GSkyB), to deliver eight new satellite TV channels.

Employment in British television has become very much less secure than in the 1980s. Independent production companies now make up to half of all prime-time programming. Even the largest independent producers typically only have two or three continuing series; most independent companies are really insecure freelance producers.

Local television and radio

The main providers of local television in Britain are the regional ITV companies. Some companies provide several different half hour daily news shows in their regions; for example, Central provides quite separate local news offerings each day in Oxford and in Nottingham as well as in Birmingham. Although there are 14 different regions within ITV, there are 28 geographically separate daily news offerings. These local offerings average some 350 hours each per year, with a total of 10 000 local ITV hours. The BBC does some 5000 television hours in Scotland, Wales and Northern Ireland and in its three English regions. Meanwhile Channel Four in Wales transmits another 1650 hours of Welsh language programming to a core audience of about 150 000 Welsh-speaking people, mainly in central inland Wales. This annual output of over 16 000 hours of non-national television is seen by audiences most of which number between 30 000 and 300 000 people; it is an important example of 'public service' in British television.

In radio a compromise, or division, of labour has been arrived at by which the BBC specializes in *national* radio and has the cream of the national FM output. Meanwhile, although there are three national commercial channels, only one (Classic-FM) is on FM.

The main local radio provision in Britain comes from commercial radio, with the total of commercial local stations passing 200 in 1996. Most of these stations still retain some public service elements, with an obligation to provide news and other material for local and ethnic communities. Most of the local commercial stations operate a music-and-talk format, and this is especially true of the 46 BBC local stations.

Programming exports and imports

British television in financial terms is a net importer from the USA and a (somewhat larger) net exporter to the rest of the world.

Most of the exports go to such places as northern Europe and Africa, which do not pay substantial prices. The BBC sells about 600 hours of programming each year to the USA; almost all of this appears on low audience PBS, or upmarket cable channels such as Arts and Establishment. Documentary, natural history and drama accounts for most of these hours. A common financing pattern for a short series is that the US network pays 25%, the BBC pays 50% and the remaining 25% comes from Australia, Germany, Japan and/or other familiar 'co-producer' networks.

In 1995 the BBC rolled out two new international offerings. BBC World is seen as a news and documentary basic cable offering (funded by advertising); BBC Prime is seen as a drama-entertainment premium offering (funded by subscriptions). Both channels are prestige-driven and seem unlikely to earn as much revenue as BBC books, magazines and videos.

In terms of TV imports, about 25–30% of all UK network programming is American. But only about two of the top 70 ratings each week are for American shows; Australian soap operas do far better at achieving high audiences. However, US shows are much stronger in lower audience time slots – especially daytime, late night and on Channel Four. Perhaps half of all British programming can be considered 100% British – this includes most news, sport, weekly drama, documentary and comedy. Perhaps as much as one-quarter of UK programming time involves British productions based on imported American formats – soap operas, game shows, talk-shows, factual crime and other 'reality' shows.

New media and convergence

Britain can perhaps be seen as the leader within Europe of convergence and new technology in two significant fields – namely news and cable telephony. The news developments include the following:

- Reuters has since the 1960s been a leader in news computerization. To the news or financial data customer around the world Reuters offers one-stop-shopping for text, audio, still pictures, video and archived world news, in addition to financial data and 'transactions' (such as large-scale currency trades).
- The *Financial Times* provides various on-line and newsletter services besides its international satellite editions printed each day in Frankfurt, Madrid, Roubaix, Stockholm, New York, Los Angeles, Hong Kong and Tokyo.
- During the 1980s ITN owned Basys, the world's then leading provider of computerized newsroom systems. The BBC now claims to be leading the next generation of such systems with its Electronic News Production System (ENPS) with a 2000 screen national and international network feeding its own television, radio and teletext services as well as news-on-demand web sites.

The second area of 'British' convergence leadership is the cable/telephony combination. This attracted American cable and telephone companies, eager to offer a combination which (previous to the US Telecommunications Act of February 1996) was not allowed at home. The great British public has long been sceptical of what cable has to offer, but the combination of cable and cheaper telephony proved attractive. In calendar year 1995 some 700 000 telephone-cable lines (almost all residential) were installed. The 'superhighway' or 'infopike' had arrived in Britain's suburban streets.

Policies for press and broadcasting

In all European countries separate press and broadcasting traditions and mythologies, plus the short-term partisan concerns of politicians, seem to lead to some fairly idiosyncratic and self-contradictory policies. But Britain's 1980s media policies under Margaret Thatcher may have been even more ineffective, idiosyncratic and contradictory than those of France under François Mitterrand.

Some traditional aspects of British media policy were quite successful. From 1922 to 1982 British broadcasting policy moved slowly and carefully through a traditional policy sequence which took a decade or more to introduce any significant innovation. But British policy in general, and the 'public service' approach in particular, was much less adept at dealing with commercial competition, with new technology, and with the United States.

The British media have been most commercially successful in areas where government policy did not intervene. The British music business has a bigger positive trade balance than television and film combined; advertising is another commercially successful area, which – like music – is little affected by government policy. *The Economist*, the *Financial Times* and Reuters have established London as the European centre of financial news without any specific public policy assistance.

British media policy has been ineffective when it has focused on media technology. In both satellite and cable the early 1980s high technology obsessions of French and German official policy were present in an even more virulent form in British policy. A British policy obsession with high technology through most of the 1980s in practice meant no satellite TV and no cable. Similar difficulties may well arise in the digital period; the main 'British' digital player may well be BSkyB, whose commercial agenda is basically American. Another complexity is that a key source of British technology – the IBA's research laboratories, near Southampton – has been sold off, via a financial company, to Rupert Murdoch's News International.

British media policy-makers have seldom tried to articulate a policy towards Hollywood and American media. There has throughout most of the twentieth century been an implicit free trade policy which sees Britain as media exporter, importer and entrepôt. There is no recent British policy document or committee investigation which has looked at the wisdom (or otherwise) of allowing British film, satellite, cable and video to come under predominant American commercial control. Nor, needless to say, has much systematic thought been given to considering the significance of Europe for British media, or vice versa.

Statistics

(1 ECU = £0.83)

Population (1996)

Number of inhabitants	58 million
Number of households	23 million
Geographical size	244 755 km^2
Population density	237 per km^2

Broadcasting

Terrestrial broadcasting (1997)	
Number of television channels	5
Number of national radio channels	8

Channel share of TV audience (1996)	
BBC1	33.3%
BBC2	10.7%
ITV	35.3%
Channel 4	11.2%
Satellite/cable	9.4%

Satellite and cable (January 1996)	
Cable franchises	105
Broadband homes passed	6.0 million
Broadband homes connected	1.3 million
Homes with DTH, SMATV and cable	4.9 million
Multi-channel homes	21%

Share of television advertising (1995)	
Carlton/Central	23.5%
Granada/LWT	16.3%
Meridian/Anglia	13.3%
ITV Big Three	53.1%
All ITV	72.2%
Channel 4	19.3%
GMTV	3.2%
Satellite	5.2%
TOTAL	100%

National radio channel share of all radio listening (1995)	
BBC Radio 1	11.7%
BBC Radio 2	12.0%
BBC Radio 3	1.0%
BBC Radio 4	10.4%
BBC Radio 5	2.9%
Classic-FM	2.9%
Talk Radio UK	1.4%
Virgin Radio	3.2%
National radio total	45.5%

Commercial radio (January 1996)	
National networks	3
Local ILR radio stations	173
Cable radio stations	14
Satellite radio channels	28
Also, BBC local radio stations	46

The press

Number of newspapers (1995–6)	
National dailies	10
National Sundays	9
Local mornings	17
Local evenings	73
Local Sundays	11
Paid weeklies	526
Free weeklies	807

National daily newspaper sales (February 1997)	'000s sold
Sun	3929
Daily Mirror/Record	3097
Daily Star	755
Total down-market	7781
Daily Express	1234
Daily Mail	2156
Total middle market	3390

The Times	768
Daily Telegraph	1120
Guardian	400
Independent	258
Financial Times	306
Total up-market	2852
TOTAL	14 024

Average (mean) no. of pages in selected newspapers, 1927–95
In full page equivalents (tabloids and small size sections counted as half)

	1927	1947	1975	1985	1995
The Times	25	10	26	33	56
Daily Telegraph	19	6	28	31	54
Daily Express	17	5	17	20	32
Daily Mail	19	5	17	20	35
Daily Mirror	23	5	14	15	27
Av. page total	20.6	6.2	20.4	23.8	40.8

Source: Jeremy Tunstall, *Newspaper Power* (1996)

Advertising expenditure (1994)

Percentage of total advertising expenditure	1994
National newspapers	13.1%
Regional newspapers	18.4%
Consumer magazines	4.9%
Business and professional directories	8.1%
Directories	5.8%
Press production costs	4.7%
Total press	55.1%
Television	28.3%
Direct mail	10.3%
Outdoor and transport	3.4%
Radio	2.4%
Cinema	0.5%
TOTAL	100.00
Total expenditure	£10 169 m

Source: Advertising Association

References

BBC (annual) *Report and Accounts*. London.
Butler, D. and Butler, G. (1994) *British Political Facts, 1900–1994*. London: Macmillan.
Channel Four (annual) *Report and Financial Statements*. London.
ITC (annual) *Annual Report and Accounts*. London.
Negrine, R. (1994) *Politics and the Mass Media in Britain*. London: Routledge.
Peak, S. (ed.) (annual) *The Media Guide*. London: Fourth Estate for The Guardian.
Seymour-Ure, C. (1996) *The British Press and Broadcasting since 1945*. Oxford: Blackwell.
Tellex Monitors (annual) *The Blue Book of British Broadcasting*. London.
Tunstall, J. (1993) *Television Producers*. London: Routledge.
Tunstall, J. (1994) *The Media Are American*. London: Constable.
Tunstall, J. (1996) *Newspaper Power*. Oxford: Oxford University Press.

Government publications

Department of National Heritage (1994) *The Future of the BBC: Serving the Nation, Competing Worldwide*. London: HMSO, Cm 2621.

Department of National Heritage (1995) *Media Ownership: the Government's Proposals*. London: HMSO, Cm 2872.

Department of National Heritage (1995) *Digital Terrestrial Broadcasting: The Government's Proposals*. London: HMSO, Cm 2946.

Home Office (1981) *Direct Broadcasting by Satellite*. London: HMSO.

Monopolies and Mergers Commission (1994) *The Supply of Recorded Music*. London: HMSO, Cm 2599.

Peacock, Alan (Chairman) (1986) *Report of the Committee on Financing the BBC*. London: HMSO, Cmnd 9824.

Index